Summersdale Publishers Ltd
46 West Street
Chichester
West Sussex
PO19 1RP
UK

www.summersdale.com

Printed and bound in the Czech Republic

ISBN: 978-1-84953-221-1

Substantial discounts on bulk quantities of Summersdale books are available to corporations, professional associations and other organisations. For details contact Summersdale Publishers by telephone: +44 (0) 1243 771107, fax: +44 (0) 1243 786300 or email: nicky@summersdale.com.

KEEP CALM

YOU'RE ONLY

30

KEEP
CALM

YOU'RE ONLY

30

summersdale

CONTENTS

ANOTHER
YEAR
OLDER

Thirty? Flirty and dirty!

Anonymous

Time and tide wait
for no man, but time
always stands still for
a woman of 30.

Robert Frost

Thirty was so strange for me. I've really had to come to terms with the fact that I am now a walking and talking adult.

C. S. Lewis

The way I see it, you should live every day like it's your birthday.

Paris Hilton

There was a star danced, and under that was I born.

William Shakespeare,
Much Ado about Nothing

When you turn 30,
a whole new thing
happens: you see
yourself acting like
your parents.

Blair Sabol

Thirty-five is a very attractive age; London society is full of women who have of their own free choice remained 35 for years.

Oscar Wilde

Age is just a number. It's totally irrelevant unless, of course, you happen to be a bottle of wine.

Joan Collins

Few women admit
their age. Few men
act theirs.

Anonymous

When they tell me I'm too old to do something, I attempt it immediately.

Pablo Picasso

Men are like wine.
Some turn to vinegar,
but the best improve
with age.

C. E. M. Joad

Eventually you will reach a
point when you stop lying
about your age and start
bragging about it.

Will Rogers

You're not ageing...
You're marinating.

Anonymous

The best birthdays
of all are those that
haven't arrived yet.

Robert Orben

All the world is a birthday cake, so take a piece, but not too much.

George Harrison

A birthday is just the first day of another 365-day journey around the sun. Enjoy the trip.

Anonymous

No woman should
ever be quite accurate
about her age. It looks
so calculating.

Oscar Wilde

Every year on your birthday,
you get a chance to
start new.

Sammy Hagar

JUST
WHAT
I
ALWAYS
WANTED

We know we're getting old when the only thing we want for our birthday is not to be reminded of it.

Anonymous

Why is birthday cake the only food you can blow on and spit on and everybody rushes to get a piece?

Bobby Kelton

A gift consists not in what
is done or given, but in the
intention of the giver
or doer.

Seneca

A gift, with a kind countenance, is a double present.

Thomas Fuller

A true friend
remembers your
birthday but not
your age.

Anonymous

God gave us the gift of life; it is up to us to give ourselves the gift of living well.

Voltaire

I think, at a child's birth, if a mother could ask a fairy godmother to endow it with the most useful gift, that gift should be curiosity.

Eleanor Roosevelt

I'm not materialistic.
I believe in presents
from the heart, like a
drawing that a
child does.

Victoria Beckham

A hug is the perfect gift;
one size fits all, and nobody
minds if you exchange it.

Anonymous

Youth is the gift of nature, but age is a work of art.

Garson Kanin

There are 364 days when you might get un-birthday presents... and only *one* for birthday presents, you know.

Lewis Carroll,
Through the Looking Glass

Birthdays are nature's way of telling us to eat more cake.

Anonymous

Birthdays are good for you.
Statistics show that the
people who have the most
live the longest.

Larry Lorenzoni

The best way to remember your wife's birthday is to forget it once.

E. Joseph Cossman

GRIN
AND
BEAR
IT

Getting old is a fascinating thing. The older you get, the older you want to get.

Keith Richards

I'm kind of comfortable with getting older because it's better than the other option, which is being dead. So I'll take getting older.

George Clooney

A woman never
forgets her age – once
she has decided
what it is.

Stanley Davis

If you carry your childhood with you, you never become older.

Tom Stoppard

There is an anti-ageing
possibility, but it has to
come from within.

Susan Anton

I think all this talk about age
is foolish. Every time I'm
one year older, everyone
else is too.

Gloria Swanson

Age is an issue of
mind over matter.
If you don't mind, it
doesn't matter.

Mark Twain

There is always a lot to be thankful for, if you take the time to look. For example, I'm sitting here thinking how nice it is that wrinkles don't hurt.

Anonymous

You are never too old
to set another goal or
to dream a new dream.

Les Brown

No one can avoid
ageing, but ageing
productively is
something else.

Katharine Graham

The only time you really live fully is from 30 to 60. The young are slaves to dreams; the old servants of regrets. Only the middle-aged have all their five senses in the keeping of their wits.

Hervey Allen

When it comes to age
we're all in the same boat,
only some of us have been
aboard a little longer.

Leo Probst

Age is a number and mine is unlisted.

Anonymous

DO
A LITTLE
DANCE
MAKE
A LITTLE
LOVE

You know you're getting old when your idea of hot, flaming desire is a barbecued steak.

Victoria Fabiano

No one grows old by living – only by losing interest in living.

Marie Ray

If wrinkles must be written upon our brows, let them not be written upon the heart. The spirit should never grow old.

James A. Garfield

The more you praise and celebrate your life, the more there is in life to celebrate.

Oprah Winfrey

Live your life and forget your age.

Norman Vincent Peale

You know you're getting old
when you have sex with
someone half your age –
and it's legal.

Dan Savage

Sex in your twenties?
'Yes, yes, yes – again.'
Sex in your thirties?
'Ow, my hip.'

Caroline Rhea

Let us celebrate the occasion with wine and sweet words.

Titus Maccius Plautus

To resist the frigidity of old age, one must combine the body, the mind, and the heart. And to keep these in parallel vigour one must exercise, study, and love.

Charles-Victor de Bonstetten

Do I exercise? Well I
once jogged to
the ashtray.

Will Self

Early to rise and early to bed makes a man healthy, wealthy and dead.

James Thurber

It's important to have a
twinkle in your wrinkle.

Anonymous

He has a profound respect
for old age. Especially when
it's bottled.

Gene Fowler

You know you're getting old when the first thing you do after you're done eating is look for a place to lie down.

Louie Anderson

I can still rock like a
son of a bitch.

Ozzy Osbourne

YOUNG
AT
HEART

I can still cut the mustard…
I just need help opening
the jar!

Anonymous

If you obey all the
rules, you miss all
the fun.

Katharine Hepburn

You know you're growing old
when the light of your life is
the one in the fridge.

Hal Roach

I have the body of an 18-year-old. I keep it in the fridge.

Spike Milligan

Bashfulness is an ornament
to youth, but a reproach to
old age.

Aristotle

Anyone who stops learning is old, whether at 20 or 80. Anyone who keeps learning stays young. The greatest thing in life is to keep your mind young.

Henry Ford

I'm happy to report that my inner child is still ageless.

James Broughton

Old age is like an opium dream. Nothing seems real except the unreal.

Oliver Wendell Holmes Sr

True terror is to wake up one morning and discover that your high school class is running the country.

Kurt Vonnegut

Youth is the time for adventures of the body, but age for the triumphs of the mind.

Logan Pearsall Smith

Inside every older person
is a younger person –
wondering what the
hell happened.

Cora Harvey Armstrong

Like many women my age, I am 28 years old.

Mary Schmich

Age does not diminish the
extreme disappointment of
having a scoop of ice cream
fall from the cone.

Jim Fiebig

The secret to eternal youth is arrested development.

Alice Roosevelt Longworth

Middle age is when you're
old enough to know better
but still young enough
to do it.

Ogden Nash

Nobody grows old merely by living a number of years. We grow old by deserting our ideals. Years may wrinkle the skin, but to give up enthusiasm wrinkles the soul.

Samuel Ullman

When you're a young man, Macbeth is a character part. When you're older, it's a straight part.

Sir Laurence Olivier

The ageing process has
you firmly in its grasp if you
never get the urge to throw
a snowball.

Doug Larson

OLDER
AND
WISER?

Everything I know I learned after I was 30.

Georges Clemenceau

The older you get the more important it is not to act your age.

Ashleigh Brilliant

Minds ripen at very
different ages.

Elizabeth Montagu

You can judge your age by
the amount of pain you feel
when you come in contact
with a new idea.

Pearl S. Buck

Age considers;
youth ventures.

Rabindranath Tagore

Ageing seems to be the only
available way to live a
long life.

Kitty O'Neill Collins

The first sign of maturity
is the discovery that the
volume knob also turns to
the left.

Jerry M. Wright

Take care of the
minutes, and the
hours will take care
of themselves.

Lord Chesterfield

A man is not old until his
regrets take the place
of dreams.

John Barrymore

Knowledge speaks,
but wisdom listens.

Jimi Hendrix

No one over 35 is worth meeting who has not something to teach us – something more than we could learn by ourselves, from a book.

Cyril Connolly

We have no simple problems or easy decisions after kindergarten.

William Dean Howells

As one young man leaves his twenties behind, idealism gives way to practicality. Almost.

Rabbi Boruch Leff

To know how to grow old is
the master work of wisdom,
and one of the most difficult
chapters in the great art
of living.

Henri-Frédéric Amiel

You've heard of the three
ages of man – youth,
age, and 'you are looking
wonderful'.

Francis Cardinal Spellman

The secret to staying
young is to live
honestly, eat slowly,
and lie about
your age.

Lucille Ball

Good judgement comes from experience, and often experience comes from bad judgement.

Rita Mae Brown

We are young only once, after that we need some other excuse.

Anonymous

LIVE
LOVE
AND
LAST

If I had my life to live over again, I would make the same mistakes, only sooner.

Tallulah Bankhead

Never be afraid to try
something new.

Bob Hope

He who laughs, lasts!

Mary Pettibone Poole

I've finally reached
the age where my wild
oats have turned into
All-Bran!

Tom Wilson

The follies which a man
regrets most in his life
are those which he didn't
commit when he had
the opportunity.

Helen Rowland

As we grow older, we must discipline ourselves to continue expanding, broadening, learning, keeping our minds active and open.

Clint Eastwood

I'm not ageing. I just need re-potting.

Anonymous

If I'm feeling wild,
I don't floss before
bedtime.

Judith Viorst

The problem with the world
is that everyone is a few
drinks behind.

Humphrey Bogart

As men get older,
the toys get more
expensive.

Marvin Davis

Seize the moment.
Remember all those women
on the *Titanic* who waved off
the dessert cart.

Erma Bombeck

You are only young
once, but you can be
immature for a lifetime.

John P. Grier

The key to successful
ageing is to pay as little
attention to it as possible.

Judith Regan

Everything slows down with age, except the time it takes cake and ice cream to reach your hips.

John Wagner

The best thing about getting old is that all those things you couldn't have when you were young you no longer want.

L. S. McCandless

Age does not protect you from love. But love to some extent, protects you from age.

Jeanne Moreau

ILLS
PILLS
AND
TWINGES

They say that age is all
in your mind. The trick is
keeping it from creeping
down into your body.

Anonymous

Being a father is like doing drugs – you smell bad, get no sleep and spend all your money on them.

Paul Bettany

Life would be infinitely
happier if we could only be
born at the age of 80 and
gradually approach 18.

Mark Twain

My doctor told me to do something that puts me out of breath, so I've taken up smoking again.

Jo Brand

As for me, except for an occasional heart attack, I feel as young as I ever did.

Robert Benchley

Doctors are always telling us that drinking shortens your life. Well I've seen more old drunkards than old doctors.

Edward Phillips

I keep fit. Every morning
I do a hundred laps of an
Olympic-sized swimming
pool in a small motor launch.

Peter Cook

Men, like peaches and pears, grow sweet a little while before they begin to decay.

Oliver Wendell Holmes Sr

You're not old until it takes you longer to rest up than it does to get tired.

Forrest Clare 'Phog' Allen

I don't do alcohol any more – I get the same effect just standing up fast.

Anonymous

Passing the vodka bottle
and playing the guitar.

**Keith Richards on how
he keeps fit**

If you rest, you rust.

Helen Hayes

I'd hate to die with a good liver, good kidneys and a good brain. When I die I want everything to be knackered.

Hamish Imlach

CHIN
UP
CHEST
OUT

After 30, a body has
a mind of its own.

Bette Midler

You know you're getting old when you look at a beautiful 19-year-old girl and you find yourself thinking, 'Gee, I wonder what her mother looks like.'

Anonymous

I like the idea of growing old gracefully and full of wrinkles... like Audrey Hepburn.

Natalie Imbruglia

To my eye, women get sexier around 35. They know a thing or two, and knowledge is always alluring.

Pierce Brosnan

I don't want to be one of those middle-aged guys who turns up with the baseball hat on the wrong way around.

Elvis Costello

You know you're getting old when you can pinch an inch on your forehead.

John Mendoza

I remember the day I turned 30… The way I saw it, I was never going to age; I'd just look up one day and be old.

Terry McMillan

Cheerfulness and content are great beautifiers, and are famous preservers of youthful looks.

Charles Dickens, *Barnaby Rudge*

Let us respect grey
hairs, especially
our own.

J. P. Sears

Time may be a great healer,
but it's a lousy beautician.

Anonymous

Wrinkles are hereditary.
Parents get them from
their children.

Doris Day

How pleasant is the day
when we give up striving to
be young or slender.

William James

As you age naturally, your family shows more and more on your face. If you deny that, you deny your heritage.

Frances Conroy

Alas, after a certain
age every man is
responsible for
his face.

Albert Camus

One day you look in the
mirror and realise the face
you are shaving is
your father's.

Robert Harris

As we grow old, the beauty steals inward.

Ralph Waldo Emerson

You know you're getting older if you have more fingers than real teeth.

Rodney Dangerfield

Age is whatever you think it is. You are as old as you think you are.

Muhammad Ali

KEEP CALM AND DRINK UP

£4.99

ISBN: 978 1 84953 102 3

'*In victory, you deserve champagne; in defeat, you need it.*'

Napoleon Bonaparte

BAD ADVICE FOR GOOD PEOPLE.

Keep Calm and Carry On, a World War Two government poster, struck a chord in recent difficult times when a stiff upper lip and optimistic energy were needed again. But in the long run it's a stiff drink and flowing spirits that keep us all going.

Here's a book packed with proverbs and quotations showing the wisdom to be found at the bottom of the glass.

www.summersdale.com

KEEP CALM AND DRINK UP

£4.99

ISBN: 978 1 84953 102 3

'In victory, you deserve champagne; in defeat, you need it.'

Napoleon Bonaparte

BAD ADVICE FOR GOOD PEOPLE.

Keep Calm and Carry On, a World War Two government poster, struck a chord in recent difficult times when a stiff upper lip and optimistic energy were needed again. But in the long run it's a stiff drink and flowing spirits that keep us all going.

Here's a book packed with proverbs and quotations showing the wisdom to be found at the bottom of the glass.

www.summersdale.com

Old Colonists now living in Manitoba or Saskatchewan are descendants of families who have lived in Mexico.[38]

The Migration to Alberta

In 1934 several Old Colony families left the Hague Old Colony settlement for Fort Vermilion, in northern Alberta. Prior to the migration, in 1932, a delegation of four men had been sent to the Fort Vermilion area to inspect the land. They negotiated with the land office in Edmonton, which advised them not to begin a settlement since the area had not yet been officially opened for homesteading. Nevertheless, several families moved to the area in 1934 despite the very primitive conditions which led to near starvation and death by freezing during the first winter.

This migration took place without the official sanction of the Church since negotiations had not been completed with the provincial government. Although at one point the Alberta government had threatened to jail the leaders for homesteading before the land was officially opened, ultimately the technicalities were taken care of, and migration to the area increased. By 1948 the settlement had a population of 377, of which about one third were returnees from Mexico.[39]

The basic motivation for the trek from Saskatchewan beginning in 1932 was the continuing dissatisfaction with the school situation in Saskatchewan. During the migration to Mexico in 1922, a sizable number (5,326) stayed in Saskatchewan for several reasons: (1) many could not afford the move; (2) many felt that the school situation might correct itself; and (3) as was true in Manitoba, many were interested in migrating, but they did not want to go to Mexico. After it

38. These estimates are based on official Church records, but these are not entirely dependable since the records are not complete. One randomly chosen section shows that eight out of forty-six families returned to Canada. In the Rosenort church, over 50 per cent of the members in 1965 were families returned from Mexico.

39. See John A. Hostetler, "Pioneering in the Land of the Midnight Sun," *Mennonite Life*, III (April, 1948), 5–9.

appeared that freedom for the Old Colony to conduct its own schools would not be found in Saskatchewan, the more conservative leaders and members began to feel the urgency of moving to a more promising land. It was the candid hope of the leaders of the conservative element that by moving to Alberta, "away from the school inspectors," they would be able to evade the school problem.

The Migration to British Honduras

The next major Old Colony migration began in 1958; British Honduras was its goal.[40] (See Map 2 for location of British Honduras settlement and Appendix K for the official agreement between the Old Colony and the British Honduras government.) By 1958 the pressure for new land in Mexico was becoming so great that general unrest prevailed. The possibilities for expansion into the area around the settlements in Chihuahua and Durango had been fully exploited, and many were landless in every village. For example, in 1958, in the village of Hochfeld, twenty-three of fifty-eight couples, or 40 per cent, were without land.

There were other reasons for migration to British Honduras. Relations between the Mexican natives and the Old Colony were poor: stealing and other overt unfriendly acts on the part of Mexicans were on the increase. (See Appendix D.) Many Old Colonists wanted to get away from the Mexican mentality. Others wanted to get out from under the authoritarian hand of the Church. Others were in search of adventure and new experience, corroborating Schmiedehaus' idea that adventure was one of the reasons for Old Colony migrations.[41] In short, there were many reasons for migration, as is indicated by an Old Colony minister in Mexico:

40. See Leo Driedger, "From Mexico to British Honduras," *Mennonite Life,* XIII (October, 1958), 160–66.

41. Schmiedehaus, *Ein Feste,* pp. 254ff. Since so many things are considered worldly, it is logical to presume that the activities that are condoned, such as emigration, would be undertaken by all who could.

The reasons for leaving were as different as the people themselves. Many stated that they were tired of Mexican government and culture and wanted a change. This is phony, since Honduras is run by Negroes and is not really a British country; further it is bordering Mexico and there are rumors that it may unite with Mexico. Others are not satisfied with the way they have been treated by the Church so they want to leave its clutches. Others state that land is their motive, though often old people, who should retire, move. This is the case in at least three or four families that I have heard about. They are past retirement age, and still they clean up everything and leave. Others leave because of relatives.[42]

Though the Church leaders had wanted only twenty families to begin the settlement so that an orderly and efficient settlement could result, eighty-seven had moved by September, 1958, despite conditions hardly conducive to successful homesteading. The dense jungle made it tremendously difficult to lay out villages in the traditional fashion. For the second time in the history of the Old Colony, people were settling in a climate substantially different from what they had known earlier. There was much sickness and disease. By September, 1958, twenty-nine people had died. In the first six-week period, before the immigrants had learned how to protect themselves against mosquitoes, twenty-five children had died. They soon thereafter learned to sleep under mosquito netting and to protect themselves from disease-bearing insects.

Because the emigration met with so much hardship and discouragement, there was a constant stream of returnees to Mexico. Out of the eighty-seven families that had migrated (after having sold all their belongings and land, if they had any, in Mexico), twenty-four had returned to Mexico within six months. Many of these had lost everything and had to start from the beginning. Some of the returnees moved on to Canada, thereby achieving freedom from the control of the Old Colony leadership, which had been one of the objections to life in British Honduras.

42. Material gathered by the author during field research.

The Migration to Bolivia

The most recent migration, one that promises to become a major one, has Bolivia as its goal. The reasons for the migration are generally the same as those given for British Honduras. The major impetus for the migration, however, came from the Nord Plan, which is the most conservative of the Mexican settlements. In September, 1966, a delegation of five men from the Nord Plan went to Bolivia. Later that year four other men, including two ministers, made another visit. They were assured the privileges of exemption from military service and freedom to conduct their own schools.

In March, 1967, the first group set out. They hired a truck to take them to Bolivia but did not get very far into Guatemala before they realized that they could not make it by car. They flew the rest of the way. The majority have migrated by bus and ship, though some took jets from Mexico City, the latter being something of an incongruity for the Old Colony way of life. By December of 1967 it was reported that there were over 500 persons already resident at the new settlement, about 40 miles south of Santa Cruz. In August, 1968, it was estimated by a minister that about 950 persons had emigrated to Bolivia. A number of families have already returned to Mexico, giving the same reasons the returnees from British Honduras gave. Several families were so poor that they barely managed to reach the Mexican settlements and "home."

The land was purchased at a very reasonable price—three dollars an acre, which covered mainly the legal costs. A total of 100,000 acres of uncleared scrub land was bought. Villages have been laid out in the traditional manner, with the general organization being greatly similar to that of the mother settlements.

Other lesser migrations that took place cannot be described in detail here. Table 1-1 provides the basic information about each, although a few minor migrations are not listed. It remains undisputed that the migrations have played a very important part in the life of the Old Colony. The causes for the many migrations are as follows, in order of importance:

(1) freedom to conduct schools in the way to which they had been accustomed, since they knew that schools were the surest instrument to break down the barriers between the Old Colony and the "world"; (2) freedom from military service and government programs of various kinds (e.g., the *Segura Social* episode in Mexico, described below); (3) population pressure creating need for more land than was available in the immediate area; (4) desire on the part of dissident elements to break away from the strong group disciplines and restrictions; and (5) desire for new experiences and adventure, aroused mainly because of lack of contact with the outside on-going world.

The consequences of the various migrations will be discussed briefly here but expanded in a later chapter. The freedom to conduct schools has been achieved only temporarily. The Mexico settlement appears to be the most successful, but even there the time is rapidly running out; the Mexican government is beginning to bear down.[43] In the Fort Vermilion, Alberta, situation the school inspector has already arrived! The Old Colony schools have been closed, and provincially approved teachers are teaching school in the Old Colony. The Old Colonists who have moved on to Fort St. John, British Columbia, will not have many months to live in peace before the inspector arrives there, too. On the other hand, freedom from government interference in nonacademic matters is being granted. Less success has been achieved in the quest for more land, for only temporary alleviation by migration has been possible. The number of landless couples in the villages in Mexico has remained about the same in the period since the migration to British Honduras began. The fourth aim, the desire to break away from strong controls, has not been achieved in Honduras, but there has been a softening of the strict discipline. (See Appendix E for details.) The migrations to Aylmer, Ontario, and to the old established centers in Mani-

43. See Schmiedehaus, *Ein Feste,* pp. 201–22. Schmiedehaus says that all other privileges will be granted the Old Colony in Mexico: "Nur ein Punkt ist da, der sich nicht halten lassen wird: das Schulprivileg!" —"Only one situation will not continue in freedom—the school privileges" (p. 213).

toba, Saskatchewan, and Alberta have resulted in more freedom, as will be shown later.

The desire for new experiences has certainly been met beyond all expectations. Undoubtedly the most prevalent topic of conversation in the Old Colony—in Canada or Mexico—is the British Honduras story. Because many have relatives there and visits are constantly exchanged, there is an endless stream of stories—some true, others legendary—about the experiences in British Honduras. Included in the exaggerated versions are accounts of flying insects that upon striking the skin bury themselves under the skin, of snakes that are less than five feet long but can strangle a man, of the richness of the soil which allows banana trees to produce a full crop in six months after planting, and so on. (See Table 1-2 for brief descriptions of environments of the various settlements.)

Conclusion

This then is the Old Colony in brief. It is a *religious ethnic minority*. The Old Colony is a *religious* ethnic minority because the basis for the emergence of the ethnic group and for its minority status is the religious dynamic, which stems from the Anabaptist movement. If it had not been for the peculiar beliefs which brought the ancestors of the Old Colony people together, the Old Colony could not have emerged. The Old Colony continues to be a religious ethnic minority, although many people would question whether there is a religious dynamic operative in the Old Colony today. An objective scientific view, however, has to maintain that the Old Colony is still motivated and guided by what the Old Colony members think is a religious faith.

Through historical events it has come into being as an *ethnic* group with beliefs, behavior patterns, and memories that are distinct from its Mennonite siblings and considerably different from other groups. The Old Colony members have inherited a rich tradition of memories, experiences, attitudes, and feelings. They have developed strong relations among themselves, to the exclusion of others. They have developed into a genuine *ethnic* group because they feel that they are a people. There

Table 1-2 *Physical Environment and Agricultural Features of Old Colony Settlements*[a]

	Manitoba	Saskatchewan	Mexico		Alberta	British Honduras	Ontario
			Chihuahua	Durango			
Altitude in feet (average)	850	1,700	7,500	6,000	2,400	250	1,100
Mean temperature in degrees Fahrenheit							
year-round	36	33	61	59	33	78	33
summer (range)	55–79	60–65	64–80	64–80	50–76	64–80	76–80
winter (range)	−13–7	−20–0	32–48	32–48	−14–11	64–80	−11–11
Precipitation in inches (average annual)	19–21	15	18–20	20	13	80	30
Soil types	pedocal blackearth	pedocal brownearth	pedocal highland	pedocal blackearth	pedocal blackearth	pedalfer redearth	pedalfer podzol
Predominant crops	mixed grain wheat	wheat, oats	beans, corn forage crops	beans, corn forage crops	oats, barley forage crops	fruit	cereal oats forage crops
Predominant livestock	cattle, hogs	cattle, hogs	cattle	cattle	cattle, hogs	chickens	cattle hogs

[a] Official Departments of Mines and Interiors of Canadian Provinces, personal correspondence, 1964. Department of Meteorology, Institute of Geophysics, National University of Mexico, personal correspondence, 1964. "British Honduras," *Encyclopaedia Britannica* (Chicago: William Benton, Publisher, 1965), Vol. IV.

is a most pronounced awareness of belonging, of *we* as opposed to *they*. There are a common past and a common future to which each member subscribes.[44] This common tradition has produced a language, a way of looking at things, and a way of doing things which set them apart from all other groups.

The Old Colony is a *minority* because it has experienced difficulty in being accepted or tolerated by the larger society, as expressed most clearly in its relations with the state. The Old Colony is a minority because of some of its practices: it has refused to submit to some of the "nationalizing" demands expressed by the state, such as learning the national language and participating in its educational processes;[45] it has insisted on perpetuating some of its own practices which are considered undesirable by the larger society, as exemplified by the perpetuation of the "German" culture in other lands; it has refused to participate in the national culture, which has caused the loss of voice in determining what will happen to the Old Colony.[46]

The Old Colony is moving to the last available frontiers in its attempt to protect its existence. Migration has been the simplest and most natural technique for survival, but the frontiers are rapidly vanishing across the entire globe. The Old Colony may need to stop and fight it out. It is beginning to do just that.

44. Milton M. Gordon, *Assimilation in American Life* (New York: Oxford University Press, 1964): ". . . we shall refer to a group with a shared feeling of peoplehood as an 'ethnic group'" (p. 24).

45. John A. Hostetler and Calvin Redekop, "Education and Assimilation in Three Ethnic Groups," *The Alberta Journal of Educational Research,* VIII (December, 1962), 189–203.

46. Ethnic group and minority are discussed in Ch. 9. For a working definition that will be used at this point, see John Milton Yinger's definition, which states in part: "A minority is a group which, regardless of where it is on the class ladder, faces barriers to the pursuit of life's values that are greater than the barriers faced by persons otherwise equally qualified." *A Minority Group in American Society* (New York: McGraw-Hill Book Co., 1965), p. 22.

Chapter 2

THE PEOPLE OF
THE COVENANT

The roots of the Old Colony can be found in the Reformation. As was shown earlier, a religious motivation was the original force in the development of the Old Colony. The consequent emergence of a "consciousness of peoplehood" was equally important, however, for it produced a particular set of values and patterns of thought which can be defined as an ethnic tradition. This system of thought can be classified to include some basic motifs, including beliefs, values, and norms.[1]

The Old Colony Belief System

The beliefs of the Old Colony have been fairly homogeneous, even though one finds considerable differences in actual practice in the Canadian and Mexican groups. According to the available evidence, the most widely held and significant belief is that the Old Colony is God's chosen people, the elect: "We are gathered here today to renew our covenant with God and our *Gemeent*.[2] The covenant consists of a promise to remain true to God and our *Gemeent*, to serve the Lord with righteousness and holiness."[3]

1. The following discussion is based on evidence gathered in the settlements at Cuauhtemoc in the province of Chihuahua and the settlement in southern Manitoba. These have been used because 1) the author spent three months in residence in the Old Colony in Manitoba in 1958 and five months in residence in the Chihuahua settlement and is thus much better acquainted with these than with the other settlements, which were visited only briefly; 2) the Manitoba and Chihuahua settlements most fully characterize the Old Colony, both in similarities and differences. Since the Old Colony has produced practically no written material, the analysis is based almost exclusively on transcriptions of verbal material.

2. *Gemeent* is Low German for *Gemeinde*, which means "church."

3. See Appendix C for the full text of the sermon quoted briefly here. Delivered in rededication by one of the most able bishops of

An unsympathetic outsider provides still more pointed comment: "I think the Old Colony's biggest problem is that they think they are God's elect. There are no other people around but them. They think that they are the special people of God, and no matter what others do to them, they think it will all come out right for them." [4]

While other religious groups and non-Christians displease God by their "worldly" ways, the Old Colony members believe that they are being obedient to God, as the ordination sermon illustrates: "Oh, beloved brethren and sisters, according to the evidence, we are living in the last time, and signs are being fulfilled so that we can with truth say with the Apostle John: Children, it is the last hour. Oh! that we might all be ready, as the wise virgins, if suddenly in the middle of the night the voice will say, 'The Bridegroom comes! Go to meet him.'" [5]

The belief in punishment for unfaithfulness is clearly evident in the Old Colony system: "God will punish us for not remaining pure from the world. Just as the children of Israel were punished when they mixed and intermarried with the world, so God will punish us for being impure and immoral." [6]

Another belief germane to the Old Colony is trust in the providence of God. God is their personal benefactor and will take care of them in every area of life as long as they are faithful to Him. The prevailing attitude even during the difficult and costly migrations is incontrovertible proof of this belief: "When I was down there [in Mexico] and saw the hopeless situation and the tremendous hardship of moving again [a new trek to British Honduras because of population

---

the Old Colony to the Canadian group after the emigration to Mexico, it includes the history of the separation of the Mexico-bound Old Colony segment and the resultant disorganization, and typifies most sermons preached by Old Colony ministers. Sermons constitute the only written sources available in the Old Colony.

4. Material gathered by the author during field research.

5. See Appendix C for the full text of the sermon quoted briefly here.

6. Material gathered by the author during field research.

pressure], I asked a bishop whether it did not look impossible. He said, 'Yes, it is impossible—if we were to do it with our own hands, but we have a Father in Heaven who cares for us. He will do it for us.' They have a complete trust in God. God has taken care of them in the past and will take care of them in the future." [7]

Beliefs cannot persist indefinitely unless they are tested and proved. The process of validating beliefs is therefore important to the Old Colony. That they are the chosen people of God is validated by their paralleling the Old Colony's history with that of the children of Israel, who were punished or blessed according to their behavior. Old Colony preachers often use this argument in their sermons to explain the Old Colony's good or ill fortune.

The belief that the Old Colony is living under the blessing of God and that other groups are frustrating His will is further validated by comparing their place with that of non-Old Colony members: "It does not matter if the outsider is a better Christian and adheres to the Bible twice as much. He belongs to the world. There is no hope for the Mexicans to ever come out of the world." [8]

The belief that God will take care of His people is derived from a study of past experience. The successful migration from Canada, which has to date resulted in the Mexican group's religious freedom and the government's noninterference in their school system, is considered concrete proof of God's care for them. The Mexican Old Colony group's ability to retain its conservative way of life when the Canadian group has lost much of its distinctiveness indicates to the Mexican group that God has rewarded them for their faithfulness. Their assurance is reinforced by their knowledge that other Mennonite groups with similar historical origins are now indulging in things which suggest that they have been forsaken by God and their consequent belief that God has forsaken these worldly individuals.

Many of the beliefs espoused by the Old Colony are ulti-

7. Material gathered by the author during field research.
8. Material gathered by the author during field research.

mately based on the Bible, the source of authority for the preachers and the bishop. The laity, little informed about the Bible and able only to educe a few biblical passages in support of a behavior pattern such as nonresistance, assume that the clergy is using the Scriptures correctly, that the truths long embraced and taught continue to be valid.

Thus, tradition also serves as a guide to and source of Old Colony beliefs. That which has been adopted by the forefathers and has stood the test of time must be true. There is no use in continually re-evaluating past behavior. In fact, as can be noted in numerous transcriptions, re-examination of past decisions is a source of severe tension.

Old Colony Values

The Old Colony social system is supported by a complex system of feelings and sentiments. The Old Colony member feels that his way of life is holy and God-ordained. The emotional tenor prevalent at formal events such as baptisms, weddings, and funerals manifests a deep reverence for the Old Colony way. The spirit of solemnity and awe that characterizes the two- or three-hour worship services reflects the respect felt for God. The minister, bishop, or deacon is held in high regard, because he is the spokesman for God.

There is also a great deal of respect for local officials such as the village *Schult* (mayor) or village clerk. The Old Colony member feels that these people and the offices they hold are part of the total Old Colony order which demands loyalty; the same applies to the mundane aspects of farm and village life. The Old Colonist feels an obligation to support his village and is happy when he can make a contribution. Although the Old Colonist does not speak of the "good life," it seems that happiness or joy is experienced when he conforms to the religious, social, and economic norms of the Old Colony.

Conversely, lack of conformity creates tension and misunderstanding. The attitude toward the adoption of new technological devices is a case in point. In Mexico, for example, the use of rubber tires on tractors has been tabooed because of the fear that Old Colony youth would use the tractors to go to town, where they would mix with the Mexican people.

To control the tensions and restore a salubrious sentiment, the Old Colony benefits from certain rites of passage. Catechism and baptism are rites that signify the safe admittance into the brotherhood of those whose status has been at best unstable and at worst outside the group. These emotion-filled occasions are high points in the life of the individual, as well as in the entire Church. Marriage is another rite of passage, for only then does the male become a bona-fide member of the responsible and decision-making group in village and Church life; the female is also accepted as a mature member of the village community and Church upon her marriage.

Funerals serve to bring the bereaved closer to the bosom of the Church and to convince everyone that the solidarity of the community has not been weakened by the death of a member; though this is a rite of passage for the deceased, it is really a rite of intensification for the community. The sermon at the funeral is normally quite emotional and is an occasion for recounting the virtues of the deceased and for admonishing the entire congregation to live faithfully. The funeral meal of coffee and bread is served to reintegrate the broken family into the healing of the normal and the routine. It is customary for the minister and the bereaved family to express their sorrow freely, thereby dissipating the emotional tension and sorrow.

Although the Old Colonists are not articulate about the symbolic value of many aspects of their life, the carefully laid out villages and fields, and the architecture of the houses, barns, and church communicate the ordered Old Colony way of life. The steel wheels on the tractor, the use of the horse and buggy for transportation when modern conveniences could easily be afforded, and the similarity of house furnishings express the adherence to a way of life that is willingly shared by others. The similarity in foods, dress, and social activities likewise demonstrates obedience to the Old Colony way.

Not only are the cultural artifacts themselves representative of the community's values, but so is the behavior that is observable in relation to these artifacts. A well-kept team of horses or a clean buggy in good repair communicates to others the attitudes and feelings of the Old Colonist. The pride exhibited in the way the farms are maintained and repaired exemplifies the basic identification with the Old Colony way of life.

The attendance at religious services speaks of the willingness to be faithful to the Old Colony. Men and women communicate their awe and respect for the worship service by coming into the church building and sitting quietly for as much as thirty minutes before the service begins. It does not take long for an outsider to reach the conclusion that the Old Colony member belongs to his Church with a deep sense of loyalty and commitment.

The ritualized behavior observable in the Old Colony also symbolizes loyalty to the Old Colony way. The *Gesangbuch,* the official songbook of the Old Colony, is kept in a special place at home and is carried to church in a reverent fashion, often boxed in a special container. The ritualism of the wearing of hats in the Old Colony is another example. There are special racks for the hats in the living room and in the meetinghouse. The hats are carefully and formally hung on the racks when the men enter the church or the home.

The similarity in cultural artifacts, behavior patterns, religious beliefs, and sentiments suggests the Old Colonist's sense of his covenanted relationship to God, his commitment to a larger force, the people of the Covenant. It speaks of the agreement of many persons on what is considered ultimately important, what is desirable and good. Though the outsider might gain the impression that the Old Colony is a group that is drab, uninteresting, and undesirable, there is much to indicate that for the insider the "good life" is entirely present within the confines of the Old Colony. The deep reverence and commitment for the Old Colony way of life is proof that here is a life worth living.

Old Colony Norms

Norms are goals which are to be achieved by a society and the means by which the goals are to be reached.[9]

GOALS

The Old Colony group subscribes to a number of goals or objectives which derive from its belief and value system. It is possible to categorize the goals into hierarchies or levels: ultimate or final goals; intermediate goals, or those which help in the achievement of the ultimate goals; and immediate goals. Achievement at one level serves to assist in achievement of the goals of the next higher level. As a matter of fact, some of the lesser goals exist mainly for the achievement of the highest goals.

The highest goal is the goal of salvation, which is understood as acceptance by God as faithful people rather than as faithful individuals. Salvation is not the narrowly conceived, fundamentalist-pietist notion of an emotionally toned religious experience. Neither is there any understanding of the inditeristic of American Protestantism. The salvation of the Old vidualistic nature of the religious experience which is characColony affects all of its members; therefore, it is important that there be no deviants to spoil the chances of the whole group.

A second ultimate goal, important particularly since non-Old Colony patterns of life are profane, is to live the Old Colony way of life, or to be in full fellowship with other Old Colony people. The desire for group affiliation is evident even at very practical levels. For example, in the village of Hochfeld there were only two farmers out of a total of seventy-four who did not own John Deere tractors. One of the seventy-two conformists said he had changed from a McCormick Deering to a John Deere because the former was too expensive to run. On other occasions, however, he had expressed his

9. See Robin Williams, *American Society* (New York: Alfred A. Knopf, Inc., 1951), pp. 24–25: "Cultural norms therefore include both cultural *goals,* and the approved means for reaching those goals."

wish to have a McCormick Deering because it had more power for its fuel consumption. His decision to act with the majority would seem to indicate that the farmer, like most Old Colony members, wanted to live the Old Colony way of life. There is no evidence of a desire to move up in the world. The Old Colony way of life is ultimate; hence, there is no attempt to keep up with the world, though there is a status struggle within the Old Colony system which will be commented upon later.

There are a number of intermediate or secondary goals which energize Old Colony life. One of the most important, already implicit in both ultimate goals, is the goal of conforming to Old Colony norms. It is a means to an end, not an end in itself. Conformity has several legitimations. The most important is that one can influence fellow members to live the Old Colony way of life only when there is uniformity or a core of similarity. Another is that discipline can be practiced most easily when there is conformity: correction can best be applied when deviance is most clearly seen. One Old Colonist said that the reason there is such a strict regulation in dress is that when an Old Colony member is tempted to stray, he will feel conspicuous and thereby refrain. There is certainly no mistaking an Old Colony member in a city such as Chihuahua. Finally, conformity is a goal because it will preserve the Old Colony way of life and contribute to its quest for salvation. As soon as there is too much deviance, Old Colony solidarity begins to suffer. One Old Colony member was excommunicated in Mexico because he bought a truck. His defense was that if an Old Colony member could get drunk, he could own a truck. Another member stated that the reason he had purchased a car was that he knew of an Old Colonist who had a truck and was somehow getting by with it. Disruption is at a minimum when there is the least opportunity for invidious comparison.

Another intermediate goal which assists in the achievement of ultimate goals is the maintenance of separation from the world. The need for realizing this goal is verbalized freely in sermons, in workaday conversations, and in periodic meetings held in various meetinghouses. The following account of one meeting was given by an Old Colony member in Mexico: "At this meeting many lay people got up and lamented the sad plight of the *Gemeent,* how it had gotten worldly, how it had taken on more of the world's show, and how it was necessary to return to the old truths. . . . Some of the worldly things mentioned were rubber tires, wrist watches, ties, belts on trousers, and cars." [10] There is a great deal of disagreement as to what constitutes separation from the world, a subject to which bishops and ministers devote much time in their attempts to interpret worldliness and enforce the norms. Briefly stated, however, separation implies not mixing with "worldly people" and not adopting "worldly practices."

One of the goals of the Old Colony which occupies much of the energy and time of the members is getting the youth to join the Church. To the outsider there seems undue anxiety about this matter, for it would appear that since the Old Colony is a complete society, a young person, Church member or not, would be an Old Colony member through kinship, economic ties, and socialization. It becomes clear upon further analysis, however, that the ultimate sanctioning power resides in the Church, which can excommunicate and ban members from the group. If any sizable number of young people should refrain from joining the Church, the excommunication function would lose its force, and religious appeals to conformity and obedience would become inoperative. The practice of parental or guardian sponsorship of application for Church membership for each neophyte suggests the anxiety surrounding the desire that each person will join the Church. Sponsorship carries two safeguards: if a youth does not evidence interest in joining the Church, the sponsor must exercise his legal role as admonisher; and if the sponsor himself shirks his duty, he is admonished. Church membership gains an added measure of support by virtue of its having been made a prerequisite for marriage. In the minds of some young people, this is the only justification for joining: "The young peo-

10. Material gathered by the author during field research.

ple are brought into the Church purely on the basis that they can not marry outside the Church. There are no other girls from which to choose, so the 'jig is up.'"[11]

Immediate goals, sometimes means to an end but often ends in themselves, are numerous. One such goal is productivity, valued as a means and an end. The concept of productivity ranges from the usefulness of everyday objects to the size of the Old Colony family: "The Church is officially against birth control. We are supposed to have large families, as many as the Lord gives us. But there are a few families who have not adhered to the ruling, some of whom have gotten into trouble for it."[12]

Although many outsiders feel that the Old Colony way of life is rigid and unpleasant, happiness and enjoyment are actively pursued goals, as evidenced by the pleasure sought in and derived from social relations. Sunday afternoons and holidays are occasions for friendly visits. Even during the work week, older couples often spend a whole day or several days visiting relatives or friends throughout the villages. The topics of discussion leave little doubt that the Old Colony people delight in humor and mirth. It is said by those having visited the Old Colony that it thrives on gossip and rumor, normally at the expense of fellow Old Colonists since they know no one else. It must be realized that for these people gossip and rumor serve as a source of entertainment, as the following example will illustrate: "Duerksen [one of the visitors present] said he had been gypped [by voting for the minister] because the new minister was now preaching against drinking and smoking. Friesen responded with: 'But he is preaching against drinking as such, not against drinking beer.'"[13]

MEANS

Human goals are achieved by "rules of action," by some normative orientation.[14] That is to say, goal-directed social

11. Material gathered by the author during field research.
12. Material gathered by the author during field research.
13. Material gathered by the author during field research.
14. See Talcott Parsons, *The Social System* (Glencoe, Ill.: The Free Press, 1951), p. 251.

behavior is controlled by a set of rules, "oughts" and "ought nots." For example, a complex set of limitations upon thought and action resulted in the development of the Old Colony way of life. There is now an elaborate system of prescribed means by which ends are to be realized in the Old Colony.

In the area of *beliefs,* a number of rules apply. It is considered very dangerous to doubt; in fact, it is undesirable to be too much concerned with beliefs: "One time I asked the bishop something about one of the seven churches mentioned in Revelation. He told me that I should read what I understood, and what I did not understand, I should leave alone." [15] This norm applies to all except the *Lehrdienst* (the ministers and bishops). The degree of enforcement for all others depends upon the "heretical" belief held. No rule is explicitly formulated; that is, the minister does not state from the pulpit that the laity should limit its reading and speculation to understandable sections of the Bible; but it is informally stated and widely understood, to the extent that there is strong emotional feeling regarding a deviant who is considered suspect.

Another limitation forbids the emotional expression of beliefs by all but the minister during the religious services. The laity expresses its beliefs through informal discussion, in singing, in reciting the catechism, in participating in the special services, such as communion, and in living the Old Colony life.

Belief, which is collective, incorporates faith in the Old Colony as the people of God. The *Lehrer* (individual minister) represents the needs and obligations of faith before God and in turn interprets and declares God's will to the congregation. Disbelief is regarded as a demon possession or a mental illness. Extreme disbelief results in excommunication.

The few prescribed patterns governing the expression of *sentiments* are also closely controlled. The most prevalent and least controlled form applies to informal visiting, the interaction in the village. Normal sentiments of day-to-day desires, hopes, and fears are easily communicated. The evening visit

15. Material gathered by the author during field research.

in the home, the chance meeting at the village store, the village meeting of the married men—all serve the expression of sentiment. The auction and other co-operative activities such as road maintenance serve communication of sentiment on a wider basis.

There are very explicit rules concerning communication between people of unlike status. Young people are not allowed to sit with the parents in discussions with neighbors. The oldest people present are shown deference, and their expressions are given most weight, even though they may be wrong. Women are given equal status when several families visit informally in the evening, but during more official visits, such as on a Sunday afternoon or when a minister is present, women are segregated from the men. Lay people may pay visits to ministers, but rarely do lay people visit the bishops. Ministers of course are expected to share problems with bishops.

Negative attitudes toward the Old Colony way of life, such as criticisms of the leadership and of village activities, may be expressed; but extreme negativity or antagonism is disapproved openly, sometimes to the point of social ostracism. In Hochfeld, a family that was extremely critical of and dissatisfied with the way others in the village were violating Old Colony norms was openly ridiculed and socially ostracized. Attitudes of disloyalty are condemned in the religious services as well.

Disloyalty is often curbed by the circulation of a rumor: "Things are never done in the open, for if they were, then the younger ones would overthrow the system. I had rubber tires on my Oliver until yesterday, but Dad and I decided we had better take them off. The rumors were beginning to buzz that the leaders were going to clamp down on me in several weeks if I did not conform. That is the way you always find out if you are supposed to be in the wrong." [16] Disloyalty in the form of deviation from the *Gemeent* evoked criticism from a faithful member of whom I asked help when my car broke down. His attitude toward a less

16. Material gathered by the author during field research.

loyal community member who chose to enjoy the convenience of a truck and electric lights was more than clear: "Yes, there are several who have trucks here, who are outside of our *Gemeent*. They like to drive very much. They will be more than tickled to help you. Here is Jacob Penner. He will be glad to help you. Look at his yard—all lit up. They are still up and around, whereas most other people are already in bed." [17]

The management of tension is similarly accomplished within a range of accepted behavior. Physical violence as a means of expressing feeling is disapproved, although it is practiced when hostility gets out of hand: "Peter Penner told of a fight he had had on the street of Hochfeld some time ago. A Franz Duerksen from Blumenhof, the traditional rival of Hochfeld, had wanted some money from Peter, which apparently he did not have coming. They came to blows and Peter walloped Duerksen so that some thought he was dead. Some people in Blumenhof had been very glad that Peter had done this and wished he had beaten Duerksen up much more." [18] This sort of violence is condemned by the *Lehrdienst*. Violence against Mexicans is less vehemently condemned, however; the Old Colony members are even known to have fired weapons at Mexicans.

Tension or hostility that emerges in the interaction in the village is managed ideally by reconciliation of the parties concerned. In normal day-to-day misunderstandings, the parties involved almost need to become reconciled because their paths cross so often that it is impossible to maintain hostility for very long. In cases where tension erupts between people of different villages, the deacons and ministers are called in to settle the matter. For an individual to appeal to the outside system of justice would be a severe misbehavior, perhaps resulting in excommunication.

The Old Colony *goals* can be achieved only by adhering rigidly to the *norms* that pertain. It is impossible to be in good standing in the Church while the norms are being violated. The main goals—salvation and realization of the Old Colony

17. Material gathered by the author during field research.
18. Material gathered by the author during field research.

way of life—can be reached only through adherence to Old Colony beliefs and practices, an increasingly difficult achievement. According to a bishop in Mexico, "At this point there are few activities which do not relate to farming among us, but the time may well come when we will mix more with the world. Just as the children of Israel were punished when they mixed and intermarried with the world, so God will punish us for being impure." [19]

From this excerpt it is clear that there are well-defined limitations on the means by which goals can be achieved. There is to be little deviance from established practices, since ultimate goals can be achieved only when the norms are not violated.

There are numerous character demands which are designed to help achieve ultimate goals. Honesty and integrity are two such demands. The Old Colony has been noted for its honesty and integrity, but the record is not spotless. A Mexican official states: "The morals of the Mennonites have shown a steady decline since they came here. The break comes between those that came here and those that were born here. The younger generation is not as honest and punctual in paying debts and the like. We have much more work here at the Presidencia [municipal office] than we used to. Ten or more years ago we never had a Mennonite in here, but now we have many who appear here. Often the Mennonites fail to pay on the date promised; they break contracts and misrepresent merchandise." [20] The Old Colony members are not blind to their shortcomings, any more than outsiders are. One member reflected: "The moral life of the Colony is not too good. There is a lot of lying and bribery, especially when hauling machinery from the United States. But the *Gemeent* does not like it and even last Sunday we heard from the pulpit that the machinery dealers should be honest in their dealings. Yes, there are even some who avoid coming to church so they will not become liable to the admonitions." [21]

19. Material gathered by the author during field research.
20. Material gathered by the author during field research.
21. Material gathered by the author during field research.

Among Old Colony people, violations of integrity and honesty are blamed on the way the Mexican political system operates. As one member related: "One time I was going to play it straight and declare everything I was bringing in from the U.S. At Kilometer 28 the officials wanted money, but I told them to show me what they wanted the money for, since I had declared everything and had paid duty on it. Then he tore into me and accused me of trying to starve them. He said, 'We want to be able to pass on illegal goods so you can pay us, for we cannot live on what we earn here.'" [22]

There are many norms which apply to the intermediate and immediate goals. Separation from the world is a goal that affects many aspects of community life. Interaction with "worldly" people is strictly forbidden. Marriage with outsiders is not allowed. Cars and trucks are forbidden because they would bring the world closer. Telephones and radios are forbidden for the same reason. Clothing is simple and austere, with styles and patterns closely regulated. The men wear clothing without such adornments as ties, belts, and jewelry. Women wear clothing which is dark and which prevents any exposure of the body. According to one Old Colony member, aware that clothes do not make the man, "The Old Colony is not all that it is supposed to be. Just because you wear a black shirt and no tie is no sign you are holy." [23]

The utilization of technology is carefully guarded. Living in Mexican towns or villages, especially in the conservative settlements, would be considered a serious violation. Owning a car or truck or tractor with rubber tires has occasioned excommunication. Use of refrigerators, lights, radios, and telephones is forbidden in the villages. But it is considered permissible to hire a car or truck owned by a Mexican in order to have some hauling done. Mexican products such as food and soft drinks, ice cream, and other things such as baskets can be purchased.

The Mexican Old Colony limitation on the use of technology is amply vindicated by observing what they maintain happens

---

22. Material gathered by the author during field research.
23. Material gathered by the author during field research.

to those who do adopt forbidden practices. When an Old Colony member buys a car, he soon begins to establish friendships elsewhere and eventually marries an outsider. When an Old Colony member buys a refrigerator or obtains electric lights he is proud of his achievements. There is thus a clear relationship, for the Old Colony member, between adoption of some technological practices and remaining a genuine Old Colony member.

The Old Colony establishes its attitude toward technology on several important premises. The first is the premise of being a "separate people." All beliefs are integrated by this principle. New artifacts, ideas, and practices are integrated or rejected by this principle. The logic is clear: What is the point of planning if the very corpus by which the planning is done will change?

A second important premise is that of perseverance. There is no point in trying to make progress, or to increase one's understanding of the world. God's will is for His people to be faithful to Him till the end. Fear of losing out in the struggle to remain faithful is an influential guidepost by which the understanding of the world of events and beliefs is gauged. The world, they say, is not getting better; it is, in fact, getting worse. There is nothing to be gained by becoming more modern or more conversant with the new. The ultimate decisions have been made, and faithfulness to these truths is what should motivate human aspiration.

Rules concerning the ranking of people dictate that there shall be no difference between the laity and the preachers. The preachers are the *Lehrer* but are otherwise not superior. There is to be no ranking of importance in village relationships, so that the cowherd and the *Anwohner* (landless tenants) should be on the same level with the landowner. In Canada the farmer, the day laborer, and the wealthy farmer should be ranked as equals.

Normally, rank has no reference to wealth but rather to piety and good will. To an observation made by the writer that wealth does make a difference in marriage patterns, a deacon replied, "Often the rich family has decided feelings about whom to marry, and this creates hard feelings. We do not like this. There should be no differences between families." Rank also determines eligibility for some positions to be filled by members. The bishop should be elected from the ministers. The village offices in Mexico are filled from the ranks of the older men who have proved themselves in local affairs. Young men are not given the status of full-fledged village fathers until they are married.

The regulations governing decision making are fairly similar in Canada and Mexico. The bishop and ministers are considered responsible for decisions relating to spiritual matters. The other officers, such as the *Vorsteher* (steward of Old Colony affairs), should take major problems of this sort to the bishop or ministers, rather than make decisions on their own.

The *Schult* (mayor) should call village meetings, and he is the one to whom complaints in village matters should be addressed. In Canada, the responsibilities of governing local affairs are being transferred to various public offices. The local schoolboard, often composed largely of non-Old Colony people, has the power to decide what curriculum will be followed and when school will start. In Mexico, the opening day of school, the schedule of classes, and the hiring of the teacher are all decided on by the village fathers.

As indicated earlier, the premises that underlie and determine the Old Colony's decisions are based upon biblical authority, but the Bible is not directly consulted in making decisions. Rather it is assumed that the traditions that have developed are just as significant a blueprint for understanding human experiences as are the abstract principles upon which the traditions are based.

The beliefs, sentiments, goals, and norms for the various settlements have been described as being quite similar. As will be seen later, however, the actual behavior patterns adopted to achieve these ends are quite different. The explanation for this phenomenon will be dealt with in later sections of the book.

Old Colony Personality Systems

Since this is a sociological analysis of the Old Colony, it is not possible or necessary to include a discussion of the "modal personality" of the Old Colony members. Describing a modal personality for a society is difficult because there is considerable haziness concerning the validity of the concept.[24] Providing a modal personality description is difficult in the Old Colony because Old Colonists are amazingly individual in spite of the rather homogeneous nature of the culture.

However, it may be useful for a fuller understanding of the Old Colony system to include several case studies of Old Colony members. These vignettes are not intended to illustrate the modal personality of the Old Colony, if indeed there is such, but rather to illustrate the diversity and individuality of typical Old Colony members.

LIFE HISTORY OF HENRY NEUFELD

Henry Neufeld was born in Canada in 1908 in the village of Hochfeld. He was the second child in a family that included three boys and three girls. When Henry was fifteen years old, his family migrated to Mexico and settled in the new village of Hochfeld. Though Henry did not have any choice in moving to Mexico, he thought it was a great adventure and remembers the trek very well. Henry recalls the tremendous hardship and near starvation of the first decade. His father had been quite wealthy in Manitoba but somehow was not able to make the transition and never became well-to-do in Mexico. Thus he could not bequeath much money to his children. When Henry was nineteen years old he began to pay especial attention to a vivacious girl in Hochfeld. Helena Dyck was the only daughter in a family of six children. She was Henry's second cousin. In 1928, when Henry was twenty years old, he married Helena. Since Helena's par-

24. Anthony F. C. Wallace, *Culture and Personality* (New York: Random House, Inc., 1961), pp. 109–11. The entire problem of portraying personality in societies is ably discussed in the chapter "The Cultural Distribution of Personality Characteristics," pp. 84–119.

ents were old and ready to retire, they moved into the "large room" and gave the rest of the house and the home farm to the new family. Helena's older brothers had all been safely established on farms by the Dycks, who were quite wealthy.

Henry and Helena have five children, the first one born a year after their marriage. They wanted a dozen, but were able to have only five, one of whom died at birth. Their oldest daughter has been married eight years and has five children.

The Neufelds have lived in the same place since they were married and are quite prosperous. Henry owns approximately five hundred acres of land, which is above the average by a considerable amount, though he has divided almost all of it among his children. Henry has been active in the life of Hochfeld, having been the *Schult,* the manager of the cheese factory, and the village clerk. At present he is the fire insurance secretary. Henry is considered one of the "fathers" of Hochfeld and is one of the main voices in local decisions. His status results partly from the fact that Helena belongs to the Dyck family, which is the most powerful family in Hochfeld. Her three brothers and their sons own about one half of the land in Hochfeld.

Henry does not conform completely to the norms. For example, he has electricity and a gas refrigerator in the house. This deviance is explained in part because Henry has been a professional machinery importer for many years. He has made as many as ten trips per year to the United States. He imports used machinery which he overhauls and sells at a profit. Often he spots bargains in home appliances, and thus he has not been able to resist the temptation to bring home a refrigerator and light plant for his farm home. The nature of his job has resulted in his learning English and becoming more sophisticated in "worldly affairs" than most people in the Old Colony. Henry likes to read and has read a number of books, most of them dealing with the history of the Mennonites in Russia and Canada.

Henry would like to live on a farm in Nebraska; of all the farm areas in the United States, he likes it best; and if he could, he would emigrate there. He would not go there alone, however. Only if the *Gemeent* would set up a settlement would he think of moving. He feels that the settlement in which he lives at present is a very undesirable place, from both an economic and a political standpoint, for he does not trust the Mexican government. He has consistently opposed the migration to British Honduras, for he knows enough about the climate and conditions to believe that it would be a fiasco.

Henry is sophisticated, but essentially he is a product of the Old Colony. He belongs to it and cannot conceive of belonging to any other group. He is loyal to the Old Colony, though he is too intelligent not to criticize it for many problems. He bows to the official position of the Old Colony and supports it in all its decisions. He does not entertain any doubts or animosities about the *Gemeent*. He chooses to stay with the Old Colony because he thinks it is right, because it is the only meaningful thing to do.

But let Henry speak for himself:

> When the Mennonites got here from Manitoba, they had to improvise everything for themselves. We could not afford to go to a doctor for everything, so we learned to do things ourselves. I have given the hypodermic needle to hundreds —no, thousands—of people. There were many epidemics when we first came here. It seems to have been caused by the shallow wells that were dug at first. Now we have deep wells with curbing so there is little disease anymore.
>
> We are not intimidated by the Mexicans. We have learned how to handle them. I have a gun and I would not hesitate shooting a Mexican in the hams if he bothered us. I would not like to be here if a revolution took place, but I think we could take care of ourselves. . . . I think the Catholic Church has made the Mexicans shiftless. They are not responsible as they should be.
>
> I have rubber on the front wheels of my tractors, but I am not supposed to have it. There is nothing wrong with rubber as such. There is nothing in the Bible that says rubber is wrong, but the thing it leads to is wrong. As soon as the tractors have rubber tires, the young fellows will get on them and drive them to Cuauhtemoc or other towns and get mixed up in all kinds of wrong. When the Old Colony in Canada first got rubber tires on their tractors, they would go to town

with people piled high on trailers, and would get terribly dirty—this was depraved behavior. The object is to keep the young people on the farm. Else they will run away. We believe farming is the only way of life. Our group would disperse if they did not stay on the farm.

I have only six years of school, as all the rest of the people do. I guess I ought to have more. But for farming it is not necessary to have much. I guess I should have more education so I could know more about my environment, about the country in which I live. I would like to do more traveling, but one needs more schooling for that.

In a sense it is true that we force our people to stay in the Colony, for if a person leaves he is considered an *"ungehorsamer Bruder"* and is not given a Church letter and is left pretty much to himself. Often somebody visits him, but he is, so to speak, given the ban of silence. No one is literally forced to stay, but he is made to feel uncomfortable, as if he has sinned and needs to come home to repent. . . . If our people got more training they would probably become so high-minded that they would not come back, but we want our young people to come and live among us.

The young people are beginning to want to sit in the driver's seat and are not satisfied with the way things are run. The old bishop is too old to take an active part in Church affairs, but will veto anything of an innovation. There is no hope of electing a new bishop in the near future, for the old one would not work with anyone. So the matter is left to lie until he dies. Sooner or later the break with the past must come. It seems to be in times of emergency or lack of alternatives that concessions are made. It is not considered permissible for a brother to go along with a worldling [in a vehicle], at least in Canada before we moved. But when the Old Colony moved to Mexico, in the scramble to get moved, many of necessity availed themselves of the use of cars driven by worldlings. The use of rubber tires on wagons was considered wrong until their use became necessary on account of the hard ground over which all the produce had to be hauled. And so it goes with all things that are considered worldly.

Reimer has been out of the *Gemeent* several times for a week or so until he repented and promised he would quit drinking. But soon he would begin again. The *Gemeent* does nothing about it, only throws him out if someone complains.

Better they would work with problems like this than with rubber tires.[25]

LIFE HISTORY OF PETER FRIESEN

Peter Friesen belongs to the more recent generation, having been born in 1923, the third child in a family of six. Peter was born the first year after his family moved to Mexico. Peter's parents moved around quite a bit, having lived in at least five villages before Peter married. Since Peter married (at the age of twenty-one), he and his family have lived in Hochfeld, moved to Ontario, lived in Oklahoma, lived in Hochfeld again, moved to another village, and at present live in Hochfeld. Peter operated a store in Hochfeld for three years. Later he operated a welding shop, and more recently he has engaged in implement importation from the United States. Peter's parents-in-law and his family moved to Ontario when there was a sporadic migration from Mexico to an area in northern Ontario. This migration was not officially sanctioned by the Old Colony Church; those who left for Ontario were deviants. When things did not develop in Ontario as had been hoped, they gave up their holdings at considerable loss and left Canada. Peter's parents-in-law returned directly to Mexico, while Peter and his wife and four children went to work for a farmer in Oklahoma. The farmer wanted Peter to remain permanently; but since Peter knew he was working in the United States illegally, he stayed only long enough to pay for a new car. Upon their return to Mexico, they decided to make a trip to British Honduras to see what conditions were like there in the new Old Colony settlement. They did not like it and returned to Hochfeld, where Peter is now specializing in importing light plants and selling them at a sizable profit to Old Colonists. The light plant is not completely forbidden by the Old Colony Church: the *Gemeent* allows light plants to be used for lighting chicken barns and for providing power for machine shops and for general utility. Thus Peter's occupation is marginal, since he

25. Material gathered by the author during field research.

sells many plants that are used for lighting homes, which is clearly forbidden.

Peter is quite uninvolved in the life of the *Gemeent*. He attends church normally only on communion Sunday or on special occasions. His life is not regulated by *Gemeent* policy, as will be seen by his attitude on birth control, for example. Peter knows many Mexicans and is involved in many business deals with them. Peter knows English and Spanish very well. Peter is in a sense a marginal person. He lives and belongs in the Old Colony, but he has a mixed set of objectives and values. He likes American things, such as cars and radios; he likes to hunt; he would like to become well-to-do and retire. He enjoys comfort and solitude, and he does not allow himself to be pushed around by anyone. He believes that it is impossible to live exactly like an Old Colonist and still enjoy life. He continually chafes under the restriction against owning a car. Peter would like to live in a rural community in the United States, but he does not know where. He thinks he would like to live in a community of more sophisticated Mennonites, but he does not know whether he and his family could make the cultural transition.

Again, let Peter Friesen speak for himself:

> Once you have owned a car and have been able to run around at free will, it is difficult to settle down to the life here in the Colony. The principle about cars is that you are allowed to own one when you are traveling outside the Colony, but when you settle in the Colony you must sell your car. The reason we did not stay in Oklahoma was the *Gemeent*. It was the problem of communion and baptism of the children that helped us decide to return. My brother has been in California for quite a while. He was doing well and apparently was on the way to getting his papers. He worked a long time for the permission to enter the United States and apply for citizenship. Now he is coming back. He is coming back since they do not consider any other Mennonite Church where they could fit in, so they feel they have to return here. . . . When the new applicants for membership take catechism, they have to promise that they will stay true to the

Old Colony Church, or when they leave, to migrate to an Old Colony-sponsored settlement. It is hard to break this promise.

I am looking forward to the geese hunting season. If the Americans do not come to spoil it, we can get a lot of geese. About twelve geese make enough feathers for one pillow, which sells for about 160 pesos. I will need to smuggle a gun across before the season starts. You are supposed to get a license, but we do not bother with it. Sometimes when they catch us, they take our guns away. Normally they will take a bribe, and the police compete for the money, so they have rivalries among themselves. . . . I have traveled thousands of miles in the United States. I have only had to pay speed fines twice, once when I was speeding and once when I jumped a stop light.

I wish we could have buried several of our children. [This was said with the children present.] Two or three is not bad, but when it is five, then it is too much. The time for large families is over. [To this the mother-in-law replied, "But that is nothing compared to the families we used to have. I have suffered all my life because of having been the oldest in a large family. I am the oldest girl in a family of fifteen, and we children practically had to raise the family ourselves. I had to work so hard raising the children below me that I have a nervous condition, especially in my left hand."] We have lived for thirty-five years in Mexico and are tired of it. If we could we would move away from here as fast as possible. . . . The Church is officially against birth control. But there are some who are not adhering to the ruling and have gotten into trouble for it. There is a couple, good friends of ours, who have a very rough time, because she is an epileptic. She is pregnant all the time, and when she is pregnant has the epileptic seizures almost continually. The doctor has been warning them for a long time she could easily die from shock. He says he has the pills so all they need to do is agree and he can prevent further pregnancies for a number of years. So the couple went to the bishop and asked for permission. The bishop said no. The health of the woman was in danger, but much more dangerous was that "they would murder many souls by preventing them from being born." He said, "You are responsible for every soul which you kill." There are an increasing number of younger couples who are learning more about the process and how to prevent births. There are some who are practicing it in open defiance of the Church. We do not feel it is right to practice sex as it is being done in the Colony. The usual practice is to behave like an animal, namely, when you are in bed with a woman, to discharge yourself and not concern yourself about the woman or any implications. I do not believe this. The woman is human and deserves consideration. We do not like large families. The more children you have, the more there are to get into fights and give you headaches. Our children are fighting all the time, and we have to be bossing continually.

I like to import implements by myself, because then I can get all the profits. One time when I had a Mexican along I found a good bargain in a threshing machine, but I could not load it. So I intended to pick it up on the next trip. But this Mexican went to some other Mennonite and told him about it and they went and got it before I could return. You cannot trust the Mexicans or the Mennonites when it comes to business dealings. Mexicans especially are deceitful. They are born dishonest. A Mexican doctor said that you have to be careful where you lay the scissors after you have cut the umbilical cord of the baby, for the little devil will steal it if you do not hide it. At first the Mennonites were honest when they declared their goods when crossing the border, but the Mexican officials bawled them out and told them to use their heads, since they only stood to lose if they were honest. The officials said, "Smuggle whatever you like, for we like to be able to overlook some things which you are taking in, so we can take money as a price." The officials have told me this numerous times.

Trucking is difficult; it causes a lot of worry and a man with weak nerves cannot take it. That is why Kroeker quit. He cannot take the war of nerves when crossing the border. The Mexicans intentionally try to scare people into either not crossing or paying dearly for the privilege. There is corruption in the government from top to bottom. Another example of how one is forced into being dishonest is the following: When my brother and I started up the store here in Hochfeld, we had about 60,000 pesos of inventory. We had to go to Cuauhtemoc to register stock for income tax purpose. We told the clerk in charge exactly what we had and he blew his top. He asked whether we were crazy and said that it was impossible to make a living if we declared full value, since the income tax for that amount would eat up the business. "You do not have more than 8,000 pesos of stock. That is how you should report it." He of course took some money for this. Then some time later a man came to our store and looked at the stock and was shocked to learn we had declared only 8,000 pesos. He said this would become a court case, but he let it be known that for a couple of hundred pesos everything would be in order. So we paid it again.

A shocking practice is cutting across fields when traveling from one village to another. This whole area is crisscrossed with these trails, which have been here from the time the area was settled. They cut right across nice fields and deprive many a farmer of land. There is not much that can be done about it. It seems the philosophy is that the common good is more important than the individual. It also happens that the one who protests a trail across his fields will very naturally cut across someone else's field. There is one way that a stop can be made and that is to get an official order prohibiting travel across fields, which can be obtained from the Mexican municipal offices, but few want to go to that trouble. The *Gemeent* is silent about the problem, in one sense feeling that it is good that short cuts can be made, for travel by buggy is long the way it is, and secondly it is best to let a sleeping dog lie, for to raise such an issue would be a real troublemaker in the Church, for it would raise the issue of travel and its inconveniences.

Several weeks ago I finally had to mete out some justice. Blumenhof has always given Hochfeld a lot of trouble. There is always warfare between the young people of Blumenhof and Hochfeld. An old friend of mine, Cornelius Dyck, loaned me some money one time. I paid it back to his wife because he was not home at the time. Some time later he came to me and wanted the money, but I told him I had repaid him and showed him the check receipt. He went away grumbling. Then several weeks ago I was walking down the street [the main road of the village] when Dyck stopped me. He was in a buggy and had a friend with him. Dyck said he wanted that money. Then I got mad and told him he should never mention that money again. So he got out of the buggy and slapped my face. I warned him that if he did not stop he would end up in poor shape. He kept slapping and boxing me so I finally let him have it. I knocked him out. His companion came to his rescue and took him off to Blumenhof.[26]

26. Material gathered by the author during field research.

Chapter 3

THE ORGANIZATION OF
THE PEOPLE OF GOD

If the Old Colony is to realize its beliefs, values, and norms, some aspects of daily life must be integrated and managed. The interrelated sets of norms that deal systematically with solutions to recurrent human problems such as religious behavior, provisions for subsistence, and reproduction are termed institutions. Not all norms in a culture are organized around a recurrent general need, but many are. It is to these important clusters of norms that we now turn.

Religion

The Mennonite ethnic minority emerged as a result of a religious conflict with Catholic and Reformation Churches over the question of restitution of the "pure Church."[1] The differentiation of the Old Colony group was based on the development of a frame of mind which conflicted with the larger Mennonite society, as shown above. This conflict was presumed to be entirely religious; but as pointed out earlier, it was predominantly the development of an ethnic group consciousness based on certain symbolic and behavioral patterns that produced the Old Colony.

Nevertheless, the Old Colony ethnic minority is centered to a large extent around the religious impulse. As we have seen, the ultimate reason for being an Old Colony member is the need of being in God's favor. Membership in the Old Colony *Gemeent* is considered a primary requisite for belonging to the Old Colony. The process of becoming a member is uniform in the Old Colony settlements: when a young person is able

1. See Franklin H. Littell, "The Anabaptist Concept of the Church," in Guy F. Hershberger (ed.), *The Recovery of the Anabaptist Vision* (Scottdale, Pa.: Mennonite Publishing House, 1957), pp. 119–34; see also Franklin H. Littell, *Anabaptist View of the Church* (American Society of Church History, 1952).

to feel and understand the need for and desirability of becoming a church member, he is given a sponsor who in-
forms the *Lehrdienst* of the youth's readiness for membership.

Usually the prospective church member applies for church
membership when he is ready to marry, the impetus being
the requirement that a person must be a member of the
Church before the marriage ceremony can be performed. Only
in cases in which the applicant will probably not marry is
the desire for admission motivated primarily by religious
concerns.

After the sponsor's announcement to the *Lehrdienst,* the
applicant joins the catechism class. Taught by a minister, the
applicants study a confession of faith, which has taken the
form of a series of questions and answers. (See Appendix F.)
When the applicants have sufficiently "understood" the catechism, they are presented to the congregation on a Sunday
morning. The minister asks them to rise and answer in
order the questions studied in class.

The object of the ceremony for the applicant is to recite his
answers flawlessly. For the congregation, the object is to see
how well the applicants have learned their catechism. "The
saying of the catechism is the very important event. It is the
thing the young people dread most. Most young people
memorize it by rote, not knowing what is going on as far
as meaning is concerned." [2] The baptismal service follows
the completion of the catechism.

Membership in the Church requires attendance at the
Sunday services, which can last from two to five hours. (One
service in the summer of 1964 in Kronsthal [Mexico colony]
lasted from 8:00 A.M. until 1:30 P.M. The occasion was the
first sermon of the newly elected bishop.) The members ride
to church by horse and buggy except in Manitoba and
Saskatchewan, where cars are allowed. There is usually one
centrally located church building for about four to six villages.
(See Figures 2 and 3 for exterior of church building.)

The members enter the church building in silence and with
bowed heads. At a certain point, when it appears all the

2. Material gathered by the author during field research.

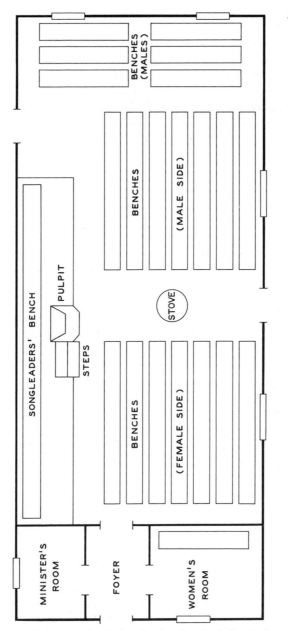

Chart 1. Drawing of a church interior in the Manitoba Settlement, Mexico

members who will be attending that day have arrived, the *Vorsinger* (songleaders numbering six to eight) march in from the anteroom and seat themselves on the *Vorsinger* bench. (See Chart 1 for interior of church building.) The leader of the *Vorsinger* announces a song and leads the *Vorsinger* group in starting the song. Slowly members in the audience begin to sing.

An old *Gesangbuch,* without musical score, is used; the melodies are sung from memory. There are about two dozen basic songs of Reformation derivation which are correlated with the various groups of verses. The songs are sung extremely slowly, so that one verse normally takes from three to four minutes. After about twenty minutes of singing, six or eight verses from a song having as many as fifteen verses, the *Vorsinger* stop.

After a few minutes of silence, the ministers walk in from the anteroom and take their places. The minister for the morning moves to the pulpit and begins to read his sermon. All sermons are read from small black notebooks. Because sermons are collected and handed down from one generation to another and are rarely composed by the ministers delivering them, sermon books are carefully distributed to the ministers after a minister dies.

The sermon is punctuated by several pauses during which the audience is told to kneel for silent prayer. The people turn and kneel, with heads on the benches. The first section of the sermon normally consists of a lesson from the Old Testament. The second section, delivered after a prayer, deals with a parallel passage from the New Testament. At the end of the sermon, the *Vorsinger* lead in a closing song, and the members rapidly file out. A church service in the Manitoba settlement has been described as follows:

> Dozens of faces turned toward the south door as I opened it cautiously and looked for an empty space. With no usher to show one to the proper place, I took the nearest seat, which was in the back row at the entrance end. Later I noticed that it was not unusual for a latecomer to walk between two full rows to arrive at an empty seat at the far side, close to the "men's side." The bashful women evidently found it

more proper to fill in their side as far away from the men as possible, thus leaving empty seats at a very inconvenient place for latecomers.

The three front rows on the women's side were filled by round-shouldered older women wearing black kerchiefs with beautiful floral borders. Their dresses were also of a dark color and were of a heavy material that made coats unnecessary. The younger girls, hair frizzed, sat on the three back rows, in sharp contrast to the black-hooded mothers and grandmothers. A few light-colored kerchiefs were scattered throughout. The young girls wore nothing on their heads. Their faces were pale without make-up, but I could imagine that in several months the summer outdoor work would make them appear robust. No skinny girls in this crowd. I missed the squalling youngsters and found later that Bible lessons were held for them in an adjoining building. And the very small ones must have stayed at home.

The absence of children is one factor that makes the service still and reverent.[3] There was no whispering among the girls or women. (I can report only on the female side of the audience since my seat did not allow me to see or hear the men.) They sat close together, rather slumped, and did not seem to look directly toward the front where the *Vorsinger* sat. These five men who led the singing came in from a side room and marched to their places on the left side of the platform and pulpit. The leader announced their numbers and led out in a loud, nasal, most unmusical tone. Everyone had a songbook which was brought in a carrying case. These five men sang heartily; I could hear only a few other voices, mostly men's. The girls did not participate, at least no lips were moving, but they did follow the songs through every one of the five to ten verses.

After two songs another door to the south opened and in strode the minister, dressed in black shirt and long black frock coat. His soft melodic voice was in sharp contrast to the nasal twangs of the *Vorsinger*. The minister appeared to

3. The stillness was as complete as the plainness of the interior of the building. The white walls and benches were spotless, and the only jarring note was a stovepipe, ugly black, running from the stove on our side to the ceiling and then along the ceiling toward the middle chimney. A similar stovepipe joined the chimney from the stove on the men's side.

deliver his sermon from notes but did not read it. He looked earnestly at his congregation as he delivered his mixture of High and Low German. The sermon was about forty-five minutes long and dealt with the various subjects of confession, conversion, life everlasting, and the last judgment. After some admonition to the young people especially to "make it right with God," he turned to the catechism, after which he again exhorted the young people to become converted—*bekeerri.* The service was punctuated with several brief prayers, the first one silent. I heard the word *bede,* and before the word was translated in my mind, the whole congregation was prostrate, faces flat on the benches. The silent prayer was soon ended with the minister's amen. The second time I was better prepared but then we only bowed our heads. The third time we again knelt.

The response to the minister's closing word was as prompt as to his call to prayer. The rows of women pushed toward the door, and since I was close to the aisle, there was no time for deliberation or observation. We marched, almost ran, to the outside where I thought surely they would stop to greet each other and talk. But the car motors were already running, and the people on their way home. I walked toward our car and, looking into the church windows, saw that some few men had remained.[4] The *Vorsinger* were especially evident from their perch on the platform. In the churchyard some dozen cars with few or no occupants waited for the after-service to break up. Fifteen minutes passed before the west door opened and the men marched out and into the waiting vehicles. The time was now almost eleven o'clock; two hours had passed since we entered the almost-full church building.[5]

4. This assemblage after the service was a *Bruderschaft* (a meeting of male members), held to discuss the new applicants for Church membership. There was a short admonitory talk by the minister in which he encouraged the brethren to make themselves available to the young people if they came for help, and then the prospective names of the candidates were requested. Fathers and various others gave the names, and the minister recorded them, listing the parents' names as well. The minister promised to make a personal visit to the applicants and urged the brethren to be of assistance where possible. The group knelt in prayer and then was dismissed.

5. Account prepared for this publication by Mrs. Calvin Redekop.

The religious ceremonies which express the beliefs, values, and norms of the Old Colony include not only the regular church services held on Sunday mornings but also the communion services and the Easter, Christmas, and Thanksgiving services. The latter are called "rites of intensification," since they serve to renew faith in and dedication to the sacred world. The communion services are conducted twice a year, once at Pentecost and once in the fall. All members are supposed to attend to demonstrate their basic commitment to the Church. Those who have been excommunicated or who voluntarily refrain from attending are under censure and are dealt with.

The other intensification services such as Easter and Christmas are characterized by "double holidays," or two days of cessation from work, a feature now disappearing from Manitoba and Saskatchewan. In the other settlements a church service is held on the first day; the second is reserved for family gatherings and visiting. Christmas holidays probably are the most festive occasions for revels and sprees, with heavy drinking reported from time to time.

The religious activities of a society are directed and conducted by persons who have been assigned to the institutional offices. The Old Colony religious offices are few in number but heavily loaded with authority and meaning.

The bishop, who is elected from among the ministers by the Church membership, is the leader of the Old Colony. He alone can administer the rites of communion and baptism, although ministers can conduct marriage ceremonies. The bishop carries the responsibility of seeing that the Old Colony remains true to the sacred objectives, though the ministers, of course, are equally concerned. The bishop is in a very ambiguous position in relation to the membership: the Old Colony member realizes the necessity of the bishop as an "office" to hold the Old Colony to its objectives, but there is often great hostility and aversion to the office as embodied in the person:

The Bishop wants us to have little if anything to do with the world. We are not supposed to read anything besides the

Bible and the *Martyrs Mirror*. We should not even read the *Steinbach Post*. He does not read anything and remains intentionally aloof from anything that happens outside the Colony. He will not ride in a car and would like us to avoid it too, but for that he does not have enough power and does not know how much we depend upon automobiles. He is quite inconsistent though, for he takes a bus when he travels to the other settlements. But when he returns and there is no buggy or wagon in town in which he can go home, he will rather walk than ride in a car and has done this on occasion.[6]

The ministers are elected by ballot at a special *Bruderschaft*. Any brother in good standing is eligible to vote and hold office. The minister's role includes preaching to and exhorting the membership during church services, performing weddings and funerals, conducting catechism, dealing with disciplinary problems at *Dunnadagh* (described below), and carrying out personal counseling and visitations. Ministers and the bishop are self-supporting farmers who perform their work without remuneration. One bishop reported spending as much as 90 per cent of his time in church work and carrying much of the travel expense himself.

The *Vorsteher* (overseer) is elected in a manner similar to the minister. He is to be of high integrity and character. His job is to take care of all official Church matters within and beyond his community. When a new area is to be settled, he negotiates for the land, takes care of the legal matters, and arranges for the payment of the money. Within the community he arranges for the collection of money to buy the land, organizes the allocation of land parcels, and supervises the settlement. Other duties include collection of money for any relief given to a sister or daughter colony and the collection of taxes demanded by the state (except in Manitoba and Saskatchewan, where farmers are individually responsible).

In addition to other officers, each plan (see Table 1-1 for a listing of all plans and their dates of settlement) has several deacons elected by the membership. Deacons and ministers are often elected at the same meeting, the one with fewer

6. Material gathered by the author during field research.

votes being elected deacon. Deacons are commissioned to look after the material and social welfare of the members. Instances of hardship are referred to them.

My job as deacon takes quite a bit of time. Many people come to me with their problems, and I have to try to iron them out. Mostly they concern hardship, such as sickness and poverty. Theoretically, everyone who wants help should come to me first, but in practice, many go to the hospital or doctor in Chihuahua, for example, and pay for the bills and then come to me for reimbursement. This is not too good, for first I can usually get a cheaper rate if the hospital knows it is a charity case. Secondly, there are cases where the recipient uses the money for something else, which is not desirable, so we do not want to give anybody cash. I have accounts at several places, such as the San Antonio *Drogeria* where the needy can pick up their items and the proprietor then sends me the bill and I pay. Most are legitimate cases, but once in a while there is a person who can pay or who uses the help for the wrong purposes.[7]

Deacons have some funds available from the so-called alms fund, and in cases of great emergency they can appeal to the Church members to give money to help. An earlier practice of collecting several bushels of wheat from every family and storing it above the church meeting room until needed by poverty- or misfortune-stricken families has been abandoned, though the poor remain:

It is said that there are quite a few Mennonite families who are quite poor. There are also some beggar families. A man, wife, and eight year old daughter appeared on the yard and asked if Dycks did not have some grapes, apples, vegetables, or meat to sell. They stayed quite a while, focusing their interest on whatever they thought they might get for nothing. Mrs. Dyck gave them some fruit, vegetables, and other things. They offered to pay, but it was clear that they did not intend to do so. Upon leaving they asked of other places where certain things could be "bought." The entire Dyck family and several neighbors laughed heartily, so that the family could have heard it as they were leaving. This family was well

7. Material gathered by the author during field research.

known in the entire colony. They lived in Campo 72, but traveled all over the valley, staying where they were asked, and accepted whatever was given to them. They are reported to be lazy and temperamental.[8]

The *Waisenamt* is an important organization which has been alluded to above at several points.[9] It is a type of trust organization which manages the estates and funds of orphans, widows, and elderly people, and which loans money to individuals for various purposes. Its officers, the most highly respected and trusted men in the Old Colony, the *Waisenmänner,* are men elected to serve as the trustees of the funds and records. They must act impartially in the settlements of estates and inheritances and must concern themselves with the collection of borrowed money and other such duties. Even though the *Waisenamt* has economic functions, it is derived from the biblical command to be concerned about the widows and the fatherless.

The *Waisenamt* is an effective and efficient organization. It has provided for a competent and peaceful settlement of many estates and has taken care of many financial problems. In a letter to the Manitoban government appealing for exemption from the provincial school attendance, the following paragraph appeared: "We work together in the normal activities and work responsibilities; we help each other in that we seek the material well being of each other; we assist all those who want to become self-reliant and independent. We have our own savings and trustee system—the *Waisenamt.* The trustees receive the members' monies and loan it to others, giving 5 per cent interest and receiving 6 per cent. We trust the integrity of the borrower, and we are happy to tell you that we have not had any losses so far." [10]

The administrative and disciplinary affairs of the Old Colony sacred world are conducted at the *Dunnadagh* (Thursday,

---

8. Material gathered by the author during field research.

9. See J. Winfield Fretz, *Mennonite Colonization in Mexico* (Akron, Pa.: Mennonite Central Committee, 1945), pp. 28–29, for a full description of the *Waisenamt.*

10. Material gathered by the author during field research.

literally "day of thunder" in the Low German) meetings held every other week. Here various decisions are reached by the *Lehrdienst* which have to do with the administration of the *Gemeent*. Here also the recalcitrant member is summoned to appear before the *Lehrdienst* to answer charges of laxness or disobedience. "When the leaders heard that I was driving a car and a truck and rubber-tired tractors, they called me to account at *Dunnadagh*. They told me the crawler was o.k., but not the cars or trucks. Further, the bigger offense was working for a *Weltmensch* ['worldling']. I had to quit the job, and then was allowed to come back in." [11]

Problems of disobedience or defiance that concern the Old Colony at large are discussed and implemented in the *Bruderschaft*.

> The most powerful people in the *Gemeent* are the *Vorsteher* and the preachers, with the bishop as the supreme authority. They feel it is their job to hold the *Gemeent* where it is, or try to keep it to its decisions that have been made earlier. Many times we know that things would be changed if this group let it become a popular topic or let them vote on it; but to avoid this, they simply do not call a *Browdaschaft* [Low German for *Bruderschaft*] to discuss it. When a *Browdaschaft* is called, the issues are frankly discussed and the average layman often speaks his mind. But the crucial matter is to have a *Browdaschaft* called, which only the *Lehrdienst* can do.[12]

Despite the existence of individuals and organizations who control Old Colony religious life, not all community members can be kept in line. Deviancy is controlled in the Old Colony society by excommunication and the ban. When a deviant has appeared before the *Lehrdienst* at a *Dunnadagh* and is not successfully rehabilitated, he is excommunicated. This punitive action is designed to bring him back to his senses and help him to submit to the religious and social behavior patterns, though it does not always work. Excommunication is normally accompanied by the ban, which involves complete avoidance of

---

11. Material gathered by the author during field research.
12. Material gathered by the author during field research.

the person—socially, economically, and of course religiously. Theoretically the ban involves even the avoidance of contact between husband and wife, but this is rarely achieved in practice. The ban is imposed when it becomes apparent that excommunication is not proving effective in bringing the deviant to repentance. Persons who ignore the ban and associate with the banned person are severely reprimanded and on occasion themselves excommunicated.

The continuing ban of a person who does not recant is still practiced in Mexico, but in Manitoba and Saskatchewan it has not been applied for many years. Very few persons remain under the ban very long. There are a few who have been under the ban and have managed to remain in the settlement, banding together to give each other support.

The Family

The family is still a strong unit of the Old Colony social structure, as it is in other traditional societies. The families are large, with an average of eight children per family in Canada and nine per family in Mexico. Families with fifteen children are common. One family known to the author has thirty-five children, a combination of the children of a widower, a widow, and their joint offspring. Large families are considered to be the will of God. One mother of seventeen said, "We have as many children as God gives us. We accept what God decides." [13]

The father, provider and spokesman, is the head of the home. During visits with neighbors or relatives, the fathers eat first and are served by the wives and daughters. They then retire to the *groti Schtov* (living room) to visit while the women and children eat and clean up. The husband can expect respect and obedience, support and encouragement, from his wife; he also expects that she will meet his physical needs, from preparing his food to washing his clothes to providing sexual gratification, the latter without consideration for

13. Material gathered by the author during field research.

her wishes or regard for the extent to which a pregnancy may have progressed.

The father's obligations include the conventional responsibilities prevalent in Western society. He is responsible for making available in adequate supply to his family all the material provisions for sustenance. In so doing, he can expect the help of all male offspring, until they marry and go out on their own, in farm work and economic transactions. A father is proud if he produces male offspring, particularly in large numbers, and envious of others if he does not. The economic advantages are as great as the emotional ones: "He will be a good farmer with all those boys growing up."

The wife is conservatively dressed with regard both to fabric and design of clothes and to the extent of body exposure. Her hair is long and braided; her head is covered except on the hottest summer days. The woman is a hard worker. She must take care of the garden, though the males in the family will cultivate and plow the ground; and she is obliged to help with the farm chores during the harvest and during her husband's absence. Her daughters are very useful to her, for they are responsible for many housekeeping chores.

Except in Manitoba and Saskatchewan, the wife must perform all household duties with the most meager facilities and work without the aid of running water, electricity, and refrigeration. Washing is done by hand. All the food that is preserved for winter must be canned in the old-fashioned way. Meat is preserved by smoking and salting. Bread, jam, and butter are made at home, as is soap.

The nature of the woman's work offers one kind of limitation; attitudes toward the woman result in other limitations on her freedom. Although ministers forbid the use of alcohol, tobacco, and crude language for all Old Colony members, only the woman is bound to observe the rules which are stretched for the male because of his superior authority.

The role of the child carries with it the obligation of complete obedience to parents. The Old Colony youth must request permission for any activity which involves leaving the farm. Until they are married, children cannot sit in the living room while visitors are present. They do not have any money of their own, since they work for their parents or give them any money made elsewhere. The range of things the youth could buy with money is so limited that money would be of little use anyhow. In Mexico the average Old Colony youth probably owns a flashlight, a wristwatch, a knife, and small miscellaneous items. A girl owns few luxury items but begins early to collect things for her hope chest.

Male children can expect some assistance in getting started on a farm when they marry. They are able to borrow machinery and tools, as well as money, to get set up in business. Daughters can expect a dowry which may include several cows, money, or even some land.

The Old Colony family is a semi-extended family. Often the married children live with the parents until they find a place of their own. Often the youngest married child, especially if he is a male, lives with his parents until they retire. After retirement many parents live out their remaining days with their children, usually giving their home to the children with whom they will stay in return for the care the children will provide. The other children in the family have been given their share of the inheritance, which is often handled by the *Waisenamt.*

Grandparents, providers of advice and knowledge of the past, are treated with respect and reverence. They can expect to be cared for by the children as long as they live. Except in Manitoba and Saskatchewan, grandparents are never sent off to old people's homes. Since they have served the Old Colony earlier in life, later they may reap the benefits of their labors. The most important obligation the grandparent has is to give affection and attention to his grandchildren.

In courtship the male takes the initiative. Courting begins in a group context. Groups of boys spend most of their evenings visiting in the village street. (See Chart 2 for a diagram of a typical village.) Girls also assemble in groups and visit in the streets. When a fellow becomes interested in a certain girl, his peer group's interaction with the group of girls allows him to talk with the girl he likes.

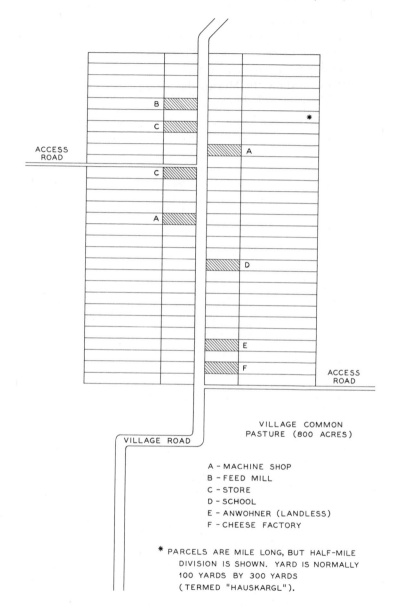

Chart 2. Schematic drawing of a typical Old Colony village

Then soon you are able to arrange to see her alone somewhere and then the personal courting starts. When you are interested in a girl, you just let the talk go around that you are interested in a certain girl and the informal gossip takes care of the rest. The girls do the same thing, and we fellows soon know who is interested in whom. When you are seriously interested in seeing a girl, you go to her home and visit with her in the house. The parents will not allow you to take her out in a buggy. Not until you are engaged are you allowed to go out together. After you are engaged, then you can do what you want to, since you are getting married soon anyhow.[14]

Occupational choices are very limited for the Old Colony family. As indicated earlier, farming has been considered the only real way to achieve the objectives of the Old Colony way of life; thus, the role most Old Colony young men assume is that of farmer. The extent to which this is true was in evidence in Hochfeld, Mexico, in 1964, where there were fifty-six family heads, one of whom was the schoolteacher, another the blacksmith, and a third the cowherd; the rest were farmers. The blacksmith was also a farmer, owning 160 acres.

The conflict between the need to conform to the accepted occupation and the desire to try other things is illustrated in the following statement by an Old Colonist: "Many fellows are beginning to think of doing other things, such as Banman, who has started up a machine shop and is known for his good work. None of the farmers that started something on the side were good farmers. . . . There is truth to the suspicion that most of these men are hanging on to farming as a mark of their loyalty, but they really have their hearts in something else."[15]

The farmer's role demands that he manage the farm well. He needs to know the best farming methods (within the limitations of the total system). A successful farmer is one who is able to pay off debts, pay for his farm, keep things in order, and accrue more land which he can give to his children

14. Material gathered by the author during field research.
15. Material gathered by the author during field research.

so that they can get started on the farm. The Old Colony male's status is dependent upon his diligence in the one trade actually open to him.

The only occupational role for the Old Colony married woman is that of housewife. If a woman does not get married, she remains in the parental home, caring for her parents when they get older. She often becomes a house maid for another Old Colony family in need of help. If she is fortunate, she will marry a widower. The job of kitchen maid (*Kjiacschi*) is fairly popular for the girl before she marries, especially if she comes from a large family or if her family is poor and needs the income.

The only real relaxation, recreation, or social activity in which the Old Colony member engages is visiting with friends and relatives, sometimes in other villages. The family does go to church on Sunday mornings, although rarely does a whole family go at once—the buggies are not big enough! Sundays after dinner are spent in sleeping and visiting. The typical conversations focus on relatives, friends, migration, unusual experiences, weather, and farming. The most popular topic is other people in the Old Colony.

The School

The Old Colony is concerned with the socialization of its offspring, just as any society would be which considers its way of life worth preserving. Despite the presence of this common goal in each of the colonies, differences exist in the way formal education is conducted in the several colonies. In Manitoba and Saskatchewan, the Old Colony groups have acquiesced to the demands of the provincial department of education. By their decision to remain in Canada and come to terms with the demands of the state, they recognized that education was one of the areas in which adaptations were necessary.

Accordingly, since 1922 the Old Colony groups in Manitoba and Saskatchewan have agreed to send their children to the provincial schools, paid for by taxes levied by the municipality. They have agreed to submit their children to the provincially prescribed curriculum and procedures, as well as to the college- or university-trained teacher. To insulate their off-spring as much as possible from the secularizing and as-similating influences, they exercise their legal right to choose the teachers for their children.

The local schoolboard in an Old Colony village in Canada is composed almost entirely of Old Colony members. This board has the responsibility for building and maintaining the school grounds and buildings and for hiring and paying the schoolteachers. Almost invariably, the schoolboard hires a Mennonite schoolteacher who understands the Old Colony way of life or a non-Mennonite who is sympathetic to the Old Colony. In the six schools this author visited in Manitoba, all of the eight teachers were Mennonites, three belonging to the Mennonite Brethren Conference.[16] These teachers are retained and given good salary increases as an incentive to promote the Old Colony way of life.

In other settlements, the school system is vastly different. It is a traditionalized form of the school system as it existed in Russia, though in many ways it is a seriously degenerated form. The school system is under the direct supervision of the *Lehrdienst,* which places responsibility for its control in the hands of two ministers and the village *Schult,* who visit the schools yearly, unannounced. Informal communication in the villages provides the ministers information about any deviant forms of education that are being practiced in the schools. If a teacher is found guilty of deviancy, he is called before the *Dunnadagh,* referred to earlier.

> I have suggested that we change from this [inadequate material] to more story-like type of material, but have been rebuffed by the *Lehrdienst* and the *Gemeent.* It is a *Gemeent sach* [Church business matter] and they are the final arbiters. It would be impossible to introduce it on an experimental way in a *Darp* [Low German for *Dorf*], though there would

16. In some instances, the Mennonite teachers have used their positions to proselyte, thereby creating tension. When it was learned that a Mennonite Brethren teacher was having evening services in the school basement, the schoolboard went to check but apparently found nothing offensive, for they let him continue.

be many who would be friendly to the attempt. But the schools are under the strict supervision of the *Lehrdienst*. Every spring before school is out, each school is visited by two preachers and the *Darp Schult*. They listen to recitations and if they are adept, will themselves conduct some type of contest or exercise. Often they will have written exercises from the last year and they will compare them with this year's work to see if there has been any change.[17]

The school is built on village ground reserved for it when the village was laid out. This plot consists normally of about ten acres, on which the school, teacherage, garden, and little pasture for the cow or horse are situated. The school facilities are supplied and maintained by the village, administered through the *Schult* meeting. Thus, if a well is to be dug, the allocation of work is made at the *Schult* meeting (village council), in which one farmer will pledge the work of two Mexican laborers, another will send his son and some tools, and so on.

The administration of the schools is illustrated by the notes taken of a discussion at a *Schult* meeting concerning the beginning time for the school:

> Someone raised the question of when the school should start. Some thought the teacher should decree this. The teacher said he was only a servant, while another retorted that the servant could state under which conditions he would serve. Another said there were not enough to decide. Then the majority said that since the slip [announcing the school starting date] had gone around, the decision would have to be binding. Some wanted the school to begin this month; others felt they needed the children to pull beans, but they would be done by the last week of the month. It was left tentatively for the first Monday in November, but it was not a fast decision.[18]

The teacher is hired by the local village and is often a person who has interests other than farming. "The teacher is usually a person who cannot make a living in any other way and has

17. Material gathered by the author during field research.
18. Material gathered by the author during field research.

to be supported by the village," said one villager.[19] There are no female teachers, although often a teacher's wife will assist him.

The teacher receives a cash salary, approximately 12,000 pesos per year, which is equivalent to $1,000, and gifts of food and clothing from the village. The cash salary is raised from levying a tax on all the land in the village and a tax on all the children who attend school. These taxes are decided by the *Schult* meeting and collected by the village *Schult*. The teacher also has free pasture rights for his cattle, if he has any; and the crops on his ten acres are planted and harvested free of charge by the village farmers, who take turns in meeting this demand.

Classes are conducted five days a week for six months of the year. They normally commence early in November, depending upon harvesting conditions, and end in March. Then in May or June, again depending upon the local situation, classes are resumed for a month to finish out the school year. The hours are 7:30–10:30 A.M. and 1:00–4:00 P.M.

The student goes to school for six years. The variations from year to year are minimal, with limited development in terms of materials and subject matter. The three subjects taught are reading, writing, and arithmetic. The instruction materials consist of the following pieces: the primary spelling and reading book, which has been adapted from an old German primer (*Vibel*); the catechism used by the Church; and the Bible, both Old and New Testaments. The fourteen-page booklet contains the ABC's, exercises in pronunciation, the Lord's Prayer, the Confession of Faith, the Ten Commandments, and similar materials. (See Figures 6 and 7.)

All the classes follow a similar schedule for the day. The school day opens with prayer and song, followed by recitation of sections from the catechism, the Bible, and the arithmetic tables. Then follow reading, writing, and arithmetic. The day closes as it opens. Twice a week there are exercises in penmanship, letter writing, and letter reading.

The practice that is most surprising is that the classes all

19. Material gathered by the author during field research.

focus on a subject simultaneously, although on different levels. The individual and graded attention given in many American schools is missing, a fact which seriously limits student achievement. With an instructional system almost totally lacking in intellectual stimulation for the student, Old Colony members are poorly educated and have little, if any, intellectual curiosity.

The school is designed by the Old Colony *Lehrdienst* to provide only those skills necessary for useful service to the community. Many teachers, therefore, are frustrated by and eager to improve the quality of the schools:

> The teaching level in the colonies is pathetic. There are many schools in which the students know as much as the teacher. I make it a point to visit other schools, and at one school the teacher was saying that a certain word was capitalized because it was a noun. But the students said it could also not be capitalized, and so the argument ran. . . . There are some new students from some other villages in my classes this fall, and since some of the oldest students still do not know how to read or spell, I will need to start them with my first graders. I hate to do it, but what can you do? There are many who try to improve themselves, and I have had a number of teachers who come to me for help. I do what I can, but with the limited facilities that are allowed, I cannot do much. I have tried to use booklets printed in Germany which have pictures making the learning process much easier, but this is quickly forbidden and is called worldly. Anything with pictures or in booklet form is worldly. So I have been making copies on a typewriter and putting my own hand-drawn pictures in. Even this is considered worldly.[20]

Other teachers attack the attitude that what has been established by tradition should be acceptable for the present: "I have often said that our schools are far too low, but our *Ollash* [derogatory name for elders] cannot be convinced. They say we have gotten by for thirty years and can get by for thirty more. In a sense it is true, but they ought to know more than some of our people now do." [21] It is maintained

20. Material gathered by the author during field research.
21. Material gathered by the author during field research.

by some teachers that many of the Old Colony students never really learn to read and are "functionally illiterate." "The learning is by rote, where the child has to memorize the ABC's and then goes over into words, with no helps or guides whatever. It often happens that a child has learned to read well, but will not know half of what he is reading." [22] Whether the schools have been any more successful than others in handling behavioral problems is also questionable:

> Klassen had been a holy terror in school and had always gotten a black card reporting his work and deportment in school. But he decided to trick the teacher; so one week he behaved especially nice, so that with much arguing the teacher gave him a red report card. He took it home, and Monday morning he told the teacher he had lost the card. It was just the same, for from then on the teacher gave him black cards for his deportment, but did not know that the little scoundrel had not lost the red card at all, but was dutifully showing it to his father each week, who in turn could not understand what had happened to his son, but nevertheless was very proud of his sudden change.[23]

Attitudes toward education are mixed. In private, many Old Colony members confess their ignorance and their desire for more education; in public they are more self-satisfied:

> The two things that have made and kept us who we are, are the schools and the belief that farming is our responsibility. We feel that farming and higher education are not compatible. We feel our calling is to till the soil. This keeps us together and keeps us in the simple life. If the six years that we conduct are done well, the person learns all that he needs to farm and be successful at it. If he can learn to read, "figure" [*reaknen*] and read the Bible, he has all he needs, for farming need not be learned out of books. It can be learned by practicing. Look at how well the Mennonites have done here. They are being copied wholesale by the world. And this was not learned out of books, but through diligent work and practice.[24]

22. Material gathered by the author during field research.
23. Material gathered by the author during field research.
24. Material gathered by the author during field research.

Social Organization—The Village

The Old Colony religious and social units became separate entities on the basis of geographic differentiation. The Fort Vermilion group, for example, became autonomous when the first minister was sent, in 1936. The religious and social organization of this area thence became a self-conscious group, and though there has been exchange and visitation with other Old Colony entities, it is a separate body. The force that binds the groups together and provides for similarity in objectives and means of achieving these objectives is the ethnic nature of the Old Colony—the common heritage and common stance toward the world outside—a consciousness of peoplehood.

When a new area was settled, as for example in Mexico, the land was parceled off in 160-acre units. Though the number of units per village varied, usually there were twenty farms of 160 acres each. Then the village street was delineated. A plot was set aside for the school and for the church, if a church were to be placed in the particular village. A village cow pasture of two sections of land (1,280 acres) was set aside at one end of the village. Some reserve land for later population expansion was usually set aside, as well as a small acreage on one side of the village to be used for indigent families (*Anwohner*). (See Chart 2.)

Historically, Old Colony life has been synonymous with village life. Except for some farmers in Manitoba and Saskatchewan, and the Fort Vermilion settlement, all Old Colony members have lived in villages. The deviant pattern in Manitoba and Saskatchewan developed after the great migration to Mexico, when the social control was so disrupted that no *Lehrdienst* existed. The individual settlement type now found in the Fort Vermilion area resulted from the fact that land had to be bought from individual owners.

The basic farmstead unit of the village is the *Hauskörgl,* which consists of a uniform strip of land three hundred feet wide, extending from the village street back to the first kilometer line. The land behind the line was then divided into larger blocks and distributed to the farmers in such a way that no one got the best or the poorest land. A village farmstead of less than 160 acres is evidence that the owner has sold the land or divided it among his sons. If a farmer has more land, he has been able to increase his holdings through inheritance or fortunate farming operations.

Ownership of the land is semi-private, with the Old Colony *Gemeent* negotiating for the land, owning the title, and exercising final control of the land. If, for example, an Old Colonist in Mexico should try to sell his land to a Mexican, he would be swiftly dealt with by the *Lehrdienst.* The church ground and building belong to the Old Colony as a totality, though the villages that comprise the "parish" are responsible for the construction and maintenance of a church building. Offerings are held in all the churches of the settlement when a new church building is planned, so as to equalize and share the costs. The cow pasture and the school building are local village property, as is the road, which is the responsibility of all the farmers in the village. Each farmer must do his share of the *Shoavoak,* which is a stipulated amount of labor, and provide his share of horses and men. The road connecting the villages is *Gemeent* property. Maintenance of these roads is the responsibility of the villages which the road connects.

The officers of the village include the *Schult,* the village chief; the secretary; the *Brandschult,* fire insurance secretary; the teacher; and the cowherd. Any negotiations with the outside world are made through the *Schult.*

Then a letter from the President of Rubio was read by the *Schult.* It contained a request for 100 pesos for a bench in the park. If the *Darp* Hochfeld gave the 100 pesos, it could have its name imbedded in the bench. There was some discussion on it—what use a Mennonite *Darp* had for benches in the park in Rubio, why they could not pay for it themselves, why they had to continually milk the Mennonite villages and the like. The *Schult* stated that another village had a bench in the park. One said, "If they promise to keep their bums off our places at night, we will fill the whole park with benches." Another stated that if they would only keep the bandits off the farms during the day, they would be happy. Then one stated that it might be good for relations to buy a bench. But since the villagers were not all here, he should instruct the President that the response had been fairly favorable, but that it would take time and that he should wait till the next *Schult* meeting.[25]

In Mexico at present the *Schult* is elected for a two-year term and gets about thirty pesos a year for his services. He is the executor of village decisions and delegates all the necessary responsibilities. He calls for a *Schult* meeting by sending a note (*Zaddel*) around the village, which announces the meeting and instructs the reader to send it on to the next neighbor. The *Schult* is the official communication channel from the Church organization, as is illustrated in the records of a *Schult* meeting called in Hochfeld, October 13, 1958:

> The meeting was called because the *Gemeent* had decided to aid flood victims in the Torreon area. The decision had been made at the *Browdaschaft,* held Thursday, October 9. [The normal pattern for such an action as this is for the bishop to receive information of a disaster area by various methods and channels. Since the present bishop does not read any newspapers or other "worldly" communications, he has to depend upon letters written by his people who happen to be in the area, or from his Church members. In this case, the Old Colony settlement at Durango had sent the information. Sometimes a Mexican official appeals directly to the Mennonites. The *Browdaschaft* had approved the collecting of funds for the needy and had instructed the *Schults* to collect the money. It was voluntary; no one was forced to give anything, nor was it decreed what anyone should give.] Only about fourteen villagers showed up, which was less than a third of the total in the *Darp.* The *Schult* expressed some dissatisfaction at the turnout. There was no formal meeting, since all there knew what the purpose was. The *Schult* and his secretary sat at the table and took down the names and the amount of money that was given. Several asked what they should give. It was a personal matter, the *Schult* said, but he did say that a worker at the cheese factory had given thirty pesos. Then there was some discussion that

25. Material gathered by the author during field research.

the workers like that had more money and could afford more than the farmers. The matter of the money getting to its destination was discussed. Kroeker, the schoolteacher, was rather unhappy and wondered why they always had to send the money to Mexicans, which was a sure way of losing it. One said that they had sent money to the Governor of Chihuahua, and another then said, "The higher they stand, the greater is their crookedness." There was a suggestion that it be given to the Mennonite Central Committee [a relief agency of the Mennonite Church]. Then someone suggested that one of their own people might be sent down with the money. But nothing conclusive came out of the discussion, since apparently they could not do anything.[26]

The secretary's responsibility is to keep the records, to take the minutes of *Schult* meetings, and to be an adviser to the *Schult*. He is also to keep the records of all the marriages, births, and deaths in the village, as well as other vital statistics. His records are forwarded to the deacons, who keep a master list of all persons who are born, die, get married, join the Church, or leave the Colony.

The *Brandschult* is the secretary of the fire insurance association. Every village has a *Brandschult* who collects the "tax," decided on the basis of the past year's losses or gains, on the property of each farmer. This money is sent to the head *Brandschult* for the entire settlement, who keeps track of all the income and expense of each village and makes an annual report to the Old Colony. (See Table 3-1.) This form of mutual fire insurance originated in Russia, where every village was enrolled in a fire insurance system. There is no insurance for weather losses. The reasons given for this are that it would be trying to secure man against the acts of God and that it would be hard to administer.

The village cowherd is given a yearly sum, usually around 500 pesos, for caring for the village cattle. (The communal pasture has been disbanded in Manitoba, Saskatchewan, and Fort Vermilion.) He is also given the right to graze a number of cattle free on the village pasture. (The number varies,

26. Material gathered by the author during field research.

Figure 1. Village of Reinfeld, Manitoba, Canada

Figure 2. *An Old Colony church in Manitoba, Canada*

Figure 3. *An Old Colony church in the Manitoba Settlement, Mexico*

Figure 4. A traditional Old Colony house-barn in Manitoba, Canada

Figure 5. An Old Colony family in Mexico

Figure 6. A school in the Old Colony in the Manitoba Settlement, Mexico (photograph by Ken Hiebert, courtesy of Mennonite Life)

Figure 7. An Old Colony classroom (photograph by Rohn Engh)

Figure 9. The approach to an Old Colony village in Mexico (photograph by Rohn Engh)

Figure 10. An Old Colony religious leader and family

Figure 8. A Mexican Old Colony village (photograph by Rohn Engh)

Figure 11. The village leaders in Hochfeld, Manitoba Settlement, Mexico

though Hochfeld allowed the cowherd to graze eight head of cattle.)

Table 3-1   Insurance Statistics in Old Colony, Mexico (1957)

A. Village of Hochfeld, Manitoba Plan, Chihuahua, Mexico
   1. Total assessed valuation of property   1,102,170.00[a]
   2. Dues for one year in village   551.08

B. Entire Manitoba Plan, Chihuahua, Mexico
   1. Assessed valuation   14,437,861.00
   2. Dues for one year   23,238.01
   3. Expenditures   10,064.94
   4. Net gain   13,173.07

[a] In pesos.

Every spring morning, after the village *Schult* meeting has decided that the pasture is in shape for grazing, the cowherd, who lives at the end of the village nearest to the pasture, sets out on horseback through the village blowing a high, melodious horn. Each farmer chases his cattle to the street and the cowherd picks them up on his return through the village. He takes them to the pasture and is responsible for the welfare and safety of the cattle. In the evening he brings the herd into the village, again blowing his horn, notifying the farmers to get ready to receive their cattle. It is a curious sight to see the cattle (a herd amounting to as many as 500 head) returning down the village street, each farmer's herd automatically veering into its respective *Hof* without any direction. Even a new calf going to pasture for the first time experiences little difficulty since its "relatives" know where to go.

Life in the villages is normally peaceful and calm. However, conflicts do emerge, and interpersonal relations become strained. Family feuds and feuds between villages are well known, and sometimes exist for generations.[27] Usually, however, the village takes care of these problems; if the individuals involved cannot come to terms, the village fathers in

27. See Calvin Redekop, "Toward an Understanding of Religion and Social Solidarity," *Sociological Analysis,* Vol. XXVIII (Fall, 1967), for an analysis of how social solidarity is affected by competition and conflict in Old Colony social systems.

Schult meetings try to decide what must be done. Deviance which involves religious factors is referred to the clergy. There was an office termed *"Kroagah"* which means "inviter" which was instituted to "invite" offender and offended to the *Dunnadagh* described above. It has fallen into disuse because of sociological forces which will be described below.

The Old Colony village social structure is closely integrated into the religious norms and institutions. The Old Colony village organization cannot be considered secular, since Old Colony members do not make a distinction between the sacred and secular, especially in their world. Their total way of life is sacred: they live the way God wants them to live. Therefore, it is accurate to speak of the entire Old Colony system, including village life, as a theocracy, a kingdom under the direct rule of God.

Economic Institutions

Though the Old Colony may be seen as a collectivity under the direct rule of God, it depends upon a particular material base for its achievement. As the youth grows up in the Old Colony system, he comes to the conclusion that farming is an inherent part of the Old Colony way of life. Farming is in fact the basic option open to the youth, though there are other things he can do if he does not succed in becoming a farmer, because of the continuing competition for land.

Through the factors of dividing land among children and of moving from one village to another or to another settlement, land is constantly being added to or subtracted from a farm. Thus the amount of land owned by the farmers in the villages is illustrated by the land holdings in three villages chosen at random. (See Table 3-2.) In a random sample of nineteen villages in the Manitoba Plan, 23 per cent were landless (*Anwohner*). This figure is indicative of a Colony member's marrying without inheriting land from parents or of his being unable to buy land when it is offered for sale. The landless in Manitoba and Saskatchewan are normally employed in nearby towns, so that they are not in pressing economic need. In the other settlements, however, a landless couple is normally rather poor, since the husband needs to work for other farmers at a very low wage (about twenty-five pesos per day in Mexico at present) or for village industries that also pay low wages.

Table 3-2   Landholding in Three Villages in Manitoba Plan, Mexico[a]

Acres per Farm	Number of Landowners[b]
0–19	2
20–39	2
40–59	4
60–79	7
80–99	15
100–119	3
120–139	2
140–159	1
160–179	9
180–199	4
200–219	6
220–239	2
240–259	2
260–279	1
280–299	2
300–319	2

Total number of acres	10,950
Total number of farmers	77
Average number of acres per farm	142.2
Average number of acres per village	3,650

[a] Chosen at random in the Manitoba Plan.
[b] These data do not indicate the number of landless in these villages.

The activities involved in making a living on an Old Colony farm are basically those of the conventional Western type. The farmer produces foodstuff, animal feeds, and certain other products for home consumption and for the open market. The greatest difference from the conventional Western farmer is that the Old Colony farmer produces a greater proportion for his own consumption: thus each farmer raises and slaughters animals for his own meat supply; eggs, milk, and meat are produced by the farmer as a part of his normal operations; even if a farmer has no other livestock, he keeps a sufficient number for table needs. The farm always produces enough for sustenance, though it may produce little else at times. Of course, there are some things which are bought in season as supplementation and variation, such as watermelons and bananas. The farmer and his family need other things that cannot be raised at home, such as cloth from which to make the family's clothing.

The farmer must produce crops for market in order to purchase necessities. He relates the Old Colony to the cash economy through his need for cloth and clothing, especially men's work clothing and dress suits; cash for land, building materials, and labor; and machinery and tools for farming operations. Though bartering is practiced, a money standard is absolutely necessary for the exchange of most values. It is clear, then, that the Old Colony farmer must produce in excess of his demands for physical survival.

In all the settlements, machinery of various kinds is used, except that the tractors until recently were not equipped with rubber tires in Mexico for fear that they would tempt users to drive to town. In Mexico the major crops are oats, corn, beans, and some rye and barley. Livestock consists of dairy cattle— predominantly Holstein—hogs, and chickens. The livestock is not generally purebred, though in recent years purebred chickens have been purchased.

According to the estimates of a half dozen farmers during an informal interview, the average income of the Old Colony farmer in Mexico might be around twenty thousand pesos per year, with expenditures of around fifteen thousand pesos per year, leaving a net of five thousand. Of course, many make less and a few much more. The interviewees felt that in their village there was a farmer who netted as much as one hundred thousand pesos per year.

Combines are slowly making their way into Mexico. Silos have only recently been introduced there. Their presence has stimulated a range of responses typical of the Colony's feelings of ambiguity in the face of progress:

The talk [at a *Schult* meeting] then turned to the corn silage and silos. There have been a few last year who tried the new method, and a number more this year, so that in Hochfeld last year there was not a single silo, and this year there are at least five. The common statement, if you do not have a silo this year, is, "I want to wait another year to see how it is, whether it can prove itself useful." Many humorous questions were asked, such as, "How is it possible to throw out the last silage at the bottom of the silo in America? Can he throw it clear up to the top?" One farmer, not the most aggressive or progressive in the village, felt the pressure of the talk upon him and began to give reasons why silage was not so good. He said he had heard from someone that in the States they do not feed it to dairy cattle, since it rots the teeth; thus it is only for steers. Further, he said, he had watched his brother's cattle, who had silage last year, and they were not as good as his. He said further, "Here when someone starts something everybody does it. They do it because they also want to be on the band wagon." Counterarguments were given such as, "So and so ran out of silage last winter, and the milk supply decreased directly with the decrease in silage, even though he fed other grains." [28]

Table 3-3   *Occupational Structure of the Old Colony in Mexico (Chihuahua Settlement)*[a]

Occupation	Number of Persons in Occupation	Clientele
Dentist	2	Old Colony and Mexicans
Doctor	4	Old Colony and Mexicans
Bone setter	10	Old Colony
Storekeeper	78 (plus)	Old Colony and Mexicans
Machinist	20	Old Colony and Mexicans
Mechanic	10 (plus)	Old Colony and Mexicans
Schoolteacher	78 (plus)	Old Colony
Cowherd	78 (plus)	Old Colony
Manager of cheese factories	35	Old Colony and Mexicans
Printer	5	Old Colony
Factory worker	25 (plus)	Old Colony and Mexicans
Cheese factory employee	50 (plus)	Old Colony and Mexicans

[a] Data gathered by author in Mexico in 1958 and 1964. All nonfarming occupations depend on farming. Most of the men in the above occupations also engage in farming, either on rented or their own land. One of the dentists does no farming. All the professionals listed here are self-educated, having no formal training.

It soon becomes clear to the visitor to the Old Colony that though farming is the basic economic activity, there are many other sources of income. (See Table 3-3.) In Manitoba and

28. Material gathered by the author during field research.

Saskatchewan the crops are the well-known staples such as wheat, barley, oats, and hay. The livestock is often purebred, indicating the acculturation to the larger society. Modern farming techniques, such as the use of fertilizer, are prevalent only in Manitoba and Saskatchewan. In Manitoba and Saskatchewan, many men work for farmers, work at various jobs in town, or manage a garage or blacksmith shop. In some villages as many as one third of the resident family heads work in various types of town jobs. (In the village of Reinfeld, Manitoba, in 1958, six family heads out of a total of eighteen were laborers in the nearby town of Winkler or on farms.)

In the traditional Old Colony settlements, because working outside the Colony is tantamount to being out of fellowship with the Church, it is almost never done. There are only rare cases of Old Colony men working for "outsiders." Although partnerships with non-Old Colonists are forbidden, some Old Colony partners, because of their powerful wealth, are allowed to remain in the Church. Because most of the nonfarmers work inside the Old Colony economic structure, farming operations are the main source of income even for the nonfarmers.

In Mexico the cheese-making business is quite profitable. There were seventeen cheese factories in 1966. During the dry years in the 1930's, cheese factories were introduced in an effort to produce a cash income. It is said by many that the cheese factories prevented the Old Colony in Mexico from experiencing a famine or starvation during these years. There are two types of cheese factories, private and village-owned. The private factories (there were nine in 1958) buy the milk from the villagers and hire their employees where they can. It is claimed that the private cheese factories are run more efficiently and are more modern and clean than the village-operated ones. The village cheese factory (there were seven in 1958) is operated by a director chosen by the village. He in turn hires the working force.

The factories, whether private or village-owned, send out wagons each morning to collect the milk. A monthly check is paid to the farmer for his shipment. On the average the farmer receives about eight thousand pesos per year for his milk. An average cheese factory produces as much as twenty tons of cheese per year, most of which is exported to other parts of Mexico and sells for about thirteen pesos per kilo. The average cheese factory hires from five to ten employees.

Numerous other economic enterprises have emerged in the Old Colony, especially in Mexico. By 1958 no less than nine feed mills had emerged and were grinding feeds for use by the Old Colony farmers. There were four harness shops which repaired and made harnesses. There was a host of other shops, including two box factories, one furniture factory, and about half a dozen machine shops which were capable of fabricating things as well as repairing them. (See Table 3-4 for list of enterprises.)

Table 3-4   Enterprises Related to Farming in Mexico (Chihuahua Settlement)[a]

Type of Enterprise	Number	Clientele	Ownership
Cheese factory[b]	16	Mexican market	10 private 6 village
Feed mill	9	Old Colony	private
Box factory	2	Old Colony and Mexican	private
Machine shop	20[c]	Old Colony and Mexican	private
Furniture shop	2	Old Colony and Mexican	private
Casting factory	1	Old Colony and Mexican	private
Harness shop	2	Old Colony and Mexican	private
Village store	78	Old Colony and Mexican	private
Printing press	2	Old Colony	private
Manufacturing	5	Old Colony and Mexican	private

[a] Data gathered by author in Mexico in 1958 and 1964.

[b] The cheese factories were originally founded as cooperatives owned by the villages which they served. Through the years, experience has shown that private ownership is more efficient and profitable for the farmers selling milk and for the entrepreneur.

[c] Shops vary from very small part-time operations to large enterprises.

In the last few years several factories which fabricate machine products have appeared. There are at present two factories that produce hammer mills; one factory produces disk-plow disks, cultivator shovels, and other related parts. Up to one half of the products of the three factories mentioned here are exported to the larger Mexican markets.

The situation in British Honduras is much more fluid and indefinite at present, though several machine shops have already been developed there. All the people in the new settlement there are involved in farming since the land pressure has not created any landless. In northern Alberta the Old Colony settlement is fairly devoid of any nonfarming practices, since the economic pressures for other sources of income have not yet developed.

An "industry" that is prevalent in all the settlements in Mexico and British Honduras is the importing business. One importer estimates that there are at least twenty importers who make at least two trips a year to the United States and Canada to import machinery and tools. This businessman averages five trips a year, bringing into Mexico about five tractors, ten drills, ten binders, and numerous plows and disks. This "industry" has proved of great financial benefit, since used machinery is very cheap in the United States and Canada and with little repair is serviceable for a long time. There is no way of estimating the value of the machinery that is imported. An average load costs about $1,500 in U.S. currency and sells for three times that in the colonies, but this is still very much cheaper than the implements would cost if purchased on the Mexican market. The import taxes on new machinery are so exorbitant that the Old Colonists rarely buy any. Despite the economic advantages of importing, the stress that importation and its attendant relationships with the Mexican officials impose on the Old Colony system has created troublesome moral and social problems for the Old Colony.

In spite of the fact that the Old Colony is a traditional society, it evidences a complex system of institutions. The institutions have been rather well integrated with each other and have served their functions well. But social systems, including those of ethnic minority groups, are almost never completely integrated and efficient. There is a considerable amount of conflict, contradiction, and disintegration in most systems. The Old Colony, though it is very "single-minded," also is plagued with problems. There are tensions, conflicts, and some deterioration evident in the Old Colony system. Since the first section of the book is reserved for description, the analyses of the weaknesses in the Old Colony system will be presented in the last section.

Chapter 4

EVERY MAN
TEACHING HIS NEIGHBOR

Social relationships in the Old Colony (i.e., the behavior of social beings as they relate to each other in the prescribed Old Colony setting) will be the subject of this chapter. The nature and quality of the relations between actual living Old Colony members will form the backbone of the description of the *social structure* of the Old Colony, as over against the more objective and "skeletal" description of the values, goals, and expected behavior (i.e., culture) of the Old Colony presented earlier.

Stratification

Although the Old Colony as a group believes it wrong to classify one person as more or less important than another, a modified system of ranking exists nevertheless. Some forms of behaviors are believed to be more desirable or more prestigious than others in meeting daily responsibilities and are thus functionally more important in the persistence of the Old Colony system.

The Old Colony as an ethnic minority considers itself superior to the members of Mexican society: "All Mexicans are crooked" is a commonly expressed belief among Old Colonists, who in normal conversation refer to the Mexican as *schvoate Tjarscht* (burnt piece of toast). Especially in commercial and economic areas, the Mennonites feel that the Mexicans can offer no competition. If one views the other side of the coin, he discovers that the Mexicans consider the Mennonites their equals or inferiors. One Mexican said, "I think the Old Colony morals are lower than the Mexican. They are more secretive about it, but they persist in immorality nevertheless." [1] Another Mexican said, "Religiously and culturally the Mennonites

1. Material gathered by the author during field research.

have not made many contributions. . . . They are very dirty. . . . They stink too." [2]

In Canada, on the other hand, members of the Old Colony consider themselves inferior to the society at large. A minister in Canada mused: "I often wonder how strangers feel about our church services and how we do things. One time when I held a service at the Old People's Home there was a very highly educated man from the States present and I asked him, 'How do you find our services? Do you find anything that you can use with profit?' " [3]

Comparisons of the same sort are made within the Old Colony itself, between the Canadian (Manitoba and Saskatchewan) and Mexican systems. Each considers the other lower than itself. One Manitoba Old Colonist stated, "The Old Colony group went to Mexico to preserve the language and to keep from changing with the world. They, however, have fallen morally very much, so that the young people have few morals." [4] The Canadian Old Colony young people share the same prejudice: "The Old Colony young people here look down upon the Mexican Mennonites who return here. I do not know why. . . . It may be that they dress a little differently, or that they are poorer. It takes some time before they are accepted in our group." [5]

Those who have settled in Mexico are vocal in their criticism of the Canadian settlements. As one Old Colony minister in Mexico said, "So far we have felt that the external control method is successful and easily worked. You can see when you look at the Old Colony group in Canada that the change has gone rather quickly since the external controls have been lifted. The attire of the young girls is a clear example, as is the fact that the son of the bishop is an officer in a credit union." [6] Visiting in Manitoba, an Old Colonist from Mexico observed that "The Old Colony Mennonites here will soon be lost completely. . . . They are dressing like the world, and they are

2. Material gathered by the author during field research.
3. Material gathered by the author during field research.
4. Material gathered by the author during field research.
5. Material gathered by the author during field research.
6. Material gathered by the author during field research.

just like the world about them. . . . The girls cut their hair, wear loud dresses, and the parents do not care. . . . The Church here in Manitoba is lost." [7]

Internally the Old Colony has only a few social classes, and those that do exist are only vaguely defined. The *Lehrdienst* (bishops and ministers), *Vorsteher,* and deacons could be considered of highest rank. The second class is made up of the farmers and those in related occupations. The third class includes the *Anwohner* (landless), the teachers, and the cowherds.

The best means of determining class standing is through an analysis of the subjective feelings of the Old Colonists as they manifest themselves in informal situations. Although there is no class consciousness as such, most Old Colonists are able to state which persons in a village are more important or influential than others. On this basis, the lowest degree of prestige is awarded the landless in each village, those who occupy small houses on the one- to two-acre plots of land set aside for the poor. These *Anwohner* have limited opportunity for economic gain: they can work for the local village cheese factories; they can try to rent land somewhere and slowly work their way up; they can try to work for well-to-do farmers in the villages; they can start little service shops, such as welding and machine shops; or they can fill village positions such as cowherd or schoolteacher.

The next rung on the prestige ladder is occupied by those who are the average farmers. In this category are included those who own from forty to two hundred acres, approximately. These people are frugal, conservative, and hard working, not prone to innovate economically or socially. Above them are the prosperous farmers and the village officers and church officials, such as deacons, tax collectors, and stewards. These officers are usually elected on the basis of their over-all acceptance in the community.

The status accorded the clergy testifies to the importance of the religious goals of the Old Colony. On the top rung are the bishops and ministers, regardless of their economic posi-

7. Material gathered by the author during field research.

tion; the richest families in each village; and those older families who are well known in the colonies for their orthodoxy, industry, and ability. These people gain their status on the basis of a number of criteria, whereas the people of lower status are usually ranked according to their economic limitations or social ineptness.

The lines of distinction between classes are so loosely drawn that one can move fairly easily from one level to another. An *Anwohner* or a teacher can move into the farmer class simply by obtaining some land on a rental basis and working as a farmer. If he is able to borrow some money from a sympathetic person and buy his land, so much the better. Almost any person can meet the technical requirements for the ministry. In Manitoba and Saskatchewan a person who has attended Bible school and expressed an interest in religious affairs can become a minister if elected by the congregation. It is more difficult to become a bishop, since only one man holds this office at any given time, but a small number of ministers of ability and commitment do advance to this level.

The outward signs of class differentiation are few in number. The garb of the clergy—the dark shirt, hat, and frock coat of the Canadian minister or the Russian-type cap and knee-high leather boots of the Mexican church leader—is distinctive certainly. One can also identify several levels of the society by noting the individual's place of dwelling: the teacher occupies the teacherage; the landless are, as we have seen, set apart by the size and location of their homes.

Rank in the Old Colony is based ultimately on the behavior of individuals as they help the Old Colony to achieve its objectives. It will be seen immediately that the ministry is of highest rank. These church leaders are the people responsible for the spiritual welfare of the Old Colony; they include the bishop, ministers, and deacons, all of whom fill roles derived directly from the Bible.

The role of farmer is probably next in importance, for the reason that it means subsistence for the Old Colony way of life. The bishops, ministers, and deacons are farmers, too, as well as religious leaders. There are very few men who are not at least part-time farmers, even though they may also pursue other occupations. In all Old Colony settlements the prosperous farmer ranks very high as compared with less successful farmers. The successful operator of a store, feed mill, sawmill, or other enterprise is ranked fairly high. The machine shop operator or blacksmith who does good work is ranked above those who perform less well and above most farmers who are only moderately successful. The day laborer is ranked lowest. The *Anwohner* who is able to get land and do a little farming is ranked higher than the laborer who cannot find a farm or does not want to, though he is by no means esteemed: "The *Anwohner* are better off than we. We have to buy land, while they can rent land from the village and from the Mexicans. They live much too cheaply. The village pays for it. I wish more of them would buy land and move away. We had one who was really rich. He even kicked when we raised the rent to fifty pesos a year. They live off the village too much." [8]

In Canada the role of the farmer is less highly regarded than in Mexico. Many people are beginning to go into other occupations, and their rank is not necessarily lower than that of the farmer; in fact, in many cases other occupations are considered more worthy. In Canada, the lowest rank, occupationally speaking, belongs to the day laborer. The garage operator and the farmer would probably be equal in rank, while a successful businessman is beginning to receive considerable prestige. The roles of teacher and cowherd have historically been ranked very low. It is commonly stated that if you could not farm you could always teach. This attitude is changing in Manitoba and Saskatchewan, since the teacher's rank in the larger society is fairly high. In Mexico the attitude toward the teacher is the traditional one. In Manitoba the rank of cowherd has disappeared now that the village common pasture has been disbanded. In Mexico the cowherd still exists and is ranked with the teacher.

There is a curious difference in the rank accorded the male and female in the Old Colony system. In Mexico, there is some evidence of pride in the fact that the Old Colony people rank

8. Material gathered by the author during field research.

women higher than the Mexicans do: "The Mexican women were much lower in relation to the man or husband than they are now. This is partly because the Old Colony has helped the Mexican see it is better to treat his wife with more respect." [9] In the Old Colony in general, women are considered almost equal to men in religious matters, but they are not allowed to give public expression to their ideas, nor are Church offices open to them. They are not allowed to take part in any village public affairs, though the schoolteacher's wife is often an assistant to her husband. In the home the woman, though lower in rank than the male, often exercises great authority because of her role performance. An Old Colony family in Mexico known to the author was held together by the wife, and her status locally was higher than that of the husband. From the point of view of the children, the mother is ranked higher because she is the socio-emotional leader, while the father is the disciplinarian.

Ranking is also based on age. Generally the oldest people have the highest rank and the youngest have the least. Thus, in a *Schult* meeting one can observe that authority and power are directly related to age. In family discussions the oldest son has more rank than the youngest son. In social affairs, such as the meal at a wedding, the older men eat first, then the middle-aged men, then the older and middle-aged women, and finally the younger men and women and the children, who eat in a more haphazard order. When the family receives visitors, the oldest children, especially if they are married, are allowed to visit with the guests. Only if the visitors are neighbors or close acquaintances are the younger members of the family allowed to be present.

Wealth serves as another criterion for ranking. Wealth alone is not a criterion, however; one must prosper only in those ways consistent with the norms of hard work and honesty. Considerable antagonism is felt throughout all Old Colony settlements toward one rich farmer, probably the richest in the total Old Colony, who procured land at the expense of others who wanted to get established in farming:

9. Material gathered by the author during field research.

"There has been quite a bit of protest in his own congregation that he should divide his land, and to subdue the protest he has divided at least half of his land among his children, but the clamor still persists. . . . He got much of his land by moved to Mexico. . . . He always outbids the next fellow." [10] buying up land that was sold cheaply when the Old Colony On the other hand, in the village of Hochfeld (Mexico), for example, there were three wealthy brothers who were accorded high rank because they had become wealthy by hard work and shrewd management.

Personality factors, including power, or the ability to use other people to achieve one's own ends, are used as criteria for ranking. For example, the Bishop of the Old Colony in Manitoba ranked high because of his strong and winning personality and his kind and understanding attitude. He was not wealthy, and it was clear that wealth could not have given him the respect he enjoyed.

The ranking system in the Old Colony derives from its beliefs, sentiments, ends, and norms. Ranking is not given by achievement as much as by ascription. The rank of farmer is important because farming is consistent with the beliefs and sentiments of the Old Colony and because it helps the Old Colony achieve its goals. The latitude of ranking within the rank of farming depends upon how well the norms of farming as means to ends are fulfilled.

The low rank attributed to the teacher or renter derives in part from the assumed violation of norms about industriousness, frugality, and productivity. It is difficult for an Old Colonist to see how the teacher contributes tangibly to the welfare of the Old Colony and its way of life. Again, the renter (*Anwohner*), when he does not work on the land, seems to be violating one of the important norms even if it is not his fault that he cannot find land.

The ranking which stems from power, wealth, and personality characteristics is derived from other motivations. Since the Old Colony goals of being productive and living as an Old Colonist should live are so strong, it seems plausible that

10. Material gathered by the author during field research.

striving for these goals would develop some sort of "bench marks" by which achievement could be measured. These bench marks of the achievement of the "ideal" Old Colony way of life by overconforming (i.e., being very well-to-do) seem to be basic for the according of status.

There are thus no class structure in the Old Colony system and no consciousness of class. The differences in class standing can be attributed more to individual idiosyncrasies and personal application than to membership in a certain segment of the population.

Social Control

There is an amazing degree of conformity to the Old Colony goal system. The deviant is the exception rather than the rule. When there is a transgression from accepted Old Colony norms, the informal discussions in which the members vent their disapproval of the transgressor and his act are numerous and intense. Accordingly, deviants are usually brought into line again because the "costs" involved in continued deviance are too great. Social control resides, in other words, in the bosom of each Old Colonist.[11]

Power has been defined by Max Weber as "a person's ability to impose his will upon others despite resistance."[12] Theoretically, the Old Colony membership should be equal in power, for all are equally submissive to the leadership of God. Practically, however, there is a good deal of difference in the distribution and exercise of power to control behavior. Not all Old Colony members conform equally to the norms, and not all members have equal power to control the behavior of others.

There is a sharing of power between the Old Colony and its surrounding society. In Canada, the state has power to send

11. George C. Homans, *The Human Group* (New York: Harcourt, Brace & Company, 1950), pp. 281ff. Homans' proposition that social control is a matter of a reciprocity in interpersonal relationships is illustrated in the Old Colony and will be discussed in more detail.

12. Peter M. Blau, "Critical Remarks on Weber's Theory of Authority," *The American Political Science Review,* LVII (June, 1963), 306.

Old Colony children to school until they reach the age of sixteen or complete eight grades. It also has power to draft Old Colony young men into military service. It has the right of eminent domain. It has the power to arrest and apprehend anyone accused of crime. It has power to build roads, collect taxes, and limit production of crops and produce.

The Mexican state has similar powers, but in fewer areas. The Mexican state does not demand the power to draft men for military service, to interfere in the teaching of children, or to maintain Old Colony roads. The Old Colony concedes that the Mexican state has power to apprehend lawbreakers and criminals and to coerce payments of bills; in fact, it sometimes depends on the state in these areas. But for the Old Colony, the state is not the sovereign authority.

Within the Old Colony as a social system, the most inclusive social control resides in the Church's power over the total Old Colony life. The *Lehrdienst* has the power to settle land disputes between farmers or villages, arrange for new settlements, collect taxes, and decide which requirements of the state should be honored. The *Lehrdienst*'s power is illustrated by a message that was circulated through the villages in Mexico on July 29, 1958, which contained the information that delinquent taxes were to be paid immediately lest sanctions be invoked. (See Appendix G for full text.) The new migrations to British Honduras and Bolivia were instigated by the Church leaders, although many migrated to British Honduras before Church leaders gave them the freedom to go. The same degree of power does not exist among Canadian ministers, who are not able to impose this much control on the members.

The clergy exercises its greatest power in bringing about conformity to religious and social norms. Sermons and personal visits serve to consolidate the power to achieve obedience. Behavior is closely guarded by the *Lehrdienst*. This writer and several villagers went to see a house that was being built in a village in Mexico and saw a manifestation of social control. The owner proudly pointed to the wiring he was installing. "What will the 'priests' say?" one of the men asked. "They will not find out since I am covering the wiring over with plaster," he replied. The wiring was included in the construction in the hope that electric lights would soon be allowed.

In Manitoba the power of the *Lehrdienst* has been weakening. After one baptismal service the Bishop reminded the young people that they were to renounce the ways of the world: "This morning Rev. Friesen said that he had a few words to say to the girls. They were cutting their hair. This was not right. It was in fact against biblical injunction, according to Paul in I Corinthians. They were being disobedient by cutting their hair. . . . Also the head covering was to be worn by all the women as it had been worn in the past, of dark color and simple in style." [13] It is obvious that the ability to control behavior is slipping, for conformity does not need admonition.

Sociological theory suggests that as long as people obey, a man has power, and the person possessing it will apply it. But when people will no longer obey, the persons who have had power relax their attempts to apply it. A case in point has been the tendency for farmers in the south section of the largest colony in Mexico, the Manitoba Plan, to put rubber tires on tractors in spite of the admonitions and the threats of the bishops to excommunicate them: "The rubber tire question is settled. The showdown came this spring when the Bishop set a deadline and stated that all those who had not taken care of their situation would be excommunicated. The time is already past and nothing has come of it." [14] This Old Colony member went on to say, "I have searched the Scriptures and can find nothing stated which would forbid using rubber tires."

Another member from the area under discussion was not ready to submit to the rules of the bishops. "I also have rubber tires on the back now, but not in front. If they [the bishops] ask me, I will tell them that I do not even have rubber in front. Actually, I am not afraid. I don't bother the ministers and they do not bother me. I do not know what they will do, but we shall see." [15] It should be noted here that the

13. Material gathered by the author during field research.
14. Material gathered by the author during field research.
15. Material gathered by the author during field research.

power of the bishops and ministers is legitimatized power—
the right to exercise the power or authority is institutionalized.
The clergy never *forces* people to do anything against their
will. If deviants do not conform to the traditional patterns,
they are punished in traditional ways.

The power of religious leaders to achieve conformity in
the realm of social patterns such as dress and drinking varies.
In both Canada and in Mexico, smoking, drinking, and
worldly dress are forbidden; but as we have seen, there is not /
complete obedience.

The second general sphere of social control is that of the
village social structure. The Canadian system is changing
rapidly, but insofar as the Old Colony people there live in
villages, social control prevails. The village is organized so
that many economic, social, and ecological processes are
rigidly controlled.

One of the functional roles which ties the "secular" village
life to the life of the Church is the *Vorsteher,* a position established by the Church. It is the *Vorsteher's* responsibility,
for example, to collect all the taxes (on a prorated ownership
basis) and turn them in to the government; thus he speaks
for the Church but deals directly with the villages in collecting the money. Collecting money to pay for land in a new
area purchased for migration is another example of how the
Vorsteher carries out the *Lehrdienst's* wishes in the villages
and thus integrates the village life into the religious.

The *Vorsteher's* power is derived from the belief system of
the Church. He represents interests that have been accorded
highest rank in the total Old Colony system—the goals and
beliefs noted in Chapter 3. He does not have the power to
impose sanctions, since he does not deal with individuals, but
with villages. Yet if, for example, a local villager does not pay
his dues for resettlement, or such things, he can be taken by
the *Vorsteher* to the *Lehrdienst* for discipline; their threats of
excommunication have almost always brought payment.

Recently a full-time and salaried *Buchführer* (bookkeeper)
role has emerged in Mexico, in an effort to make more efficient
the collection of money to meet Mexican tax demands. He
reports delinquent payments to the *Vorsteher* and the *Lehr-*

dienst. Normally the village authorities try to encourage the delinquent to pay, and social pressure is often enough to make the person co-operate.

Despite attempts to expedite the collection of taxes, the system is not without its weaknesses: one of the best ways to avoid discipline for failure to pay or to cut down on amount of payments is to report lower than actual income to the *Buchführer:* "Several farmers have said that if they reported everything that could be classified as income, they would not be able to survive because the Mexican tax system is based on income alone, not allowing anything for expenses, depreciation, or improvements."[16]

The village *Schult* has power to call village meetings, to appoint people to carry out village decisions, and to reach solutions to problems not important enough to refer to the village fathers. The responsibility for general village administration—directing the repair of the village roads or repairing a dam, for example—is in the hands of the *Schult.* The village clerk does not possess much power, though possession of records of any sort is a source of power in a sense. He reports to the *Schult* any unfinished business.

The fire secretary's duty is to collect dues for fire insurance. He has the power to cancel a farmer's protection if he does not pay his dues, and the power to have the farmer make necessary improvements or to change his coverage. Arson is rare, but when it occurs, the secretary reports it to the *Vorsteher* and *Lehrdienst* who investigate the allegation.

The individuals who fill the offices mentioned above are the power bearers of the will of the local village. What power does the collective have over the individual? The Old Colony system, especially in Mexico, reveals the collective nature of power. The will of the majority rules. The village, through informal discussion and official village *Schult* meetings, determines whether a person may set up a store, a mail distribution center, or a cheese factory. The village can decide how many cattle the village farmers may graze. The village dictates how much each family must donate to the maintenance

16. Material gathered by the author during field research.

of roads and other collective facilities. The village determines the amount of taxation each family must supply for the maintenance of the local school. The village can limit the amount of water a farmer pumps out of the ground for his own crops if he acts to the detriment of his neighbors. The village has the right to eminent domain for flood control, road building, and construction of a cheese factory. Any misuse of village facilities can be called to a halt by the power of the village.

The individual is not able to circumvent the village power. He has to limit his herd of cattle to the prescribed number or pay a fine. If he refuses, he may be denied the use of the pasture. He has to bring quality, clean milk to the village cheese factory or be barred from selling milk. The only recourse the individual has is his informal power. He can influence individuals by the communication of sentiment and through his kinship system, explained below. He can also cast his dissenting vote in village meetings. But unless he gets support, he is helpless.

The third general power structure is the kinship system, which is very pervasive and strong. Especially in Mexico, but still to some extent in Canada, a partially extended family structure exists. A family of procreation coinhabits with the family of orientation in many cases, a fairly common practice because of lack of land and economic opportunity. Often new families reside with one pair of parents, though the normal pattern is for the new family to move to its own home as soon as an opportunity presents itself. But the residential pattern is not so influential in the power structure of the kinship system as is the authority pattern.

The father is the direct power-holder over his sons and daughters. With the counsel of his wife, who does not wield power of her own, the father determines what his children may and may not do, what privileges they shall have, and what rights and duties they have. The extent of the Old Colony father's power can be far-reaching and his actions severe: "I do not allow my children to go to town by themselves. They never have been in town by themselves. The furthest they have gotten is Chihuahua. I take each child to Chihuahua separately when they are going to get married and join the Church. Then I take them to town to buy them a dress or suit. I do not believe in letting them run around in the evening or go to another village when they please." [17] Another father is said to have taken more drastic disciplinary action: "There was a case some years ago of a Wiebe in village 21 who wanted to marry a girl who was quite poor. The father disapproved and forbade it. When the boy disobeyed and married the girl, the father forbade the family ever to cross his doorsill." [18]

Although the father has ultimate power in the family, the grandfather is often consulted by the father. The grandfather exerts a power of wisdom and moral authority over his sons and daughters because of his revered position. His wishes are communicated by his approval or disapproval of acts perpetrated by his children or grandchildren.

The woman has much less power in social affairs. Although she has no voice in village affairs, she does exercise considerable power in the household over her children. She can tell her daughters what to do, and the boys who are not old enough to help in the fields are often put to work by the mother. In some cases older sons are able to control the actions of younger brothers and older daughters the actions of younger sisters, but there is little evidence to indicate that males in a family are able to control the actions of females other than by enforcing some directive of the father or mother.

A fourth area of power is the informal social structure. Since the Old Colony has *Gemeinschaft* characteristics, power does not necessarily reside in institutionalized offices or in prescribed roles. That interpersonal relations are a source of power in the Old Colony is evidenced in many ways. In the *Lehrdienst,* for example, the amount of power a minister has is proportionate to his personal influence with the bishop. A young deacon is rumored to have more power, by virtue of his relationship with the bishop, than have many of the ministers. Personal influence involves exchange of one service for another, as the following example of the operation of patronage illustrates:

17. Material gathered by the author during field research.
18. Material gathered by the author during field research.

Dave Friesen complained that often when the bishop would shake hands with a circle of people, he would be overlooked. "I guess it is because we have not been very faithful in supporting the work of the *Gemeent*." John said, "No, it is rather that we have never 'bought' the preacher as so many others do. Fehr [the Bishop] is not a very good provider and is dependent to a large extent on his parishioners for his support. Many people give him a lot of gifts, and to these people he is very solicitous and kind. . . . But I have never given the Bishop anything, for I do not believe in buying his friendship or good will. Many do and get by with murder." [19]

In village affairs the *Schult* is often the figurehead for an influential farmer in the village. Frequently, as indicated in the discussion of ranking, the influential farmer is the one who has been financially successful and socially correct. An observation made about a meeting of a village *Schult* illustrates the part the informal power structure can play in regulating village affairs; it also demonstrates the fact, when seen in conjunction with the above quotation, that one need not have official sanction in order to carry considerable weight in decision-making situations: "During the meeting the ultimate decision seemed to rest with Dave Friesen. When someone suggested a name or an idea, everyone looked at Friesen. He would respond with a reason why he thought the idea or name was not suitable or good." [20] In this situation, Mr. Friesen was not an official, though he earlier had been the *Schult*.

Another illustration of the workings of the informal power structure, within a broad framework of traditional designation of a different formal authority, can be seen in some homes. Although the husband is ostensibly the head of the house, ultimate responsibility for the family may lie with the woman, who may inherently be better equipped to assume it; or a husband may be made to appear dominant because of the strength of the woman behind the scenes.

We have seen the way power is distributed in the Old Colony. The question of how power is acquired, maintained,

19. Material gathered by the author during field research.
20. Material gathered by the author during field research.

and buttressed remains. Formal power is *acquired* largely by occupying certain roles, such as bishop, *Vorsteher,* or father. A person who becomes the bishop acquires the power (authority) that the position of bishop accords.[21] A man acquires parental power simply by becoming a father. There are some powers which are granted without any effort on the part of the recipient, such as the power that goes with being a male rather than a female. This kind of power constitutes what is called ascribed status.

The power which informal leadership possesses is achieved by virtue of personal ability, age, or influence (*charism*). An older Church father may exercise tremendous power by virtue of his ability to influence and control the action of others, especially the *Lehrdienst*. A personable and able villager may acquire power by his ability to lead people, a strength based on his ability to enlist loyalty or to befriend his neighbors. In the home or family, a sibling may possess power because of his natural ability to influence others.

It is quite normal that a person who exercises informal power is shunted into positions of power posited in various roles. Thus, if a younger man in the village achieves informal power, he will usually end up as *Schult* of the village. An older person of power may already have been the *Schult,* so that his power is more diffuse; he does not need the office to establish his strength.

Power is *maintained* in numerous ways. The bishop, for example, maintains his power by carrying out his duties. He maintains it further by gaining the support of his ministers. As long as he can convince the majority of the ministers that he is representing them and the Church, he is secure. The support of powerful members in the congregation is also an important means to the retention of power. As indicated above, the bishop often accepts gifts and other kindnesses from

21. Power becomes authority when there is a voluntary submission. Thus, in a sense, institutionalized submission to power exercised in certain roles is authority and not power. Space does not allow a careful distinction in the discussion between power and authority. For a full discussion see Blau, "Critical Remarks on Weber's Theory of Authority," p. 307.

his members, a practice which indebts him to his benefactors. Any favors that are returned, however, indebt the members to the bishop, so that both persons' powers are thereby established and entrenched.[22]

In the village the *Schult* maintains formal power by virtue of his being in office. He maintains a greater amount of power, however, if he is able to influence others to support him in his endeavors, since he can then initiate acts readily rather than having to wait to carry out the wishes of the *Schult* meeting.

A father in the family maintains his power if he is able to perform the functions expected of a father. If not, it is likely that the mother will become the power behind the scenes and the father a figurehead. He entrenches his power by being a successful father and gains status in the community to the extent that he is able to control others as well.

Power can be buttressed and expanded in a number of ways. The office or role can be expanded to include other functions or expectations. A new responsibility for the *Vorsteher,* such as the responsibility for collecting tax money for the Mexican government, made him more powerful, until the work load became too large and a new role was created. Acquiring new friends or gaining support for a proposal or belief strengthens the power potential of the bishop. In Mexico, the strength of the Manitoba Plan Bishop was increased in 1958 with the election of a deacon who supported the conservative policy of the Bishop and thereby strengthened it and the Bishop.

The entrenchment of village power comes about in much the same way. An informal power-holder can increase his power by indebting others to him. For example, he may lend a sizable amount of money to an aspiring young farmer who remains a source of power as long as the loan is outstanding.

22. This illustrates Homans' theory: "The mutual dependence between social rank and performance in a certain activity, in this case, the return of favors, constitutes an automatic control of the activity." See his *The Human Group,* p. 288.

Sanctions

The social control system outlined above should theoretically be sufficient to guarantee Old Colony conformity to norms, but, as we have seen, such is not always the case. Those who have a tendency to deviate are brought into line by the use of sanctions, social approval or disapproval of certain behavior. Positive sanctions are applied to help people become more integrated into the Old Colony way of life, and negative sanctions are applied to keep deviancy from occurring, or as a punishment for deviancy.

Sanctions can be quite particular, referring to a specific act, or quite general, referring to an undefined area of behavior. Sanctions may be expressed in a warm, affective way or in an impersonal, neutral way. Withholding of approval and friendship is one of the most effective negative sanctions. If these are not effective, then more serious punishments such as excommunication and ultimately banning are tried. Positive sanctions are usually rewards of various types, such as commendations or gifts.

As in most ethnic groups, the most powerful Old Colony negative sanction is expulsion from the group. Expulsion is an unhappy experience, especially in Mexico, where the Old Colony still evidences close primary-group characteristics. Excommunication from the *Gemeent,* an official response to spiritual misbehavior, need not in itself result in the isolation of the punished individual. Excommunication means exclusion from communion and being placed under the strict surveillance of the *Lehrdienst.* Excommunication occurs as a result of the continuation of an unacceptable activity. The offending person is reinstated as soon as he "takes care of his matter" (*moakt zeeni zach*). An Old Colony member described the experience of an Old Colonist who was excommunicated as follows: "An Old Colonist from Mexico wanted to join the Old Colony in Manitoba, but did not have a letter from his bishop in Mexico since he had been excommunicated. So the bishop from Manitoba came to Mexico to see the local bishop, but our bishop would not relent and said only if this man 'takes care of his matter' would he release him." [23] Communion is considered an important ordinance in the life of the Old Colony Church, and fear of being refused it is the source of the power underlying excommunication.

It is only when the ban is imposed that the erring person is to be avoided socially and isolated spiritually, even by his mate. Banning, if enforced, is tantamount, then, to total expulsion from the community; but the ban is usually violated —except in cases of major moral lapse—by the immediate family and close friends: "David Fehr, who has been under the ban for a number of years, says that the ban is only partially practiced. He has a truck, and when they have need, those who practice the ban socially and religiously will come and borrow it to their hearts' content. . . . His brother-in-law has practiced the social ban for years, but recently hired him to take him to a village some miles away to do some business in an emergency. About 50 per cent of the village in which he lives practice the ban, but the others are sympathetic, and when they are not watched, socialize freely with him." [24]

The ban, when it is observed, is effective as a sanction as long as people feel that the Old Colony offers them the only tenable way of life, for then excommunication and banning would mean annihilation.[25] However, "There are many now being banned by the *Gemeent,* and are glad that they are. There is now no longer the dread of excommunication that once existed. They do not believe any more that the Old Colony is the only Church." [26] The lay enforcement of the ban is part of its effectiveness. When large numbers of Old Colonists cease to dread the ban, it will lose its sanctioning power. One Old Colonist who was "fed up" with the arbitrary

23. Material gathered by the author during field research.

24. Material gathered by the author during field research.

25. Direct statements of the suffering inflicted by the ban are hard to come by, since those under the ban want to minimize its effect. An informed observer stated, "The biggest lever that the Church leaders wield is the fear of being banned, which puts the banned out of fellowship of the group, but more importantly, puts them out of heaven."

26. Material gathered by the author during field research.

rules of abstaining from "worldly" activities said, "These laws have been made many years ago, and the loyalty of people who do not want to be dissenters or to cause splits makes them abide by these rules, though they were outmoded long ago. I am ready to bear the pressure of the ban and suffer social disgrace for my convictions." [27]

Another sanction, less severe than excommunication and the ban, is the appearance at *Dunnadagh*. To have been dealt with by the bishop and ministers at *Dunnadagh* is an effective sanction because of the public condemnation associated with it.

Removal from office is a sanction which serves to achieve conformity among the leadership. One minister did not want to accept the call, which requires a lifetime commitment, and did almost everything possible to avoid it, though in the end he capitulated: "John Wiens had once been called to the ministry. Later he became disgruntled and engaged in various sorts of immorality to get excused from the responsibility of being a minister. He was relieved of his office and was asked to confess his shortcomings." [28] Usually an official subjected to sanction is permitted to remain in office until his term expires; he is not eligible for re-election.

One of the most powerful social sanctions is simply public opinion. Fear of negative responses from the villagers can be a strong deterrent to misdemeanors for a person who wants to be accepted.

These sanctions apply to Church and village matters. Family sanctions are of a somewhat different nature. Sanctions of disapproval involve physical punishment until the beginning of adolescence. The father usually administers punishment, although the mother may if she is so disposed or if the father is not in a position to do so. Older children are generally reprimanded verbally. One evening when the author and his landlord were returning home, the landlord saw his fourteen-year-old daughter holding hands with a boy at the intersection of the lane and the village road. The girl received a severe reprimand and was required to remain at home for two weeks.

27. Material gathered by the author during field research.
28. Material gathered by the author during field research.

Privileges are withheld when such a punishment is feasible, but the privileges the young people possess are so few that this is not always effective.

Positive sanctions at the family level are of various kinds. Verbal praise and rewards are two types. A girl who helps in the garden or house, for example, may receive permission to take a half day off to visit her girl friend in the village, or she may be given money to buy material for a new dress. A boy may receive money, or he may eventually be given a horse. These more important gifts are usually promised long in advance and serve both as an incentive and as a reward.

Similarly, the pressure of public opinion is a force for good in that it can be positive as well as negative. Although positive sanctions as expressed by public opinion are less common than negative ones, they can be heard, just as leaders can offer praise for the obedient or *"ajcht"* person.

A highly important positive sanction is the expression of approval by the *Lehrdienst*. Oddly enough, funerals are frequently occasions for the pronouncement of *Lehrdienst* sanctions, for in this context the deceased can receive commendation and simultaneously be made an example: "Then the minister began to speak. . . . The recurrent theme was that this woman's life was as a flower that is cut off. This should be a lesson to us, that we would not go to hell, that we should live a humble, simple, and pure life as against the pride of the eye, the pride of life, and the lust of the flesh. . . . The young people were appealed to, to avoid all kinds of sinful life such as drinking, smoking, dancing, cutting the hair, and the like. The quiet, peaceful, prayerful life of the young deceased woman was held up as a standard." [29]

Primary Relationships

Members of an ethnic minority tend to experience a primary type of interpersonal relationship.[30] This is true of members

29. Material gathered by the author during field research.
30. See Milton M. Gordon, *Assimilation in American Life* (New York: Oxford University Press, 1964), p. 34.

of the Old Colony, for all members have at least a semi-personal knowledge of each other. If an Old Colonist does not know another from direct contact, chances are good that he will know of him through friends or by virtue of the fact that the two are related. Of course, one is apt to be related to or to know best those in his own settlement (see Table 4-1), but his knowledge of members in other settlements—second-hand if not direct—is fairly inclusive.

Table 4-1   Parental Interrelationships in and around the Village of Hoch-feld, Manitoba Plan, Mexico[a]

The Homes of the Parents[b]	Number of Parents	Number of Offspring in Hochfeld	Number of Offspring of Each Parental Family Living in Hochfeld
Hochfeld	15	48	3.2
Contiguous villages	2	2	1.0
Villages 1–2 villages from Hochfeld	14	20	1.4
Villages 3 or more villages from Hochfeld	18	18	1.0
Total	49	88	

[a] Based on research by the author in Hochfeld in 1958.
[b] There were 26 villages from which parents came.

Occasions for primary relationships abound in the villages. The local store, found in almost every village, is a place for many of the men to meet, especially in the evening. Here, over a bottle of beer, topics of interest varying from weather to the latest migration are discussed. The village *Schult* meetings are called for business, but often involve more personal interaction than business. One *Schult* meeting the author attended included about one hour of business and two hours of visiting afterward. Officials such as the *Lehrdienst,* deacons, *Vorsteher,* and others are acquainted on a first-name basis with most of the members of all the villages.

The various village activities—repairing the street, fixing the fences on the village pasture, digging a trench to prevent the village from being flooded—provide occasions for primary relationships. Of course, neighboring farmers have numerous occasions when they interact in a closely knit fashion, lending farm implements and generally aiding one another. The absence of fences, except around yards in the traditional village and the village pasture, creates the atmosphere where a sort of open communal ecology exists. Boundaries do not seem as foreboding and limiting as they are in the capitalistic non-Old Colony world. The close interaction pertains mainly to males. Females have less opportunity to interact with others except by means of the visiting practices prevalent in the Old Colony.

The intimate relationships in the family need hardly be commented upon, since they reflect the typical primary family relationship. In general there are no formal events in the family except the meals, during which the whole family acts closely as a unit. Most decisions are made around the table, and the gossip that develops from day to day is shared at mealtime. In some families, a formal religious worship is held either in the evening or at breakfast, but this is not general. In the warm summer evenings after supper, the family often sits outside under the trees, taking advantage of an opportunity for interaction.

There are some village events which involve the families in primary relationships. One of these is the butchering, at which time one family often helps another. It is the old traditional butchering and involves one or two other families in the village or nearby villages. The threshing ring is another such event, when the families involved in a ring provide meals for the workers and otherwise share in the threshing operation.

Although the relationships of members of the Old Colony outside the family or village context are much less primary than those within the more narrow framework of day-to-day activity, they never become so detached as the completely impersonal secondary relationships that characterize modern urban areas. Membership in the Old Colony, recognizable because of similarity in dress and in modes of living, produces a "consciousness of kind" that is very effective in creating solidarity. Among the *"Deetschi"* or "Germans," as they refer to themselves, as distinct from those outside, the terms *"Welt-mensche"* or "people of the world" constitute a threat to soli-darity: "Kroeker says the Wiebes are indignant that there is a man from the 'world' living among the *Gemeent*. This distinction between the world and us is sharply held. In my estimation you are less of the world than, for example, the drunk we have had here for several days, but that does not matter. We think the Christian kingdom is made up of our kin and the blood relationships of the clan. The others are 'worldlings.' "[31]

From this discussion, it is clear that Old Colony members are related on a primary level with many, if not most, other Old Colonists. The relationship is often a first-name one, since belonging to the Old Colony serves as a common de-nominator. Even for those Old Colonists who do not interact often, there is a feeling of common loyalty and kinship which is much greater than that which exists between Old Colonists and members of the host societies.

Even though the Old Colony now numbers over 35,000, the author's experience suggests that there is only a small chance that any one person does not have any knowledge of every other person, even if only by recognition of the family from which he comes. What is the basis for the primary type rela-tionship that obtains? In large part, it is the consequence of the demographic structure of the Old Colony.

The Old Colony as a self-conscious ethnic minority is now about one hundred years old; thus, there are only about five generations to account for. The Old Colony originated with about thirty families in 1890. Since the present population stems from these families, it is relatively easy for a person to be placed within a particular family. It must be remembered that the Old Colony does not proselytize; therefore, few new genes are being introduced from the outside. The result is that the Old Colony is rapidly becoming genetically inter-related.[32] Second-cousin marriages are very common. Apart

31. Material gathered by the author during field research.

32. Gordon Allen and Calvin Redekop, "Individual Differences in Survival and Reproduction Among Old Colony Mennonites in Mexico: Progress to October, 1966," *Eugenics Quarterly*, XIV (June, 1967). On the basis of one sample, an inbreeding coefficient of .019 was established.

from the biological consequences, the fact of multiple inter-relationships widens the capacity for primary relationships, since the family is one of the best structures in which primary relations grow. (See Appendix H for description of marriage relations in a typical village.)

Another reason for the primary relationships is the ratio of interaction with other Old Colonists as opposed to inter-action with outsiders. Especially in the Mexican Old Colony, the amount of interaction with Old Colonists is much higher than with outsiders. This high ratio of interaction, coupled with the cultural homogeneity, serves to give Old Colony members an attitude toward each other that includes a feeling of identity, common purpose, and understanding—earmarks of the primary relationship.

Abundant and strong as primary relationships are, they by no means preclude the possibility of secondary type relations. The conversation which involves unfamiliar members of the Old Colony sometimes reveals a feeling of distance and un-concern about the person. Stories about the hardships experi-enced in British Honduras evoke little sympathy in the Old Colony settlement in Chihuahua. There is some exploitation of Old Colony members by fellow members. Old Colony members who have experienced misfortune are rejected with the statement that misfortune is the person's own fault. Stories of social misfits are told with relish and enjoyed immensely. There are considerable deceit and prevarication, and worthless checks have appeared in the villages. Even though they are not welcomed, secondary relations often do prevail among Old Colonists and are the best indicator that things are not completely as they should be.

Reciprocity

Scholars have proposed that primary relations derive in part from the process of exchange—the giving of "gifts" and the re-ceiving of a "favor" in return.[33] "Although this rule is a

33. Reciprocity as a sociological concept is gaining increasing im-portance since it was introduced by anthropologists, such as Malinow-ski and Radcliffe-Brown. Originally proposed as a mechanism of social control, it has now been expanded to include functions of

general one for all interpersonal relations, it is particularly important in friendship in that it is one of the mechanisms that keeps a friendship going." [34] Indebtedness perpetuates a relationship.

In the Old Colony there are various examples of the principle in operation, mainly on the village level, though of course among friends reciprocity spans villages and even settlements. Barbering illustrates the point. In most Old Colony villages in Mexico there are men who cut hair for others in the village. When asked why he did not charge, one "barber" said, "It would never work. There are too many who cut hair as a favor for others for anyone to get customers. First, there is not enough money available for such a frivolity, and secondly, why exchange money when the actual commodity can be exchanged?" [35] If a person does not feel he can cut another's hair, he usually reciprocates for his haircut by performing a different favor—doing an errand in town, taking him his mail, and so on.

The "meat ring" is an example of reciprocity which does not involve any record-keeping yet pertains to a valuable commodity. Especially during the summer, when meat does not keep very well (this applies only to the traditional settlements of the Old Colony, where refrigerators are not allowed), the fresh meat from one animal is shared throughout the village. About every two weeks one farmer in the village will slaughter a calf or steer. The meat will be cut into as many pieces as there are members of the ring (usually made up of relatives and close friends in the village) and delivered. In order to make sure that each person gets a fair share of the good and poor cuts, they are numbered and distributed on a rotation system. In several weeks another farmer will butcher an animal and the same procedure will be followed.

---

stability and creativity in social relations. See Alvin Gouldner, "The Norm of Reciprocity," *American Sociological Review*, XXV (April, 1960), 161–78.

34. Alvin W. Gouldner *et al., Modern Sociology: An Introduction to the Study of Human Interaction* (New York: Harcourt, Brace & World, Inc., 1963), p. 352.

35. Material gathered by the author during field research.

Since the major towns in Mexico, British Honduras, and Bolivia are a great distance from the colonies, the use of a "messenger" is prevalent. When a farmer plans to make a trip to market, he lets it be known in the village so that requests can be made of him, such as mailing letters, sending an order for certain commodities, or bringing back a special order.

A form of reciprocity which operates among relatives and includes friends is the "watch." When a person is sick, some member of the family or a friend will sit up all night and "watch" the sick person. This activity sometimes will continue for months at a time, until the person dies or recovers. This favor is then returned when a member of another family is sick. Secondary benefits of this practice are that it saves hospital bills and it gathers relatives and friends around the sick one, giving him a sense of belonging and a reason for getting well.

When a new baby is born in the village, neighbors bring soups to the home so that the mother does not need to worry about cooking for the first few days. Normally there are close relatives such as the grandmother who attend a mother and her new child, but the food brought by the neighbors is a gift which is reciprocated as children are born into neighboring families. It is also customary to visit the baby and mother and express best wishes for their health.

The concept of reciprocity is related to that of mutual aid, whereby material goods are shared with more unfortunate members. This applies especially in times of disaster or misfortune. There are many instances when mutual aid is practiced in the Old Colony, though it has been waning significantly in Manitoba and Saskatchewan and declining generally as more labor-saving devices are being bought:

> When we first came here, usually four farmers went together to share machinery and work. It was a lot of fun working together and sharing life in general. But it seems this gradually has been disappearing until now no one wants to work with anyone else. In fact, borrowing is becoming quite a problem. People take advantage of you, or do not bring the borrowed item back. I have had several bad experiences where

it seemed the borrower delighted in breaking the implement and then did not feel obligated to bring it back or fix it. As people have become more well-to-do, it seems they have forgotten about the need for co-operation and will rather go to great expense than co-operate. It seems we can only work together when we are poor or in need.[36]

One area in which mutual aid has been institutionalized is the fire insurance plan that operates in all the settlements. Each farmer pays an assessment according to the fire losses of the entire settlement, though he himself may never benefit from the fund. In Hochfeld in 1957, for example, the total assessment was based on property value amounting to 1,102,170 pesos, for which the yearly premium amounted to 551.08 pesos, prorated among the farmers in Hochfeld according to their holdings.

Young farmers used to be able to borrow money interest-free from wealthy farmers, but this form of mutual aid is being discontinued: "It is quite hard for a young man starting up to borrow money. If he goes to the bank and borrows, he has to pay 12 per cent, and even then he has to have his father or father-in-law sign for it. There are occasional fellows who borrow from rich farmers, but they also have to have a co-signer who has money, so it comes to the same thing, though he can then borrow it for 6 per cent. It is becoming quite like the bank system with money loaning among our church brethren. Apparently there is more and more distrust and dishonesty associated with repayment, for it was not like this in the past." [37]

Communication

Without communication the "life line of interaction would soon be lost and the systems would quickly collapse." [38] The Old Colony member communicates with his fellows in vari-

36. Material gathered by the author during field research.
37. Material gathered by the author during field research.
38. Charles P. Loomis, *Social Systems: Essays on Their Persistence and Change* (New York: D. Van Nostrand Co., Inc., 1960), p. 31.

ous ways. The communication provided within the framework of the family has been alluded to above. Communication in the daily life of the village also needs no further elaboration, except to say that communication practices have varied recently with the use, particularly in Manitoba and Saskatchewan, of cars, telephones, and radios. It is necessary additionally merely to indicate some of the institutional patterns for the communication of ideas and feelings.

One of the clearest examples of an institution that serves communication in addition to the *Schult,* discussed above, is the farm auction. Even though auctions have the ostensible purpose of providing for the exchange of property, a fringe benefit is the opportunity they afford for visiting and gossiping. "The auctioneer got angry several times when there were great groups of men who were talking loudly and not bidding. It was obviously a social event as well as an auction. In fact Wiens and Wiebe both said they would stay at the sale until all the news had been obtained, and then they would be ready to go home. Over-all there were groups of five to ten men standing and talking about various things." [39]

The greatest source of communication is the visitation that is conducted in every village every day of the year. In the leisurely pace of the Old Colony way of life (not nearly so leisurely in Manitoba and Saskatchewan), the typical farmer makes at least one daily trip to the village store and hears the latest news. He also visits at least one or two neighbors a day with two purposes: to achieve some end such as borrowing a tool and to pass the time of day.

Family visiting has been described above, but an account of a visit will illustrate the nature of the communication:

At about 3:30 the Klassens came over. We talked about the fact that there were eighteen marriages in the colony that week [Chihuahua settlement]. They laughed about the courting that a seventy-year-old man was conducting with a lady in a neighboring village. Then the Frank Froeses arrived about 5:00. The recent robberies in the colonies were discussed. At 6:00 the Klassens left for home. After supper, at

39. Material gathered by the author during field research.

about 7:30, the Peter Penners arrived. The British Honduras settlement was discussed as were the possibilities of emigrating to Australia. At 9:00 the Froeses left. From then until about 12:30 A.M. (Monday morning) Peter Penner described experiences that the Old Colony had had with Mexicans, prompted by a recent experience Penner had with a Mexican he caught in his backyard.[40]

Sociologists have defined social interaction as a unit of activity of one person which is followed by some unit of activity of another person.[41] We have seen how a unit of activity—limited by cultural patterns—of one person affects the activities of another person and effects a cultural "design for living."

40. Material gathered by the author during field research.
41. Homans, *The Human Group,* p. 36.

Chapter 5

BREAKING THE COVENANT

The chapter on the goals of the Old Colony indicates that the Old Colony's basic goals are personal salvation and dedication to the Old Colony way of life. These ultimate goals are to be achieved by separation from the world and acceptance by the young people of the Old Colony way of life. These goals have been achieved to varying degrees by the several Old Colony groups. Differences in the degree of achievement from settlement to settlement assume importance in relation to the question: How well has the Old Colony realized its reason for being?

Separation from the World

The "world" has been described above as being composed of people, acts, and things. Thus, separation from the world necessitates isolation from or rejection of other people, their behavior, and the items they use.

The Old Colony settlements have differed among themselves in the degree to which they have separated themselves from "worldly people." In the Manitoba and Saskatchewan settlements, the distinction between "worldly people" and the Old Colony is becoming increasingly hazy; in fact, the interaction with non-Old Colony people is increasing at a rapid pace. Social interaction includes visiting other churches when there are special occasions, such as weddings and funerals of acquaintances and friends, and serving on various church committees dealing with local and regional problems, such as mental health and relief activities.

Social interaction can be inferred when there is a loss of Church members to other denominations. In the Old Colony, loss of a member is often precipitated by marriage, as indicated above. In the village of Reinfeld, eighteen out of a total of about thirty families left the Church during the 1922 migration to Mexico. Of the children from the eighteen families, only one child returned to the Old Colony. In the Manitoba settlement, a random sample indicates that thirty out of fifty marriages recorded between 1900 and 1945 involved non-Old Colony partners.

Interaction with outsiders through the schools has been kept rather minimal in the past because the Old Colony members managed to send their children to schools which were almost totally Old Colony in direction and enrollment. But there are increasing instances in which non-Old Colony children are attending Old Colony schools mainly because Old Colony villages have non-Old Colony members in them. To illustrate, in Chortitz, the village having the highest percentage of Old Colony members per total population, there were fifteen Old Colony children and thirteen non-Old Colony children in grades six to eight in 1958. In a neighboring village, Schanzenfeld, there were seven Old Colony children and twenty-five non-Old Colony children in the same three grades.

The presence of non-Old Colony families in Old Colony villages of course also affects adults and their interaction with outsiders. In Reinfeld, there were twenty Old Colony families in 1958. There were also twenty-five families who belonged to other Mennonite denominations. In Chortitz in 1958, there were twenty-eight Old Colony families, along with eighteen non-Old Colony Mennonite families. In both villages the infiltration began when the majority of Old Colony families moved to Mexico in 1922. There are even cases of non-Mennonite families living in Old Colony villages.

Social interaction which has its origin in matters of an economic nature cannot be tabulated easily. Because of the use of the automobile, telephone, radio, and television, the Old Colonist is in direct and immediate touch with the markets, the buyers, and the commercial world in general. Thus, Old Colony members can be found on boards of local banks, credit unions, mutual insurance associations, and co-operatives.

An educated Old Colony teacher who had completed high school and two years of normal school—the first Old Colonist to progress this far—described the situation in Manitoba and

Saskatchewan as follows: "Before the migration the concept of the Church or brotherhood was uppermost and all things were done as a people. During the migration, it broke down. My mother said often, 'Now it is each man for himself; there is nothing to keep us together.' Thus, I think first the fellowship broke down, and then the ties of working together broke down. We are losing many things and are sorry about it. It seems we are beginning to feel sorry about being Old Colony and want to slough it off as soon as possible." [1]

The traditional Old Colony settlements, those in Alberta, British Columbia, Mexico, British Honduras, and Bolivia, have been much more successful in avoiding contact with worldly people than have those in Manitoba and Saskatchewan. The settlements at Aylmer and Rainy River, Ontario, cannot be evaluated since they are not settlements in the traditional sense, but rather dispersed residences among other people. Because all the settlements are homogeneous Old Colony enclaves, the interaction with others has automatically been restricted very considerably. In none of these colonies are there any strangers who reside in the confines of the settlement. In the Chihuahua settlement, for example, no Mexicans live within the fairly clear boundaries of the settlement, though occasionally a Mexican may stay overnight if he is working for a farmer as a skilled craftsman and his home is a great distance away.

While the writer was living in Hochfeld, his host hired two Mexicans to build a trench silo for him. Since they lived in Cuauhtemoc, some twenty miles away, they stayed for the week, sleeping in the oats bin of the barn, which is connected to the house. The Mexicans were fed in the kitchen. The son of the landlord described the workers and their stay as follows: "The Mexicans are staying overnight. They have been given some covers and sleep in the granary. They always eat after the family has eaten, but usually get the same type of food that the family has eaten earlier. The conversation is carried on in Spanish, and the Mennonite boys talk it quite fluently. These Mexicans seem to be quite friendly and submit

1. Material gathered by the author during field research.

to the ways of the Mennonites. They even bow at the table when silent grace is said. The one knows quite a lot of Low German, probably because of his having worked in a closer way with a lot of Mennonites, since he is a specialist that demands more communication with the patron." [2]

Interaction with the "worldly people" is increasing through the employment of indigenous people by the Old Colony. In almost every village in the Chihuahua settlement, it is possible to meet Mexicans who are working for an Old Colony farmer. Often whole families are hired to pull weeds in the fields. Though the interaction is intentionally kept to a minimum, personal relationships do emerge:

> Johann Friesen has a steady hired hand from Rubio. This Mexican is young and good-looking. Friesen does not believe that the situation is as dangerous as people tell him. When he made a trip to British Honduras, he left the Mexican in charge, and left his daughters at home. The Mexican did not leave the girls alone, though they resisted and did not want to mix; but nevertheless, the condition is worsening. The girls may weaken yet. Franz Giesbrecht calls the Mexican Friesen's son-in-law already. One case like this happened already in the Swift Plan, where a Mexican had close contact; one night, when the parents were gone, he wanted to force the girl to come with him. When she refused, he shot her, but luckily, she pulled through. [3]

Transportation has also brought about increased interaction. Since Old Colony members are forbidden the use of the truck or automobile, they need to hire others to transport them. Bus lines have been routed through the villages in Mexico, and hired cars and trucks haul people and produce. In the Alberta colony, Canadian truckers are hired to drive to Edmonton, a trip of two or three days' duration. Normally two Old Colony men ride in the cab with the truck owner.

Another significant contact with the "worldly" person occurs at the marketplace. In the Fort Vermilion and St. John areas, since access to the marketplace in villages and

2. Material gathered by the author during field research.
3. Material gathered by the author during field research.

towns is limited because of the long distances that must be traveled, interaction is infrequent and is mainly limited to the male members, although occasionally females do ride in the cab with the driver. The same holds for British Honduras, though trips to Belize are more frequent than trips to Edmonton in the Alberta settlement. In Mexico, on the other hand, the trip to town is a common occurrence, especially since the roads and bus service are gradually being improved. In the Chihuahua settlement, the black-topped highway (completed in 1962) which runs through the Manitoba and Swift Plans has provided very satisfactory bus service, with four trips daily to and from Cuauhtemoc through the colonies. In Cuauhtemoc, a livery stable with a cement floor has been provided. The same has been done in Rubio. (See Figure 17.) These stables, provided by the Mexican merchants, attest to the importance of the trade and to the numbers of teams that need to be accommodated.

The Old Colonist is urgently counseled to stay out of the "world's" villages and towns. When the preacher or bishop rides through such villages or towns in his buggy, he tries to see if there are any loiterers on the streets. The *Kroagah* also keeps the ministers informed if anyone is spending too much time on the streets. The ban on rubber tires on tractors was also aimed at keeping Old Colonists off the streets and in the colonies. "There is nothing in the Bible that says rubber is wrong, but the thing it leads to is wrong. As soon as the tractors have rubber, the young fellows would get on them and drive to Cuauhtemoc or other towns and get mixed up in all kinds of wrong. . . ."[4]

There is increasing interaction with Mexicans on the Old Colony premises in the Chihuahua and Durango settlements. The Old Colony village storekeepers as well as blacksmiths and other craftsmen naturally develop business relationships with Mexicans since they provide opportunity for economic gain:

Corny Wiebe who runs the local *paleta* [ice cream bar] shop, has much contact with Mexicans and talks good Spanish.

4. Material gathered by the author during field research.

He has a little one-room house where Mexicans often stay overnight when they make their runs through the villages to the north and back delivering supplies such as soft drinks and fruit and hard staple goods. It is estimated that at least twenty-five Mexicans come into his store every day, either as salesmen or as customers. . . . Yesterday there was a sale in Kronsthal. Wiebe made nine hundred *paletas* and commissioned a Mexican from Rubio to sell them at the sale. He also sold other goods from Wiebe's store. The Mexican got a commission for selling.[5]

The development of nonfarming specialties is also increasing the contact with Mexicans. The lack of land is forcing a large number of young fathers to turn to other kinds of employment. Thus, machine shops, fabrication shops, repair shops, feed mills, and other enterprises develop. The profits in the past have come from Old Colony customers, but there are increasing gains from the exporting of products and services to the Mexicans: "In Schoenhof, Campo 115, a George Klassen operates a shop which has everything a big city garage would have, including a crankshaft lathe. He does work for the Mexican road machinery and has Mexican trucks and cars waiting to get repaired, cluttering up his yard. He is also part owner of a well-drilling outfit that is drilling an expensive hole for a big Mexican apple grower. It is safe to state that this shop is more complete than any garage this side of Chihuahua or Mexico City." [6] Engaging in nonfarming occupations, however, increases the contact with the outsiders and is condemned by the Old Colony *Lehrdienst* and the mores of the Colony. An Old Colony bishop indicated his concern about the increasing interaction of Old Colonists and Mexicans in the following statement: "The greatest problem in the colonies in relation to the Mexicans are the village stores. There is a lot of intimate and personal contact in the stores, and the temptation and opportunity for much mixing and immorality. I wish our people would not operate stores." [7]

5. Material gathered by the author during field research.
6. Material gathered by the author during field research.
7. Material gathered by the author during field research.

Despite such official protests there are even isolated cases in which Old Colony members and Mexicans have gone into partnership:

> In Silberfeld, Campo 26, there is a box factory which supplies a good proportion of all wooden boxes for Mexican fruit. It is supplied by Mexican truckers who get the lumber from the hills. There is a joint ownership of the factory, one being an Old Colonist, the other a wealthy Mexican from Chihuahua who does most of the "dirty work" of avoiding the payment of income tax and other taxes which can be avoided if the right people are known. . . . The factory was not able to function and make profits as long as only Old Colonists were running it because of the red tape and governmental interference, which they did not understand and were not able to sidestep.[8]

The low standard of living of the indigenous people surrounding the Old Colony settlements makes labor available at a much more economical rate than the Old Colony members can find within their own borders and thereby serves to increase the interaction between Old Colonists and Mexicans. The average Mexican makes fifteen to twenty pesos a day, whereas the Old Colony member makes thirty or forty pesos for the same work. An illustration further indicates the difference. For several days a Mexican had asked for work from a farmer in Hochfeld. Finally the farmer put the Mexican to work digging a privy hole, for ten pesos a day. The Mexican did not get much work done, and the farmer's two boys were sitting in the shade most of the time the Mexican was digging. Asked about this situation, the farmer replied, "We can make money sitting in the shade. We would eat up more food than he costs. The Mexicans can live on almost nothing." The economic power of the difference in the standard of living is making itself felt in unmistakable terms and will continue to do so and to result in interaction until the two societies live on similar economic levels.

The breakdown of the isolation from "worldly persons" is taking place in other ways. With the expansion of the

8. Material gathered by the author during field research.

farming areas into one-time frontiers, it is no longer possible for Old Colonists to obtain contiguous areas of land. Pockets of "natives" are being encircled by the Old Colony, thereby increasing the extent of interaction with outsiders.

One must conclude that the Old Colony systems in Manitoba and Saskatchewan have not succeeded in avoiding contact with the "world," if in fact they so intended. But it is equally clear that the Old Colony systems in Alberta, British Columbia, Mexico, British Honduras, and Bolivia have been fairly successful in restricting interaction with "outsiders." The question to be answered in this connection is whether the definition of the "world" has shifted in the Manitoba and Saskatchewan settlements so that they consider themselves no more worldly than the other groups who have drawn the line at a much more conservative place. This question will be explored below.

Another major Old Colony tactic for remaining separate from the "world" is to refrain from behavior that the "worldly" person exhibits.

Again the Manitoba and Saskatchewan colonies differ from the others. In these two settlements, the behavior of the Old Colonist is in many ways similar to that of the surrounding society. In religious behavior the similarity is increasingly evident: church services are becoming shorter; songs are sung at a faster tempo; shorter and more evangelistic sermons are being preached, and overt expressions of feelings are more prevalent. One young preacher in Manitoba was beginning to preach in a manner similar to that of evangelists who visited the area. He soon got into trouble with his elders, though the young people responded to his preaching enthusiastically, indicating a generational change in orientation.

Young people are also beginning to go to local Bible schools and beginning to behave and think in the manner typical of the region. They participate in evangelistic campaigns and attempt to promote the "evangelical" temper in the congregations. Sunday schools are being started by some leaders with the intention of increasing the knowledge of the Bible and upgrading Christian commitment. Bible study groups are springing up, as are young people's organizations that give the Old Colony youth a sense of identity and purpose.

The ethical behavior of the Old Colony member is not as rigidly controlled as it was formerly. The honesty of the original settlements before the great migration is no longer found, according to some observers:

The breakdown of the honesty and integrity as well as the more equal distribution of wealth can be attributed to the Church disorganization when the Old Colony left. The people who borrow are not as honest as they used to be. One time I sold a horse to an Old Colonist for $150 and he only gave me $20 down and said he would pay the rest as soon as he could. That fall I had the rest of the money, and we had no note of any kind. Now we are having some trouble with our Church members about paying debts. We bought a house for $700 in Schanzenfeld for a newly married Old Colony fellow. We loaned it to him without interest, but the poor fellow has not paid any money back yet. I do not know whether he cannot or does not want to; I suspect it is the latter.[9]

The regulations of the Church are no longer respected as they were before. Smoking and drinking are indulged in despite the admonitions of the *Lehrdienst*. Beer is widely sold in the village stores operated mainly by Old Colony members, though this practice, too, is strongly condemned by the *Lehrdienst*. A layman suggested the problem is getting quite serious: "The elders and ministers are unable to do too much about the drinking and smoking habits of many members. They go to the saloon at 10 A.M. and stay till 10 P.M. They drink worse than the English. They do it with a vengeance." [10] Young girls do not dress as modestly as they used to, nor are the women continually careful to observe regulations governing dress. The Old Colony once adhered to the belief that the female should worship with her head covered. Now the Church must enforce the practice: "Rev. Wiebe, at the close of the wedding service, had a word to say to the girls.

9. Material gathered by the author during field research.
10. Material gathered by the author during field research.

'Would you not please comply with the admonition that the Word gives us that you be covered? The angels see what is done and are happy and honored when they see faithful women appearing covered. This applies to all women, not just the young. They can all respond to this call. It is commanded in the Bible and we should be faithful.' " [11]

In social behavior the Old Colonist's actions are conforming more and more to those of the larger society. The young people are beginning to "carouse" as "worldly people" do. "The problem of the young people is the Saturday night carousing and always wasting time up town. This is living the world's way. In our day, that was not done. They did not learn to do this from us. It is up to the parents. Many parents do not care about their children and let them do what they want to." [12] The youth also participate enthusiastically in sports, one of the few activities allowed them, and in this way have opportunity for interaction with "outsiders," particularly through the formation of and participation in baseball leagues, some of which contain non-Old Colony members.

More young people than ever before pursue higher education. From the twenty-four Old Colony families in the village of Chortitz in 1958, twelve young people were attending the local high school. One woman, in her mid-thirties when she was interviewed, said, "The Old Colony has been negative to education by simply ignoring it. The idea was that they needed the help of the children at home. I, for example, had to stay at home until I was twenty-three, and then barely got to go to school. My parents did not refuse, like some did, but they needed me at home." [13]

The schools in the Old Colony villages are conducted largely like those of other communities, except as a Mennonite schoolteacher modifies the behavior of his charges. As indicated earlier, a Mennonite schoolteacher is hired, when possible, to retain as much of the Old Colony orientation as possible. This is to say that he is to include a Bible study

---

11. Material gathered by the author during field research.
12. Material gathered by the author during field research.
13. Material gathered by the author during field research.

hour, principally as a vehicle for the teaching of the German language.

Many young people are taking jobs in the towns and cities. Again, in Chortitz in 1964, there were twenty-six males and twenty-five females working in Winkler or more distant towns and cities. In addition eight married couples had moved to Winkler or other towns and cities.

The change in behavior is observable mainly in the young. The older generation is changing much more slowly, although the changes are observable over a longer period of time. The occasional Old Colony adult may follow the sports section of a newspaper or support the local village baseball team. It is probable that traditional forms of behavior are being observed by the adults despite changes in attitudes and beliefs, for most parents are not overly resistant to the changes in their children's behavior.

Farming patterns are almost identical to those practiced beyond Old Colony boundaries. Production, control, and price support programs are participated in by all the Old Colony farmers. The latest methods of farming are used, as are modern fertilizers and sprays against insects and diseases. The types of crops raised and the seeding and harvesting procedures are identical. The farmers participate in local cooperative marketing and production associations. There is little observable difference in the farming practices of the Old Colonists and "worldly" people.

In the Old Colony settlements in Mexico, British Honduras, Bolivia, British Columbia, and Alberta, unlike those in Manitoba and Saskatchewan, the behavior patterns are much less like those of the "world."

Religious services are conducted in the traditional method. There is still the long period of silence as the members congregate and wait for the minister. It still takes fifteen minutes to sing four to five verses of one of the songs in the *Gesangbuch*. Sermons can last as long as two or three hours, punctuated by the parade of listeners who depart the building momentarily to use the rustic outdoor facilities. The minister, whether for effect or relief, still makes use of the pulpit spittoon; and the sawdust on the floor of the church buildings still serves to absorb the spittle of the gentlemen in the congregation.

Undesirable behavior is avoided in the more conservative settlements mainly because of external restraints and traditions, not because there is inner compulsion. A Canadian Old Colonist is the source of the following: "I know of a fellow in Mexico who was very much afraid of the thunder, which is quite common and terrifying during the months of July and August. When he saw a storm coming, he would smoke as heavily as possible so that if something should happen and he would have to make a covenant with God, he would have had enough to last him. I think he was convicted, but not enough to give it up." [14]

Social behavior has not changed appreciably since the settlements began. Most of the waking moments of the Old Colonist are spent in working, even though at a relaxed pace. There are few varieties of leisure. There are no recreational activities, since most of them have been condemned historically. The family spends the little time after supper relaxing, before going to bed. In summer, supper is served so late that there is little time afterward for activities. In the winter, the longer evenings are spent visiting with neighbors, friends, or relatives in the villages. Often parents will leave the farm in charge of the children and make a two-day trip to visit a relative or friends in one of the distant villages. Those who are interested in hobbies can pursue them in the winter. Since musical instruments are forbidden, as are other types of "worldly" activities, legitimate hobbies consist of making of furniture or other useful articles. The writer has only several times come across evidence of a hobby that was not utilitarian. A clockmaker is known in the Mexican settlements, but he has made his hobby into a business and is very actively patronized.

The main reading materials of the Old Colonist are the Bible, which he peruses infrequently, and the *Steinbach Post,* a weekly German-language newspaper, which has long been the accepted source of news about the outside world, about

14. Material gathered by the author during field research.

other Mennonites, and about the other Old Colony settlements. "The *Steinbach Post,* published at Steinbach, Manitoba, is the only paper that is regularly read by the Old Colony. Almost every family gets it. Upon investigation it appears that the *Steinbach Post* early began having correspondents from all outlying Mennonite settlements. The best reason why the Old Colony read only the *Steinbach Post* is because it carries reports of 'our people who live in various parts of Mexico and other areas.' " [15]

The young people spend their free time visiting with peers in the village. During the evenings the village streets are dotted with groups of fellows or girls who are gossiping about acquaintances, escapades that have recently taken place, or problems connected with the *Gemeent* such as the question of rubber tires on tractors. The range of topics is narrow and the discussion concrete, rarely dealing with philosophical or speculative subjects.

Although the regulations of the Church are still quite rigorously applied, there is increasing resistance to, even defiance of, some of them. The schoolteachers especially express a considerable amount of impatience and opposition. About seven years ago, several schoolteachers were in a semi-excommunicated state because of their recalcitrant attitude toward some of the prohibitions affecting teaching, such as the ban on all illustrated books or use of illustrations in teaching. "I still get all sorts of complimentary copies of books from Germany which I keep to get ideas for myself, even though I ought not have anything like that. I don't think the *Darp* leaders are so particular, but we have an *Ohm* (minister) in the village, and he takes care. I use the blackboard for illustration purposes, and they cannot say much about this since it is quickly erased." [16]

Young people sometimes engage in worldly behavior, though this is not very frequent. In Mexico, occasionally some young fellows may go to the larger towns to get drunk or to rendezvous with Mexican girls. During the Christmas holidays,

15. Material gathered by the author during field research.
16. Material gathered by the author during field research.

young fellows will sometimes indulge in carousing, but this tends to be a common practice.

> Visiting on the street is the most common pastime for the fellows as well as the girls. Among us fellows one of the best entertainments is to see how crazy we can be when we get drunk. We dare each other to drink so much, and see what happens. That picture you saw of us lying on the ground was on the second holiday last Christmas. It is the custom for us to drink as much whiskey as we can stand. Then we all get sick and have to vomit terrifically. Once last year three of us went to a sale, and we bought a bottle of whiskey, and John drank so much that when we got there he talked and greeted everybody, but did not remember anything of the sale. Several times I have gotten drunk by myself and lain in the ditch till past midnight, for I was ashamed to go in, since my parents were still up.[17]

Staying out late, beyond the time the parents set as curfew, is a common occurrence, among the young men especially.

Drunkenness among older persons has been rare historically though there have been and are occasional cases. As a Mexican medical doctor who knows the Old Colony well said, "Drinking is another vice which many Mennonites have. They do not follow the Mexican pattern of drinking in public places. They are recluse drinkers who will get drunk by themselves or in isolated places. They will go on sprees that last for weeks, and become completely uninhibited."[18]

In the economic realm, the Old Colony settlements in Mexico, British Honduras, Bolivia, and the conservative Canadian settlements have retained their practices to a great degree. The basic economic enterprises are working the soil, seeding it to the crops that will grow, and harvesting the proceeds. Only rarely are cattle raised for slaughter. Hogs are fed for home consumption and for sale. Chickens are being raised on an increasingly large scale, especially in Mexico, with some flocks numbering five thousand layers. A dairy of twenty to thirty milk cows is considered large. The large

17. Material gathered by the author during field research.
18. Material gathered by the author during field research.

herds or the mass production schemes that are developing in the American and Latin American agriculture are not present in the Old Colony. Rather, the small, highly diversified family farm is the general pattern. (See Table 3-2 for description of farm size.)

Modern techniques are still not widely applied in the more traditional settlements. Modern soil conservation practices are not understood or considered necessary. Fertilizer is still not used in Mexico, after forty years of depleting the soil. Many individual farmers admit that something should be done, but in general Old Colony farmers find excuses for their failure to modernize: "What we lack is the understanding of the English language, so we could read the chicken journals that come from the States. The Mexicans are eager to sell us all sorts of medicines, but we are never sure whether it is the right or wrong thing. Sometimes we feed them exactly the wrong thing, I am sure. If we had one veterinarian in the colonies, we would be able to benefit much more from the opportunities and we would prosper much more. We do not understand enough of the technical matters of cattle and poultry raising. We would like to work more with purebred stuff, but then we need to know what is needed to produce good animals." [19]

Some new practices have been tried, but with limited results. In 1957, for example, trench silos were introduced into the Mexican settlements and built by many farmers. Since they require hard work, depend on the success of the corn crop, and contribute in no directly measurable way to the milk-producing capabilities of a farmer's cows, some have already fallen into disuse.

The contact with the "world" through interaction with its people and involvement in its activities implies the use of cultural objects that the "world" uses. In general, then, the degree to which a settlement reaches beyond its realm for contact with others and their activities affects its use of worldly goods.

The progressive settlements in Manitoba and Saskatchewan

19. Material gathered by the author during field research.

at present use almost all the objects that the "world" does. Tractors with rubber tires were utilized as soon as they were available in the 1930's and are used today. Trucks and cars are owned and operated by all the members of the Old Colony and have been since the 1930's. Electricity has been used in the homes and barns since about 1940 as have electrical appliances. Most homes have radios though they were not officially permitted until 1950, when the *Lehrdienst* decided to sanction what was being widely used. Television is still officially condemned, though a few families own sets. The reasoning behind this prohibition is, naturally, the traditional one—that television brings the "world" into the home and confuses the members' distinctions between right and wrong.

The dress patterns and clothing among the young cannot be distinguished from those of the surrounding societies, except that the Old Colonists do not wear gaudy clothing to church. The older people, especially the women, wear dresses that are homemade, or very conservative "store bought" ones. The women's Sunday garb is in many ways the old traditional garb, with a head covering, called the *Kraunz,* worn beneath the shawl. The shawl is no longer always black as it used to be and in many cases is bought in the stores. The men wear the conventional suit, though the more orthodox do not wear a tie to church services.

An interesting exception to the wholesale adoption of technology is the prohibition of the use of electricity and lights in the Church meetinghouses. The most apparent explanation is that the meetinghouse symbolizes the traditional belief system, and a too rapid change in it would create doubt as to the continuity of the Old Colony as a religious system. When the meetinghouse at Reinfeld (Manitoba) was renovated (1958), some of the members wanted to have electric lights installed in the building. This created a great amount of contention, settled finally through a compromise: the furnace would be controlled and fired by electricity; the Sunday School rooms in the basement could have lights; there would be no lights in the sanctuary. The older meetinghouses in the Manitoba settlement still do not have electricity, though it is gradually being introduced as old buildings are renovated or new ones are built.

In the traditional settlements, abstinence from "worldly" things is still much more rigidly practiced. In all these settlements, the automobile and truck are expressly forbidden, and no one who is in good standing owns one. There are cases in which a person defies the prohibition, but he is flaunting the norms and is usually in trouble with the *Gemeent*. "Today a truck sped through the village at a high speed. Corny and Henry said it was a Mennonite truck from Burwalde. The man owned the truck but did not belong in the Church anymore. 'He must have fallen by the way.'" [20] Some members own automobiles and trucks but keep them hidden in Mexican villages or at the border. These violaters are dealt with when discovered.

> I was just beginning to farm and had a crop failure. So I thought that I would buy a truck and earn some money and then sell it again. I made good money hauling, mostly for Mennonites, but this was the signal to be excommunicated. The Bishop came to me and told me that I was sinning, that I could not come into the Church again till I had confessed and repented of my sin. I told him I would not repent; I was not guilty of any sin. I came to Church as usual the next Sunday, and before the service the Bishop and the *Ohms* had a meeting and called me in. The Bishop said I had to confess much before I could get in. He said that those who buy cars and trucks and other forbidden objects usually do it to cover up much more grievous sins. They told me that I should confess my worse sins.[21]

Tractors are allowed; in fact, they were imported from Canada during the great migration to Mexico, but they should not have rubber tires on them. Rubber tires themselves are not considered evil; what they lead to is:

> Originally the ban on the rubber-tired tractor and the truck was introduced to keep the *Gemeent* together, to inhibit

20. Material gathered by the author during field research.
21. Material gathered by the author during field research.

too much intercourse and mixing with the world. Let's say we allowed rubber tires on the rear of the tractor. Soon someone would say, "C is using his tractor as a truck—I would rather use a truck than a rubber-tired tractor, so I have ample reason to get a truck." Then E would say, "D is using his truck not only for hauling but as a car. Since I would rather have a car than a truck, I have full reason to buy a car." Thus it is the fact that one thing inexorably leads to the next that we try to stop somewhere. We cannot stop it though, for rubber in front has to all practical purposes been condoned, and the foot is in the door for rubber in back, and so the story will develop.[22]

In the Mexican settlements, the agitation to adopt rubber tires had been going on for a long time. At first rubber tires were used only in front, a use finally approved by official action. The argument had been made that rubber in front facilitated steering without providing faster means of transportation. An Old Colonist concerned with the issue describes it as follows: "The whole problem of deciding what should or could be condoned and what could not is not a moral or spiritual one. It is rather the problem of drawing the line. The Bishop of the Swift Plan once said that it was easier to hold the line tight than to push the line back once it had advanced too far. It is the idea of moving too hastily and having to face the consequences of a decaying society that is feared most. Many have said time and time again that with the condoning of rubber in front, the camel's nose is in the tent." [23]

The issue is a sensitive one in the British Honduras settlement as well. From evidence available, two types of people moved to British Honduras: those who believed that the Old Colony people in Mexico were "going to the dogs," and those who wanted to get away from the "hypocrisy" of the Mexican government. When the settlement was being made, the "liberal" members obtained some tractors with rubber tires, maintaining that the need for hauling supplies from Belize demanded rubber-tired tractors. The conservative group re-

22. Material gathered by the author during field research.
23. Material gathered by the author during field research.

acted with indignation. The tension mounted and finally the rubber-tired group's young people were denied baptism. This resulted in a call to the *Lehrdienst* in Manitoba to come and conduct the catechism and baptism in the "excommunicated" group. The Canadian *Lehrdienst* responded by sending two men to British Honduras with instructions to try to harmonize the two factions. The minister and deacon would not budge. The minister stated emphatically, "I came here with a promise to the *Gemeent* that I would keep the *Gemeent* as it had always been. I am going to fulfill my vows." The leader of the "progressive" group retorted by saying, "If we had always remained as we were, we would still be in the Catholic Church." [24] (See Appendix E for further details of controversy.)

The tractor tire has been one of the most hotly debated and emotional issues that has faced the Old Colony system in the traditional colonies. Intuitively the leadership has perceived that a breakdown in the control of transportation would be the beginning of the end. Their worst fears seem to have been realized. The test case came when a group of young farmers in the southern part of the Manitoba Plan in the Chihuahua settlement banded together and unashamedly drove their tractors with rubber tires on front and back wheels. When the ministers could not do anything by personal persuasion, the bishops finally issued an ultimatum: remove the tires by a certain date or be excommunicated. The "Young Turks" called his bluff and did not respond by the stipulated time.

The final showdown with the rubber tires came some weeks ago, when the three bishops got together and decided that the time had come for a final housecleaning. So a letter was sent to the villages of the Manitoba Plan (the other Plans are not bothered with it as much). It was sent to the *Darpe* south of the tracks, for that is where the major forces lie, because of the hard and stony ground. But soon after the letter went out the bishops felt that this might prove too explosive, so they began to follow up their ultimatum letters by holding meetings in the individual *Darpe* and discussing

24. Material gathered by the author during field research.

with each farmer privately his situation and his intentions to work with the *Gemeent* or to refuse. It is known that a good majority of those who have rubber are standing pat, though some have reneged and recanted.[25]

The bishops lost, for there was a good deal of sympathy for the young farmers among the other members of the settlement. Since that time, the use of rubber tires on the rear wheels has very quickly made its way through the villages. Now the Nord Plan is the refuge for those who are trying to hold the line. Some farmers have moved there as a protest to the "worldly" direction being taken by the Manitoba Plan.

Other worldly things have been much easier to control than has the rubber tire. There is no telephone service in any of the colonies. If there is need for quick communication, a telegram is sent, or a Mexican is hired to deliver messages by car. Newspapers and magazines other than the *Steinbach Post* are forbidden and cannot be found in the homes. Similarly, books are banned from the homes: they introduce "worldly" ideas and wishes into the mind. Only old Montgomery Ward and Sears catalogs are permitted, primarily used to entertain children.

Most modern conveniences are forbidden in the traditional settlements. There are, however, notable exceptions. Many Old Colonists have had water brought into their kitchens either through hand pumps or pressure systems. Some homes have gas refrigerators. Electric lights are common in the chicken barns and other barns, and even in the kitchen, defended on "economic" grounds. Electricity is produced on each farm with a diesel light plant. Machine shops and blacksmith shops are fully equipped with electrical machines and tools.

Other products of modern society have made their way into traditional areas. In many homes one can find closets or cupboards well stocked with medicines which can be bought, especially in Mexico, without prescription. Many parents inject their children with drugs.[26] Certain types of clothing

25. Material gathered by the author during field research.
26. See Chapter 2 for reference to medical practices in the "Life History of Henry Neufeld."

have been adopted as well. In Mexico most young males wear the Mexican sombrero as part of the work outfit. The Mexican *canasta* (bag) is used widely for shopping trips. Both of these objects, however, are utilitarian and are justified on this basis. The female dress has not changed in any fashion by the adoption of Mexican articles. (The straw hat some women wear is made in Mexico, but is not worn by the general population.) In the other areas, such as British Honduras, Alberta, and British Columbia, the costuming has not changed and is similar to that worn in Mexico.

The adoption of indigenous architectural forms has been resisted for the most part in all the traditional colonies. The basic form of the house-barn is similar in Mexico, Alberta, and British Columbia, though there have been some adaptations. In British Honduras, the climate has forced the construction of two-story houses built off the ground, away from the dampness, subject to the air movement higher up. The houses there are separated from the barn, from its flies and insects.

An occasional young person possesses things which are forbidden by the Church, such as a camera or radio. Though such objects are not numerous, their existence is known among the young people, who make them the subject of discussion and trade.

However the "world" is defined, it must be agreed that the traditional settlements have achieved the goal much more successfully than have the more progressive ones. If, however, one uses the definition of the world as the progressive groups see it, then it is not clear which group has been the more successful. But this problem must await later discussion.

Propagating the Old Colony Way of Life

If the Old Colony is to achieve its own way of life, it is not enough for it to remain separate from the world. It will also be necessary for the Old Colony to retain all of its offspring to carry on the way of life, since recruitment from the outside has never been practiced lest strange ideas and practices be brought into the Old Colony and threaten to contaminate and destroy it.[27] The Old Colony, therefore, has never incorporated outsiders into the Church, even if there were interested persons.

In the progressive Old Colony settlements many young people are not joining the Old Colony Church and therefore do not remain in the community. Many young people are marrying outsiders and leaving the *Gemeent,* as indicated above. Others are leaving the Church for other reasons.

When the migration to Mexico from Canada had been completed, about 1,186 Old Colonists remained in the Manitoba settlement. In 1943, the population had decreased to

Table 5-1   Population Data for Mexico and British Honduras Old Colony Settlements for the Years 1953–1958[a]

Year	Births	Deaths	Total Popula- tion	Crude Birth Rate	Crude Death Rate	Net Increase Absolute	Per Cent Increase
1953	767	151	18,287	42.4	8.2	616	3.8
1954	909	162	18,871[b]	48.0	8.5	747	3.9
1955	899	142	19,731	45.5	7.1	757	3.7
1956	1,167	153	20,474	56.9	7.4	1,014	4.9
1957	1,019	160	19,703	51.7	8.0	859	4.3
1958	918	183	20,575	44.7	8.0	735	3.4
Totals	5,679	951	20,575	Ave. 48.2	7.8	4,728	Ave. 4.0

[a] Source: Official Old Colony Church Records.

[b] Since the immigration and out-migration are not listed in the records, the percentages are based on the excess of births over deaths, not on the totals given in the Church records as "total population." We can conclude, since births exceeded deaths by 4,728 in the six-year period, that 2,440 persons emigrated to Canada; otherwise, the total population would have been 23,015.

1,116. During the same year, 37 babies were born and 4 persons died, increasing the number by 33 persons. To this total must be added 60 persons who returned from Mexico. This amounted to a 7.9 per cent increase during the year (2.19 per cent from natural increase, 5.0 per cent from Old Colony immigration from Mexico). (See Table 5-1 for total statistics for a six-year period.)

27. See Calvin Redekop, "Postulates Concerning Religious Intentional Ethnic Groups," *Concern* (Scottdale: Mennonite Publishing House, 1959), IX, 33–37 (occasional pamphlet series).

Using a conservative estimate of a 2.5 per cent natural increase and a 3 per cent increase through returnees from Mexico, the population in 1963 in Manitoba should have been about 3,256. The actual total was 2,337. Thus, there was a theoretical loss of 919 persons between 1943 and 1963. (This figure is somewhat inaccurate since the birth rate has gone from 2.9 per cent per year in 1943 to 3 per cent in 1953.) Comparing the proportion of Old Colonists leaving for Mexico and the present Mexican population with the proportion that stayed in Manitoba, we find that the Manitoba Old Colony should have had a population of 3,674 in 1963, instead of the actual 2,337. Since the Manitoba rate of increase includes the reproduction contributed by the immigrants from the Old Colony in Mexico, this figure is more revealing. It would seem safe to suggest that an average of at least 38 persons has left the Old Colony in Manitoba each year, whether by out-marriage, lapse of Church membership, or affiliations with other denominations in family or individual units

One of the best ways to check membership loss is by an actual count of young people from completed families (families whose childbearing has been completed) who left the Old Colony Church in certain villages chosen at random. Several village samples indicate that one of seven young people is leaving the Church for reasons other than marriage. It would seem, from the evidence, therefore, that approximately 15 to 20 per cent of the young people in the Old Colony in Manitoba and Saskatchewan leave the Old Colony. This figure may fluctuate and probably is increasing. "Quite a few young people are leaving because of a self-consciousness and inferior attitude. There are three big reasons why young people leave the Church: 1) they don't want to be looked down upon; 2) they want liberty and freedom to develop; 3) they want more activities. Those, of course, that leave for the bigger cities are lost." [28]

The loss of the young people to the Church is not the only measure of success or failure in propagating the Old Colony way of life. It may be that many young people remain in the *Gemeent* without wholeheartedly internalizing the Old

28. Material gathered by the author during field research.

Colony way of life. This might have two important consequences: disloyal members in the Old Colony will probably
reveal their lack of agreement with the system; a negative
atmosphere resulting from the disloyal segment might cause
the next generation to be socialized out of the system.

There are many indications that the young people are not
accepting the Old Colony system completely and eagerly, as
the influx of worldly activities demonstrates. It would seem
logical to assume that when forbidden practice is accepted as
common, there is a resulting change in the value system or
diminished loyalty to that system. An educated Old Colony
member pinpoints the problem:

> The greatest problem that I see for the Old Colony is the
> young people. We will lose many more than we are losing
> at present if we do not do something. You cannot expect
> them to conform to our ideas completely. There must be some
> form of give and take. Further, the times are bringing with
> them greater changes, and these changes demand more
> change and openness to change on our part. . . . Since the
> war, many of our young people are not satisfied with farm
> life any more. They want to earn money and live like city
> people. They want the money so they can buy cars and other
> things. They do not want to work hard any more.[29]

An older parent described the young generation as follows:

> The young people in the *Darp* are beginning to live their
> own life pretty much. The girls are getting to be just like
> the boys. They smoke and are beginning to dress like
> them and cut their hair. They play on Sunday, and there
> is little the elders and parents can do. They want to be them-
> selves. They need things to do. They are more insubordinate
> than they used to be. This can be traced to the breakdown
> of village life. You can't do anything with the children in
> the village any more because they are all over the village. It
> used to be that the children would stay home except probably
> for one night a week. But now there is no holding them,
> and there is no respect for authority. Village life is not like
> it used to be, when there was order in the home and in the

29. Material gathered by the author during field research.

village. Rarely did childen spend any time on the street. Now they are on the street day and night.[30]

Another member, a Church leader, voiced his concern that something be done to win the support of the Old Colony's youth:

> The only way we can save our young people is to have more Church activities in which they can take part, such as evening meetings on Sunday, Bible study other evenings, and other such activities. It seems many of our most aggressive and able people join other churches, and it is precisely these people we need to challenge our young people. The introduction of Sunday Schools has done a lot already, and we are very happy for it. There are many of the younger men about my age who see the problem of our young people, but many of the older are not concerned. I think that our Church is beginning to stress more the inner experience, but to many the outer form is still the important thing.[31]

The young people are sensitive to many of the same shortcomings and are vocal about their dissatisfactions:

> Another thing I don't like is the singing. . . . Some of the songs are stuffy and sung very poorly. We had a song choir or youth choir in the village some years ago, but now there is no one to lead it. There are no organized youth activities in the village. Sometimes I wish there were, something like a Bible study evening or something. I do not think too many of the older people would be against it. There was not too much opposition when the Sunday School was introduced. There are always some who are opposed to everything, and usually they are the same ones. There seems not to be too much unity among the young people, else something might be organized.[32]

The situation is not hopeless, however, as is evidenced by the fact that the Old Colony Church membership is now increasing slightly. Also, some of the young people still attach considerable significance to Church membership, a fact which

30. Material gathered by the author during field research.
31. Material gathered by the author during field research.
32. Material gathered by the author during field research.

the leadership recognizes, as it recognizes the need to make religious experience meaningful experience:

> I am fairly well satisfied with our Church. There are some things about which I am unhappy, but in general it is all right. I plan to become a member when I get old enough. I do not like the way many people join the Church in a very light-hearted manner. They do not realize the seriousness of joining Church. Many do it to get married, though there are some who take it quite seriously. I guess they think it is necessary to get married, and nothing else.
>
> The sermon [at a baptism] indicated that the candidates might not understand the full significance of the act they were doing and probably were not entirely sincere. They were told time and again that this was the most important event of their lives. . . . The formation of the *Bund* [covenant] with God and with the *Gemeent* was also stressed. At the close of the sermon, the Bishop took the opportunity to apply the elements of the covenant to all the members. He said this was not being done for the candidates alone, but for all the members, that they would evaluate and criticize themselves, to see whether they were living according to the promises they had made.[33]

The evidence seems to indicate that the young people will become increasingly critical and exert greater pressure on adults if they choose to involve themselves fully in the existing way of life. The Bishop of the Manitoba settlement stated, "The greatest problem is protecting the children from adopting the practices of the world. . . . Parents are very important in this process." Also important is the tendency toward critical evaluation, for therein lies the means to conscious acceptance of and commitment to the traditions of the Old Colony.

The best tactic in retaining the young people would be to baptize children at a younger age, thereby divorcing the concept of baptism from marriage, but there appears to be no conscious analysis of the problem and its solution in the Old Colony.

The attitudes expressed in adult conversation about the

33. Material gathered by the author during field research.

"politics" of "inner" Old Colony life will no doubt have their influence on the young generation that is coming on.

> When some Mennonites are up for Church membership, Neufeld says to them, "You should not smoke," and he would be supported by the other preachers; but Friesen is more interested in gaining more members than he is in seeing to it that they quit smoking or drinking, though he is also against drinking. Friesen is known as the little pope among his members. He is very power hungry, wants to rule people. It is said that Rev. Epp, who would like to lead the Church to more evangelical life, cannot because Friesen has loaned him a great deal of money, so that Epp is merely a mouthpiece for Friesen. There has been a general conflict and fight in Reinfeld for the last few years. Friesen's son is the chairman of the schoolboard and some were interested in getting him out. When the election rolled around, Friesen drove around the village politicking and sewing up the votes for his son. He was able to force his congregation to stand solidly behind his son, while the other faction is composed of the members of other churches. The reason for trying to get Friesen off of the schoolboard was his dictatorial method. One time several of the board members had gone out of town for a few days, and in their absence a schoolboard meeting had been advertised, held and the business decided. When we asked for the minutes, we were given the cold shoulder.[34]

The retention of young people, both in terms of membership in the Old Colony and internalization of its attitudes, is much less a problem in the traditional than in the progressive settlements. In the Mexican Old Colony systems, the rate of intermarriage is almost nil. Only three Old Colony men have married Mexican women, as far back as the Old Colonists could remember. All three men have stayed in the general area of the Old Colony settlement, but none was allowed to settle in the villages. "Warkentine married a Mexican girl and now earns a living trucking. He was not disciplined since he married the girl before he joined the Church. He is apparently happy, but persuaded his brother, who was also interested in a Mexican girl, not to marry her. I do not know

---

34. Material gathered by the author during field research.

the reasons, but I suppose it has something to do with family relations and being left out of things. I do not know where he attends church, but I suppose he goes to the Catholic Church in Rubio." [35] Two Old Colony women are known to have married Mexican men. One lives in a neighboring town (Celulosa) and often goes into the Cuauhtemoc area of the Old Colony to beg for food and money. Persons who marry non-Old Colonists are banned as soon as they do so. The only other alternative in cases of intermarriage—acceptance of the outsider by the Old Colony—is not a possibility, even if the nonmember is willing.

It is estimated that six men and several women have left the Old Colony to live in the "world." In all cases, they were allegedly personality deviants who indulged in antisocial or asocial behavior. Most persons who leave the closely knit Old Colony are so shocked by their encounter with their new surroundings that they return to the colonics; in fact, this happens fairly often. Those who do not return are deviants who cannot adjust to the Old Colony.[36]

Sizable migrations are constantly taking place from Mexico to British Honduras, Canada, and now to Bolivia; and internal migrations occur regularly from one settlement to another. The Old Colony Church records indicate that on the average, fifty Old Colonists migrate to Manitoba and become rooted in the Old Colony communities there each year. (It is not known how many migrate to Canada and fail to join the Old Colony Church there.) This is a small migration since the other settlements formed in Canada—Aylmer, Rainy River, and Matheson, for example, all in Ontario—have in recent years attracted more of the Mexican Old Colony emigrants than have migrations to Manitoba. There are, in addition, the

35. Material gathered by the author during field research.

36. Because of the unavailability of Church records, the reluctance of laymen to discuss openly the official business of the Church leadership, and the ever-changing status of those subjected to these punishments, it is difficult to arrive at a precise figure of members absent for disciplinary reasons. The best information available indicates that six members had been banned or excommunicated in each of the two years for which I made studies—1958 and 1964.

migrations to all of the other settlements in Canada, such as the progressive Saskatchewan settlement and the conservative settlements in Alberta and British Columbia. Of the ten families that moved from one Old Colony village in Mexico in the years 1950–60, three moved to Canada.

Many of the migrations are motivated by dissatisfaction with or inability to conform to the Old Colony system, as is illustrated by a Canadian Old Colonist:

> The Mennonites who return [to Canada] are often no good. One Wiebe family which returned settled near our farm. They had nothing but a large family. It was cold that winter so I brought him a ton and a half of coal. He said he could not pay for it right away, and I said he did not need to. He was very thankful and the next day came to borrow chicken feed. This is typical of him. He owes me a great deal of money because of machinery he had bought, but he keeps on buying rather than paying off. He and his family are always in town, spending their money as fast as they make it. When they came from Mexico, though they had not enough money to buy food, they bought the eldest boy a bicycle and Mr. Wiebe and the eldest son got wrist watches. They got what they were forbidden to get in Mexico. As soon as they could afford it they bought a car and now have two. . . . The Mennonites are all very unsettled. They move from place to place. I think it is those that cannot get along in Mexico. Some of them are no good. Wiebe is no good. They will get settled, and have a good start, then pull up and move somewhere else—like Jacob Friesen. He had a good income in British Columbia, and after six years there, pulls up stakes and comes here.[37]

The migrations to British Honduras and Bolivia from Mexico and from the conservative settlements in Canada are being conducted on the same basis. A minister in the state of Chihuahua lamented the disorganizing forces of the migrations and did not know what could be done to strengthen the unity of the *Gemeent*:

> We feel we are a *Gemeent* with definite principles or faith, but we are involved in the problem of keeping the *Gemeent*

37. Material gathered by the author during field research.

together so these principles can be put to practice. I do not
know what can be done. I have said that I wish the *Gemeent*
could do something to induce the people to believe and
understand some of these things. But so many will not let
themselves be told anything. They are very stubborn and
ignorant. The example of the young fellow who said he
would move to Honduras in spite of me (or more correctly,
because of me) is met time and time again among us. They
apparently are sick of being told what to do and having
community habits and customs regulate their lives. They
want to strike out for themselves.[38]

There is also migration within the settlements themselves,
based on the shadings of "orthodoxy" that are to be found
in one settlement or another. Thus, for a long time, the Nord
Colony in the Chihuahua settlement was the area in which the
most orthodox lived and to which the most conservative from
other settlements moved. Since 1964, the Bishop of the Nord
Colony has cut off fellowship with the Manitoba and Swift
Plan and has forbidden his members to indulge in fellowship
with their members. At present, the oldest settlements—
Manitoba, Swift, Nord, in order of increasing traditionalism—
are undergoing rapid changes, while the conservative enclaves
at Casas Grandes and the conservative segment in British
Honduras and Bolivia are attempting to maintain their conservative positions. The settlements in Alberta, British Columbia, British Honduras, and Bolivia, though relatively new,
demonstrate that though the position on the dissolution scale
may be different for each of the settlements, the process nevertheless is taking place in each at a rapid rate.

The migrations offer evidence of dissatisfaction and lack of
solidarity. It is logical to propose that if the Old Colony
system were more similar to the society around it, some migrations would take the form of defections from the Old Colony
system. Unable to contemplate life in nearby but totally dis-
similar surroundings, however, the Old Colonists mill about,
only letting off enough steam to avoid an eruption.

In the midst of the confusion of migration and the dissatisfaction that stimulates it, it is hard to imagine that the

38. Material gathered by the author during field research.

youth could look with enthusiasm to their futures in the Old Colony. Still, to one not familiar with the system, the young people give the appearance of complete integration into the system. They all take catechism and undergo baptism at the same age; they marry in uniform fashion and at approximately the same age. Appearances are one thing; attitudes are another: "Especially in religious things, I do not see why our people should not get more training. I can only read the Bible for myself, I could not interpret or explain it for anyone else. It seems ironic or illogical to say that it is wrong to get to understand the Bible better. There are so many illogical things about our faith. If it was not for the relatives, especially parents, I would get out and be through with the entire mess. They are so inconsistent. One person can get by for what another gets severe punishment. It seems money or friendship makes a difference." [39]

As indicated earlier, the schoolteachers are most vocal and clear about their dissatisfaction with the Old Colony system. Their education and their contact with young people make them good barometers of feelings and attitudes: "I am not even allowed to have a map of Mexico in school so I can show them where we live. The school is kept very poor so no layman will be able to question the Church regulations or think for himself. The school system is a scandal and is the thing that will ruin the Old Colony as a group, and as a Church. There are numerous younger people who are reading quite a bit. They will be dangerous when the time comes." [40]

There is a considerable amount of disagreement and dissatisfaction with the Old Colony system, but the deviancy evidenced is still not of a degree sufficient to form a rebellion or cause a mass exodus.

The difference in attitudes and feelings between the progressive and traditional groups may not be great, since the expression of the attitudes is more camouflaged in societies which have strong external controls. Nevertheless, it is incontrovertible that the traditional Old Colony settlements have been more successful in propagating the Old Colony

39. Material gathered by the author during field research.
40. Material gathered by the author during field research.

way of life among their offspring. The progressive Old Colony offspring are, as it were, "poised" to leap from the Old Colony ship if changes are not made soon to meet their demands. There is some evidence that those changes are being made.

Conclusion

Has the Old Colony ethnic minority achieved its goal of living its inner life according to Old Colony values and beliefs? Only ambiguous answers can be given. If lack of change is taken as a bench mark, then the answer is no, for there has been change in the internal life of every Old Colony settlement. If the bench mark is the basic "charter" or belief system, then the answer could be a qualified yes. In every settlement there has been some success in living up to the basic ideal of the Old Colony way of life.

This "success," however, is a matter of interpretation. In the conservative Old Colony, the predominant definition of success would imply a maintenance of the status quo. From an objective perspective, this purpose has been achieved. The minority which believes otherwise would consider the present conditions a sign of failure. In the more progressive Old Colony settlements of Manitoba and Saskatchewan, the majority of members believe they have been successful in living the Old Colony way of life. Again, a minority which is not able to conceive of change as progress would disagree. In terms of an intersettlement evaluation, the conservative colonies feel that the progressive colonies are utter failures and do not deserve to be considered a part of the Old Colony family. On the other hand, the progressive colonies feel that the traditional settlements are "dead" and are already reaping the consequences of stagnation.

An observer of the Old Colony in Canada who has lived close to it all his life provides us with something of a concluding analysis of the Old Colony's success or failure in achieving its goals:

> The Old Colony is gradually coming to an end. It is getting worse all the time. The Old Colony is losing many young

people. Many join other churches that suit them or that will accept them with their beliefs. Parents do not believe in order. Young people are rejecting their parents' authority. They play ball on Sunday on the schoolyard. . . . The Old Colony organization and life broke down when the majority left for Mexico. The moral life of the Mexican migrants declined; they were not willing to live a disciplined life and adhered only outwardly to the standards of the Church. Leadership is the clue to the survival of the Old Colony. As the preacher, so the congregation. But preachers are no longer chosen on the basis of religious fervor. They are rather chosen on the basis of prestige, intelligence, and economic success, often one who is a friend of more rebellious or traditional elements. Religious and worldly interests must not be mixed. But the Old Colony seems to be mixing the world and religion.[41]

41. Material gathered by the author during field research.

Chapter 6

BABYLON'S SEDUCTION
OF THE OLD COLONY

One of the presuppositions undergirding this study is that it takes two groups to create a minority-majority situation. An opposing group must be present before conflict can exist. Two sets of peoples and two sets of cultures are required before ethnic relations can be conceived and developed. This has been stated effectively by Everett C. Hughes: "It takes more than one ethnic group to make ethnic relations. The relations can be no more understood by studying one or the other of the groups than can a chemical combination by study of one element only, or a boxing bout by observation of only one of the fighters. Yet it is common to study ethnic relations as if one had to know only one party to them." [1] This chapter will deal with the "other party" and the relations between the two groups, with this orientation in mind. It will focus on what the "host" societies are doing that has implications for Old Colony survival.

The Old Colony has from its earliest beginnings lived in what it has termed a "hostile" environment (the world), which has served as an adversary in its pilgrimage. If there had been no adversary, no "hostile" world from which to withdraw, there would have been no motive for the formation of the Old Colony. Somehow, the society around a new movement can always be seen as inimical to all that is considered good. The Old Colony system would be hard pressed for a reason for existence if suddenly the entire population of the world were to accept the Old Colony way of life, for the Old Colony view of life demands a "world" from which God's faithful must separate. (See the poem "Es Geht Zu Weit" in Appendix M, written by a disgruntled Old Colonist.)

The Old Colony's life has been couched in the framework of

1. Everett C. Hughes, *Where Peoples Meet* (Glencoe, Ill.: The Free Press, 1950), p. 158.

a conflict or contest with the "world." The objective has been to survive against the attacks and the inroads of the world. The "world" as seen by the Old Colony is a system that is literally "hellbent" or lost, and thus outside God's concern or care. The Old Colony has never presumed to persuade the "world" to join the Old Colony and emulate its way of life, nor has it ever given thought to the possibility of joining with the "world." Rather the Old Colony has covenanted all these years to remain separate and survive as it is. Documentation of this stance has been presented above, but it may be appropriate here to quote an eighty-year-old man who had been a faithful Old Colonist all his life: " 'He who loves the world does not love the Father.' Our call is to remain separate from the world and its sin. We must be absolutely clear on what is 'worldly' and what is commanded by God." [2]

It is self-evident that the forms the Old Colony settlements take today in the various regions are owing in large measure to the experiences, contact, and interaction with the "host" or majority society. The development of an ethnic-minority group can never be considered solely the consequence of its inner dynamics; rather it is the result of a complex interaction of internal factors, external factors, and an interaction of the two sets of forces.[3]

Institutional Relations with the Outside World

In the survey of the historical development of the Old Colony ethnic minority, its relationship to the state was shown to be very important. In Prussia the governmental attitude was shown to be one of grudging toleration, with numerous restrictions. The emigration from West Prussia was precipitated just as much by the political restrictions as by the population pressure. The migration to Russia was carried out on the basis of a fraternal benefactor's committing himself to providing certain things to the Mennonites. When these

2. Material gathered by the author during field research.

3. See George C. Homans, *The Human Group* (New York: Harcourt, Brace & Company, 1950), pp. 108–11.

personal commitments could not be carried out, the pressure for emigration again emerged.

The political environment for the emergent Old Colony in Canada was of a similar nature. The creation of a personal compact between the Mennonites and the provincial government was the condition for moving to Canada.[4] In ensuing interrelations the Old Colony took the stance which it has taken ever since: the state should personally guarantee the protection of the Old Colony in its attempt to live out its own life. The increasing infringement or impingement upon the life of the Old Colony did not result in increased interaction and negotiation, but rather served as a reminder to the Canadian government of the conditions under which the Old Colony had come to Canada. Emigration was, in fact, suggested as the alternative in case the Old Colony was not allowed to continue under the initial agreement.[5]

The progressive colonies, Manitoba and Saskatchewan, have experienced various types of encroachments by the "world." By far the greatest offensive, according to the testimony of the Old Colonists, has been the school issue. The promise of freedom to conduct the schools as they pleased was one of the major prerequisites of the migration from Russia to Canada. Freedom in Canada was short-lived, however, and the migration to Mexico followed in less than fifty years.

As indicated earlier, the Mennonites enjoyed school autonomy from 1874–83 on the basis of the British North America Act, Section 93.[6] By 1879, schoolteachers were examined by

4. There is considerable documentation of the official negotiations. For basic background see David G. Rempel, "The Mennonite Migration to New Russia," *MQR*, IX (July, 1935), 109–28; G. Leibbrandt, "Emigration of the German Mennonites from Russia to the United States and Canada in 1873–1880," *MQR*, VI, (October, 1932), 205–26; Ernst Correll, "Sources on the Mennonite Immigration from Russia in the 1870's," *MQR*, XXIV (October, 1950), 329–52.

5. Walter Schmiedehaus, *Ein Feste Burg ist unser Gott* (Cuauhtemoc, Chihuahua, Mexico: Druck G. L. Rempel, Blumenort, 1948), pp. 61ff., contains the final letter of appeal that the Old Colony leaders sent to the Provincial government in February, 1919. See Appendix referred to above.

6. E. K. Francis, *In Search of Utopia* (Glencoe, Ill.: The Free Press, 1955), p. 161.

the provincial officials, and the teachers were ordered to attend teachers' conventions to upgrade the quality of teaching. The other Mennonite groups went along, more or less, with the increasing interference from the province, but the Old Colony tried to hold firm. They simply did not comply with the orders. First, the Old Colony exploited the loopholes for ethnic groups in the amendments to the Manitoba School Act, passed in 1897, which allowed teaching of religion in schools and bilingual instruction if there were at least ten pupils who did not speak English.

The School Attendance Act of 1916 repealed Clause 285 of the original Manitoba Public Schools Acts of 1890, made English the sole language of instruction, and compelled all children between the ages of seven and fourteen to "attend public schools unless private education was provided for them in a manner acceptable to the school authorities." [7]

The Old Colony, of course, continued to send its children to its traditional schools. These schools were ultimately all declared "unacceptable"; thus, the stage was set for conflict. By 1918, many parents were fined for not sending their children to provincial schools, often built alongside the village schools. Thirteen parents spent three days in Morden jail before paying the fine during that year.

According to observers on the scene at the time, the basic reason for the migration of a large majority to Mexico in 1922 was the school issue: "They did not want to participate in the government schools, while the families without children did not want to pay for those with children. If they had supported their own schools, the state would not have imposed its schools upon them. Those that could afford it went to Mexico, while those who could not, or did not want to sacrifice their land and possessions for the school issue, chose to stay here." [8] Other members suggested, however, that the cause of the migration was not education as such, but the consequences which it brought: "But the real reason was the fear of loss of their young people. Not only the leadership but many of the laity

7. *Ibid.*, p. 183.
8. Material gathered by the author during field research.

were afraid of losing their young people. Some that stayed were not intimidated as easily." [9] Non-Old Colony Mennonites believed that the Old Colony remained needlessly rigid and stubborn, that it should have conceded to the provincial demands: "If they had been willing to take a half hour of English each day, the government would have given them absolute freedom. They were continually reassured that the original agreement stood in principle, but that learning the English language was a requirement that the country could expect of everyone." [10] For the group that stayed in Canada, the infiltration of provincial educational practices has continued. The school language is English, and the teachers have to meet the qualifications of the province. The flag is saluted and government-chosen texts are used. Some contemporary Old Colony members are ambivalent about the influence of the schools on the Old Colony: "The group going to Mexico considers us lost. But we think differently. We feel we are just as safe as they are. Education of our young people has been responsible for the development of our group, since it is demanded. There is nothing wrong with education as such, although it takes the young people from home so much." [11] A member of the *Lehrdienst* in Manitoba was less pessimistic in his appraisal of the influence of the schools:

The schools were ordered disbanded in 1921, which was the main reason for the trek to Mexico. The government then built schools and conducted them according to its rules and regulations. The flag that was to be flown and the speaking of English seemed to them to be a forecast that their freedom was lost. . . . Thus they had always tried to be not too closely identified with any country. . . . I myself am not afraid of the schools, though they have their dangerous elements. The further away from home, the greater the influence on the student. Often the young people come back with shorn hair and other evidences of beginning to adopt worldly practices. If they come back and have not lost their

9. Material gathered by the author during field research.
10. Material gathered by the author during field research.
11. Material gathered by the author during field research.

loyalty, education is fine. We have a number who have education and are active in the work of the *Gemeent*.[12]

As has already become abundantly clear, the Manitoba and Saskatchewan groups have changed more rapidly and radically than those settlements which chose to emigrate rather than to adapt to the schools required by the state (province). It is, however, impossible to prove a causal relationship between submission to state school requirements and becoming worldly, even though a causal relationship is assumed to exist by the conservative Old Colony settlements.

Although the Old Colony has never been subject to the military draft, it has long felt uneasy and has believed that the time would come ultimately when no exemption would be made. Although those who moved to Mexico were threatened by the prospect, according to a member of the Canadian *Lehrdienst*, military service has not resulted in the grave consequences feared:

> Our principles have been respected. Look at the experience in the last war [World War II]. It was a big war, and we were allowed to do alternative service. At first we were wondering what was meant by the examination by a doctor before men were drafted. So several ministers went to inquire and we were told that it was not to prepare them for army life, but simply that they did not want unfit people in the hospitals or wherever they worked. Then we were satisfied. Many fellows had to appear before a court and be adjudged. This experience has shown us that we can preserve our principles here and that we can remain trustful toward the Canadian government, which they cannot do in Mexico.[13]

The conditions underlying the government's military program have had little consequence for the Old Colony since, as the above quotation suggests, the freedom to keep a pure testimony was possible. It can even be argued that military service and the exemption for conscientious objectors served

12. Material gathered by the author during field research.
13. Material gathered by the author during field research.

to unite the Old Colony in Canada and helped to clarify its purposes. This observation applies to all the Canadian Old Colony settlements, even those which have remained conservative.

The invasion of the Old Colony world by the Mexican society was in many ways similar to the invasion in Canada, though it was more direct. In 1922, the Mexican government promised freedom in perpetuity to the Old Colonists to conduct their schools and religion as they saw fit. It was not long before the Mexican government began to chafe under this promise. By the middle and late 1920's, President Obregón began to be concerned about the Mennonite schools, although he admitted that the Old Colony schools were better than many rural schools in Mexico, especially in that the Old Colony demanded "universal" education for its numbers. Obregón wanted especially to have the Old Colony young people learn Spanish. He was further interested in getting the schools in the Old Colony more in line with the Mexican forms, but was dissuaded from putting any pressure on the Old Colony because of the implications this would have for further immigration of foreigners.[14]

In 1927, Article 3 of the new Mexican constitution disestablished religion and forbade its being taught in churches and schools. The fact that the Old Colony ignored this law and continued "arrogantly" on its traditional course antagonized the indigenous population, which registered many complaints with the government.[15] Forced closing of the schools was averted only through the co-operation of many public officials when, in 1935, the first thunderbolt struck. Without warning, a Mexican school inspector visited all the schools, made a record of all the proceedings, and declared all the schools substandard and therefore closed.

This condition prevailed for almost a year, while commissions from the Chihuahua and Durango Old Colony settlements spent many days at the state and national levels of government trying to obtain permission to reopen the schools.

14. Schmiedehaus, *Ein Feste Burg,* p. 209.
15. *Ibid.,* p. 210.

The Old Colony counterattack consisted of reminding the Mexican government that it had been promised autonomy in the schools; the Old Colonists would not listen to any other reasoning. Even though the central government officials were inclined to understand, the state and local school officials were unwilling to yield.

Finally, the Old Colony leadership sent a letter requesting enough time to emigrate to another land where their people could live in peace. In two days, a telegram was received granting the Old Colony freedom in the schools. Since that time there has been an uneasy truce. Both sides are aware that further hostilities are imminent. Schmiedehaus quotes a Mexican official as saying that almost everything can be worked out to the satisfaction of the Old Colony, but there is one point which will create further difficulties: the school problem.[16]

Recent incidents show that the issue is not dead and may, in fact, erupt anew any moment. In the summer of 1964, the author heard rumors that a Mexican inspector had been traveling around in the villages, inspecting schools and talking to schoolteachers. In 1967, a school inspector again made unannounced visits in selected schools in the settlements, presumably to see whether the Old Colony was upgrading its schools. The schools have not changed in the forty years since the Old Colony settled in Mexico. Many of the teachers feel that the hope of the Old Colony is better schools, a sentiment with which the Mexican officials agree. The Old Colonists and Mexicans differ only in their interpretations of "better schools": the Old Colony teachers want better schools so that the Old Colony youth can preserve their heritage while the Mexicans want better schools in order to make Old Colonists better citizens.

The situation in the other traditional settlements is similar to that which originally led the conservative Old Colony segment to move to Mexico. Thus, whenever the provincial officials have appeared to demand the upgrading of the schools, the Old Colony leadership has threatened to emigrate. In the Fort Vermilion area of Alberta, school inspectors have

16. *Ibid.*, p. 213.

demanded the closing of Old Colony schools and attendance at schools approved by the provincial government. The Old Colony group has submitted to the extent that it has hired some Mennonite teachers who have the qualifications demanded by the province but who are, nevertheless, sympathetic to the Old Colony way of life and unwilling to undermine it. The province has accepted this formula.

The solution is not always that easy. A conservative segment of the Fort Vermilion group "fled" to British Columbia in the hope that it could evade the tentacles of the government. This group will probably face the same ultimatum in the near future, if it is not already having to decide whether to emigrate to another land or accept a compromise. Thus each migration is in a sense the separation of the more conservative from the more "progressive" element, the more conservative trying to stay the evil day when there will be no place to which they can escape.

The problem is still to be faced in British Honduras and Bolivia. It is fairly clear from all the reports the Old Colony travelers bring back from British Honduras and Bolivia that the governments will demand state-approved school instruction before very long.

Since Mexico has never had universal military service, the Old Colony members have been free of demands in this connection. More importantly, Old Colony members have not in the past become Mexican citizens—at least not intentionally. The Old Colonists who came from Canada had British citizenship. The situation is rapidly changing, however, for many parents have not taken the trouble to register their children with a Canadian or British consulate before their children become eighteen. Thus, an increasingly large number of the younger generation are becoming Mexican citizens by default or ignorance. Should military conscription come, their right to alien status would no longer exempt many of the young Old Colonists, as a Canadian Old Colonist has foreseen: "They all say, 'It is best not to become Mexican citizens.' This is not healthy, for though they are aliens as far as military service and other things are concerned, they still demand all the protection and rights that the other people get. There is no conscious understanding of the political implications of this, and they will run into trouble soon." [17]

Though not yet successful in bringing about changes in education and in demanding military service, the Mexican government has imposed other claims upon the Old Colony. Taxation, of course, is one; and the Old Colony has not protested, except to the "arbitrariness" and "corruptness" with which taxes have been levied:

> Henry Peters reported that in the early years, there were numerous butcheries in the villages so that villagers could get fresh meat often, which was clean and dependable. The Mexican government got wise to this and imposed a heavy tax on all meat sold or animals butchered. The tax was so high that it eventually closed all the meat markets. The Mennonites had not learned to lie, nor had they wanted to at this point. Now several farmers have told me that if they reported everything that is classified as income, they would not be able to survive because the Mexican tax system is based on income alone, not allowing anything for expenses, depreciation, or improvements.[18]

Another instance of the Mexican government's penetration into the private life of the Old Colony is the area of reports of deaths and the time restrictions placed on burials. The following statement illustrates not only the problem, but also the compromise:

> The Mexican government has a requirement that all dead are to be buried within twenty-four hours of their death. The practice stems from a belief that the disease of the deceased can easily be transferred to the living. This belief may have begun in the area when plagues and epidemics were rampant. Thus, when the Mennonites moved here, they came under the same requirement. Since the Mennonites took care of their dead in a different fashion and needed to allow at least a day for the funeral ceremony and another day for the relatives to gather, etc., they were never able to bury the dead within the deadline. The Mennonites felt that their way of preserving the dead made them less

17. Material gathered by the author during field research.
18. Material gathered by the author during field research.

dangerous as far as disease or decomposition was concerned. The trouble began as soon as the Mennonites reported deaths. They reported a death . . . as much as five or six days after the event. Upon being asked whether they had been buried within twenty-four hours, the answer of course was no. This made the officials very angry, and a tax was imposed on the violators. Soon the Mexicans got tired of levying the fines and told the Mennonites to register the death within twenty-four hours of the death and to state that he [the deceased] had been buried according to regulations. This did not help either, for the Mennonites came to report the death within twenty-four hours, but would not lie by saying that he [the deceased] had been buried. Since neither the fine nor the encouragement to falsify the dates was successful in conducting the Mennonites to comply (at least legally) with the Mexican laws, the Mexican officials slowly began to realize that some other working relationship must be found. So the Mexican officials merely began to wink at the infraction of the law and filled out the records according to a method which gave them time to allow for laggards among the Mennonites and still have the records correct according to Mexican law. Now Mennonites register the dead when they are buried and do not concern themselves with the fact that technically they are breaking the law.[19]

A related demand was that the Old Colony establish a cemetery for every five villages. Since this demand ignored the existing plan, by which there were "churchyards," Old Colony burial places associated with church districts, this requirement was ignored. The Mexicans finally retracted their demand.

One of the most celebrated cases of Mexican intervention in the private life of the Old Colony is the *Segura Social* system which the Mexican government promulgated in 1955. In 1956, the state officials sent representatives into the colonies, asking for signatures for the *Segura Social* plan. In essence, the *Segura Social* program is fashioned somewhat after the United States' social security plan and involves retirement benefits as well as hospitalization and medical care. Hospitals and other facilities were also to be built with the finances this plan sup-

19. Material gathered by the author during field research.

plied. The program was compulsory for the industrial sector, but not for farmers. Nevertheless, Old Colony farmers were urged to sign up under the guise that it was compulsory.

> They sent men around asking for signers, but among the farmers in the Colony hardly anyone signed up. The cheese factories and other businesses did sign up because they felt it was compulsory. Then the authorities in Cuauhtemoc summoned the *Schults* from each village to a hearing in town to find out why they were not signing up and tried to get them to sign. They refused. Then the Old Colony had a number of *Browdaschafte* (meetings of male Church members) and decided that if they were forced to join, they would leave the country. When the government heard about this, they immediately withdrew their pressure and promised the Mennonites that they would never need to join the plan.[20]

The Old Colony prepared and dispatched a long statement on the historical beliefs of the Old Colony, including in it an expression of the belief that social security and insurance were irrelevant because the group, since its inception, had practiced mutual aid and had taken care of all its poor and infirm. (See Appendix I for copy of letter.)

> The *Segura* problem brought to the fore an interesting incident which was one of the main reasons, it is said, why Henry Krahn was asked to quit as *Vorsteher*. The incident developed when the problem of the *Segura Social* was at its height. Krahn had a personal friend in Chihuahua who apparently was a friend of the head men in the *Segura Social* in Mexico City. When it appeared that nothing could be done, this friend offered to put on the table in front of them signed papers exempting the Old Colony categorically from the plan, for a sum of 200,000 pesos. Apparently this fellow was so convincing that Krahn and the other *Vorsteher* went to see him in Chihuahua. When they came home, they had *Browdaschafte* where they told the congregation that they had reached an agreement and that they should now provide the 200,000 pesos. This was not so easily done, and many grumbled. But the fact that the sum had been promised made it a closed question, and in the end the congregations paid the sum. The money was given to the

20. Material gathered by the author during field research.

man but nothing happened, and the pressure continued until the Old Colony decided that they would leave Mexico rather than submit. Then immediately the pressure was off. So the 200,000 pesos did not help (one Mexican who disappeared was that much richer), and the old tactic of threatening to leave was used.[21]

The Mexican society is applying other types of pressure to cause the Old Colony to conform. Since Old Colony people do not drive cars, they go to town with wagon teams. These demand hitching areas, which have been supplied through livery stables in the larger towns, such as Cuauhtemoc, but the inconvenience they cause creates considerable opposition to them among the Mexicans: "For some time there has been some dissatisfaction about the unsanitary conditions. . . . There is a livery stable that has been erected for the Old Colony and which is used quite extensively. But recently some agitation from more progressive-minded citizens pressured the 'Chamber of Commerce' into closing the livery stable. It was only a threat, but it evoked quite a response from the Mennonites. They said, 'Let them chase us out of town with our horses. They will come begging to us, for we offer the livelihood of the town.' "[22]

Mexican governmental agencies want to include the Old Colony in the conduct of public affairs. The request of the President of Rubio for help from the surrounding Old Colony villages in the purchase of park benches and benches at bus stops is a representative example. (See p. 80.)

Although the Old Colonists are dependent upon Mexicans for some services and goods, particularly those desired but forbidden within the confines of the Old Colony settlements, interaction exists much more frequently as a result of the Mexicans' eagerness to avail themselves of Old Colony products and services. This may not appear significant at first glance, but when the effects of close interaction on many levels are analyzed, the degree of infiltration is staggering. It seems that Old Colony men who have special abilities are often visited by Mexicans, their yards serving as meeting places.

21. Material gathered by the author during field research.
22. Material gathered by the author during field research.

There the men engage in the friendly personal exchanges typical of any informal business relationship, their children play together, and all come to know more about the customs and folkways of the cultures represented.

The political environment, from the perspective of the Old Colony, can be seen as an overarching canopy of protection and provision. If the political system functions well, there is need for only little, if any, contact between the Old Colony and the state. If the state functions poorly, it does so by interfering in the affairs of the Old Colony or otherwise failing to allow the Old Colony to live its life.

The relationship of the Old Colonists to the British Honduras political systems has not emerged very clearly, but indications are that it is similar to that prevailing in Canada. Patterned after the British system, it does not offer special privileges but provides guarantees as granted by the constitution. (See Appendix B.) The relationship of the Old Colonists to the Bolivian government is still obscure.

The relationship of the Old Colonist to the Mexican system is somewhat more clearly defined, as the following statement by a president of a *Presidencia* illustrates:

> Now since the Mexicans see what the Mennonites have done, how they have improved the land and given the economy a shot in the arm, they are right proud of them. The Mexican government, both locally and federally, is well satisfied with the Mennonites in every respect and does everything in its power to make it easy for the Mennonites to stay here and prosper. The *Segura Social* question is an example of this. The government could have resorted to all sorts of pressures and coercion to get the Mennonites, but they have given them their way in most things, though this is in part based on the fact that the Mennonites can take care of their own problems very well.[23]

On the other hand, the Old Colony attitude toward the system, typified by the following, is not nearly so congenial: "The Mexicans have come to us often with governmental orders, but then we often become *polietsch* [underhanded].

23. Material gathered by the author during field research.

One time the government ordered all the cattle to be vaccinated. Much of the vaccination was done with Pepsi Cola, so they say. When they came to me, I took four of my cows and hid them in the barn. I only had three for them to vaccinate. I did not like the idea. It cost a lot of money and they did a very sloppy job." [24] Government intervention in behalf of its own people, particularly those who are willing to pay, does little to ease tension between the Old Colonists and the system. "George Klassen's brother had eaten some meat . . . at the Lux Café in Cuauhtemoc. Soon thereafter he died of meat poisoning. . . . The family had not pressed any charges because 'We knew how corrupt the Mexicans are. They will cover up everything so well that there is no basis for a charge.' They had a Mexican doctor investigate, but he found nothing wrong with the meat so nothing further was done. The doctor was obviously paid by the Mexican restaurant to find them innocent. Since that time several other Mennonites have been poisoned in that restaurant and still it is not closed." [25]

Certainly one of the most prevalent topics of conversation in the Mexican Old Colony settlement is the *Mexikaunishe Regierung* (the Mexican government), which has a derogatory connotation by now in the Low German. Frequently Old Colony people talk about the undesirability of the Mexican environment, referring, of course, to the poor treatment they are receiving from the government officials and the population in general. One of the most convincing rationales in support of migration to other countries is the advantage to be gained by escaping the "corruption" of the Mexican environment: "Neufeld also said that the Mexican government was responsible for the demoralization of the Old Colony. They had learned to lie and bribe because the Mexican system demanded it. He stated that if the Mennonites were to stay here another thirty years, they would lose all their principles, including nonresistance which is the strongest belief which they still have." [26]

24. Material gathered by the author during field research.
25. Material gathered by the author during field research.
26. Material gathered by the author during field research.

The economic environment of the Old Colony has varied little throughout its long history, since all of the settlements have been made in the "West." All of the lands entered—Russia, Canada, Mexico, British Honduras, and Bolivia—have welcomed the Old Colony on the premise that it would make an economic contribution to their countries.[27] They anticipated a surplus of agricultural crops, improvement in land previously uninhabited, and stimulation of industrial products and consumption.

Another similarity was that the countries have all been organized on a free-enterprise or capitalist system. (The Russian economic system of the 1880's might better be called a modernized feudal system, but certainly the effect of the Old Colony on the nation's economy was that outlined above.) In Canada, Mexico, and British Honduras the political structure and the economic organization provide for the private production of capital with minimum state interference or restriction. Thus, in all these environments, the Old Colony members have competed on the "open market" for goods, services, and survival.

The indigenous people of each country in which the Old

27. For the Russian invitations see Rempel, "Mennonite Migration to New Russia," and C. Henry Smith, *The Story of the Mennonites* (Newton, Kan.: Mennonite Publication Office, 1950), pp. 386–87. For the invitation to Canada, see the documents in Liebbrandt, "Emigration of the German Mennonites," which testifies to the intense desire of the Canadian government to have the Mennonites settle. Liebbrandt states, "In the meantime the Minister of Agriculture, very pleased with Hespeler's report on the proposed immigration, decided on his part to do everything in his power to induce the Mennonites to come to Canada" (p. 219). This included an offer to pay a Mennonite $2.00 per head for every Mennonite he could induce to come to America. The eagerness of the Mexican government to have the Old Colony migrate to Mexico is described in Schmiedehaus, *Ein Feste Burg*, pp. 74ff. See also J. Winfield Fretz, *Mennonite Colonization in Mexico* (Akron, Pa.: Mennonite Central Committee, 1945): "Avila Camacho, the present President of Mexico, has on several occasions told Mennonite delegations visiting him that Mexico desires a Mennonite settlement in every one of the twenty-eight Mexican states" (p. 33). For the invitation to settle in British Honduras, see Appendix I for letter indicating receptivity.

Colony has settled have been eager to consume the products of the Old Colony. In the Chihuahua settlement, for example, the Mexicans comprise up to one half of the clientele of Old Colony machine shops and factories. One machine shop operator felt that he had to limit trade with Mexicans because it was harder to collect from them. Another Old Colony entrepreneur stated that almost one half of the hammer mills he had produced went to Mexican buyers.

Although differences in economic factors are not great among Canada, Mexico, British Honduras, and Bolivia, there are some which have implications for the Old Colonist. In Manitoba, Ontario, and Saskatchewan the Old Colony has always lived within seventy-five miles of major cities and within twenty miles of shopping and marketing towns connected to their settlements by all-weather roads. In these three areas the Old Colony has utilized the automobile and truck, so that access to and contact with the market have been much greater. The nearest market to the Chihuahua settlement in Mexico is Cuauhtemoc, located on the south side of the settlement, at least thirty miles from the north end. The state of Chihuahua has built a black-top road through the main villages, thereby expediting the transfer of products and people throughout the entire settlement. In British Honduras, there is only one major market—Belize. As indicated earlier, a road is being constructed which will connect the Old Colony settlement and Belize. The Fort Vermilion settlers in Alberta also have a long way to travel to market. Trucks are usually hired to take produce to Edmonton, a venture which involves two days, one to get to Edmonton and sell the produce and the second day to buy supplies and return.

The British Honduras government has been building an all-weather road to the Old Colony settlement in order to facilitate the movement of produce to market. The Alberta government has recently completed (1950) an all-weather road to Fort Vermilion, a stretch of some two hundred miles over unsettled land; a railroad also has been laid to the edge of the colony, and a station at Carcajou was completed in 1964.

In Mexico the fluctuation of prices and the excessive involvement of the middleman make economic matters difficult for the Old Colonists. Much of their produce is bought by Mexican grain brokers and livestock buyers, but since the Old Colony member is intentionally not well informed, he is often the victim of exploitation or misinformation:

> Several days ago a Mennonite, Henry Peters from Eichenfeld, suffered a loss of 13,000 pesos. Peters is a poultry raiser and also buys eggs from others and resells them. A Mexican with a good line and a new truck came to him and arranged to pick up the eggs. He said he would not always show up himself, but would send a worker. So the first few loads of eggs were picked up and everything went fine. But then the Mexican picked up several loads in succession and paid for them with three checks. When Peters went to cash them, he found out that they were no good. He was not able to find the Mexican. There is a chance that he may recover some, but the Mennonites from whom he bought eggs want their money so he may go into the hole quite badly.[28]

Social Relations Processes

The processes discussed above that contribute to the dissolution of the Old Colony are based on actions initiated by the host. In this section the processes that are based upon relationships with the outside world motivated in part by inner Old Colony systemic processes will be analyzed. These processes include transportation and communication, increasing economic dependence, law and order, and rising expectations.

TRANSPORTATION AND COMMUNICATION

Except for the mass migrations, the Old Colony in its earlier days was fairly independent of public transportation and communication. In Russia, the colonies were fairly contiguous, and most communication between them took the form of personal visits. As the Old Colony migrated to different sections of the world and expanded in numbers, it found itself increasingly dependent upon outside assistance. The post offices in vil-

28. Material gathered by the author during field research.

lages serving Old Colony settlements are constantly filled with Old Colony people coming to mail and receive letters and packages and send telegrams.

Transportation needs have undergone a similar change. Visits from one settlement to another put heavy demands on the buses and trains. Not only are there bus lines within the larger settlements (Mexican settlements at Chihuahua and Durango) which bring the Old Colony members to town; there are bus lines and rail lines connecting the settlements. These are heavily used by the Old Colony.

This dependence upon the communication and transportation facilities of the outside world has increased because of the population explosion which increases the size of the settlements and makes bus travel and letters necessary and because of the migrations to new areas. The increased use of communication and transportation facilities offered by the outside is of importance only because of the consequences for the Old Colony system itself. Increasing use of communication and transportation facilities adds to the amount of personal contact with "worldly" people and serves, thereby, to break down the barriers of the Old Colony and destroy the cohesiveness of the system. A Mexican official observed,

> The greatest area of social contact is the contact afforded during travel together. The *camiones* [buses] and trucks provide for the most intimate relationship and interaction. Many Mexicans and Mennonites make long trips together, and in the buses there is often good opportunity for contact, especially for regular travelers. There is a great deal of interaction on the buses that run on local routes here. The business contacts are also important, but they are more casual. The stores in town offer opportunity to learn to know each other, but it is usually of the "Hello, how are you, what can I do for you?" variety. There will be increased interaction and contact and intermarriage as time goes by. We Mexicans would like to see this happen.[29]

Increased use of the transportation and communication systems certainly serves to acquaint the Old Colony person with

29. Material gathered by the author during field research.

the world outside, regardless of whether he has contact with others. This is especially true of transportation. Seeing the larger world beyond the Old Colony gives the Old Colonist a view which he would not have were he to stay isolated. To his delight and to the displeasure of his religious leaders, one Old Colony farmer who went on a trip to the western coast of Mexico took dozens of color pictures of bridges, factories, resorts, boats, and skyscrapers, and shared them with his friends—all richer or poorer, depending on one's point of view.

INCREASING ECONOMIC DEPENDENCE

The expanding population and total production, both agricultural and other, are making the Old Colony increasingly dependent upon the larger system. The dependence goes beyond reliance upon communication and transportation to include goods and services.

The demand for goods—clothing, household goods, and produce—is increasing at a rapid rate. Many of the goods once produced at home are now bought, thereby making the Old Colony dependent upon the outside supplier. To illustrate, some Old Colony women now buy vegetables and fruits on the market, saying that they can be bought more cheaply than they can be raised. Furniture is being purchased with increasing frequency in the marketplace. The demand for agricultural machinery grows as the equipment becomes more sophisticated and can no longer be made at home.

The demand for different kinds of services accelerates, too, as noted. More labor is needed as new agricultural practices are attempted. When corn silage as livestock feed was being introduced into the Old Colony in Mexico, a need for expert Mexican stone masons expanded rapidly, thereby increasing the number of Mexicans on farms. As other agriculturally related processes such as cheese making and manufacturing develop, there is increasing need to utilize the services of the larger economy. The making of cheese, grinding of cereal, and making of hammer mills—all taking place in the Chihuahua settlement—augment the demand. For example, the manufacture of hammer mills requires contacts with suppliers of various metals and materials. The selling of the mills creates a vast network of sales outlets and dealers. In both of the Chihuahua firms which are making hammer mills, substantial relationships have been established with larger economic structures in the Mexican economy.

In Canada one of the effects of the increased involvement of the Old Colonist in the larger economic system has been the integration of Old Colony people into various official positions and functions in the community. A number of the Old Colony people, partly as a result of their economic prosperity, have taken positions in various local and regional organizations. One Old Colony leader in Manitoba is a member of the Purebred Seed Growers Association of Manitoba and Saskatchewan. Another has become one of the directors of a vigorous credit bank in one of the towns. Another is a member of Parliament, the only Social Credit party man to be elected in Manitoba in the 1963 elections. Politicians seek the advice of Old Colony people on many matters, as the author himself was able to witness in 1958 when various candidates for public office campaigned in person in the Old Colony villages by attending the Old Colony Church services.

The Old Colony sub-system has been ultimately dependent upon the outer economy for much of its livelihood. Though the Old Colony members have been self-sufficient in some areas, in the main they are dependent for their existence upon the exchange of goods. Thus, they have needed machinery to carry on their farm program. They have utilized markets to dispose of their produce. They have depended on the consumer market because very few things were made at home. They have required transportation and communication facilities to conduct their business and social activities.

What has made the Old Colony even more vulnerable to the penetrations of the host society through its economic structures has been the almost total lack of restriction on the number of people who made contacts in the marketplace and on the degree of intimacy of the contacts. Each farmer is free to go to town, and each farmer conducts his own business directly. This is in marked contrast to the Hutterites, who control their contact with the outside world, including the economic community, by limiting the interactions to the preacher and the farm boss. Although the Old Colony in Mexico, in reaction to the threat of invasion, did develop "status-roles" that enabled the group to limit the amount of contact with outsiders, this system is rapidly breaking down.

LAW AND ORDER

As has been shown above, the social control of the Old Colony is ultimately based on the religious authority of the *Lehrdienst.* This authority stems from the belief system which ascribes to God the ultimate power and from the goals toward which the Old Colony strives. In theory, then, the social behavior of the Old Colony is governed by religious beliefs. In practice, however, the Old Colony experiences considerable deviance in religious as well as social norms, as we have seen. Much of the deviance affects only the Old Colony membership and is managed within the Old Colony society, but often it involves an individual outside the system. Such deviant behavior the Old Colony member is quick to defend on the grounds that it is impossible to survive otherwise: "Epp said if he were honest in his tax reports and other negotiations he would have to close up his store today. 'It is just not possible. They have made it imperative that we take their own tactics. I have learned to deal just like the Mexicans, and that is not good. We left Canada so that we could remain a people pure and undefiled from the world, but the opposite has happened. We speak their language, use their tactics, and are mixing ever more with them.' " [30] It is less easy for him to defend his having sexual relations with non-Old Colonists, but his lack of defense does not necessarily curb his noncommunity relations. Once when the author was walking with an Old Colonist, we saw an Indian mother with four children begging for food along the road in the village. The youngest child was of light brown complexion and had light hair. When asked if her appearance indicated the presence of mixed blood, the Old Colonist replied, "Yes, it may quite well be a Mennonite. It often happens, and nothing is said or done about it.

30. Material gathered by the author during field research.

When we came to Mexico, the idea was that we would stay completely separate and would never mix with these strange colored and acting people. But we are mixing quite a bit, so that purpose was defeated." [31]

The significance of deviance, as it relates to both internal and external relations, is that increasingly the Old Colony is compelled to appeal for help from the outside in finding solutions. This implies that the system is incapable of handling its own problems, and dependence upon the outside for the maintenance of law and order is in itself a dimension of the deterioration of the Old Colony system. The deviancy cases that cannot be handled by the Old Colony itself are turned over to the institutions of law and order in the larger society:

> Corny Dyck's store has trouble with receiving checks that are no good. He has one . . . made out for about 160 pesos and signed by a John Friesen. This fellow has been in the community often but always manages to sneak out before anybody collects. Dyck said that from now on if they find somebody that has written rubber checks, they will put him in jail, since they have obtained the power of arrest and need only to present a warrant of nonpayment, and the police will put him in jail.

.   .   .   .   .   .

> Just recently a fellow in Campo 11 made two girls pregnant. He was forced to marry the one. The other, however, was taken home. When she had her baby, it was a difficult birth which required a lot of medical attention. The father of this girl went to the President at Rubio and demanded that the father of the guilty son pay for the hospital and related expenses. This was then taken care of. The church did not get involved in this matter.[32]

Cases in which individual members take the law into their own hands, though these are not very prevalent, probably represent a transition from the intrinsic control patterns to the final stages of integration into the larger society's law and order system: "Jacob Harder, the well driller, is considered

31. Material gathered by the author during field research.
32. Material gathered by the author during field research.

very cold-blooded, and the Mexicans will not bother him. He has shot at Mexicans often and is not worried about losing his life. The Mexicans do not care much whether they die or live, but when there is such a one among the Old Colony, they stay away from him. Once a group of three was after Harder for some type of grievance, but another Mexican told them they should stay away, for Harder would do away with all three before they knew what was going on. Harder has many dealings with Mexicans." [33] The ability of the Old Colony to control its deviants seems to be decreasing, probably to a large degree because of the increasing size of the Old Colony system: the primary group aspects of the social control system are no longer operative.

WORLDLY EXPECTATIONS

Because of the complex ways in which the Old Colony system is brought into touch with the social systems of the "world," there is a general rise in the expectations of the rank and file. These expectations affect relations with the outside world to a large extent since it provides the only possibility for the fulfillment of expectations. There seems to be increasing evidence of a desire to slough off the mantle of separation and to engage fully in social intercourse with other peoples.

The wishes of schoolteachers to increase contact with the intellectual traditions beyond the barrier have been cited. One Old Colony member makes it clear that some parents share their hopes, though not without some longing for a revitalization of Old Colony values:

> I want my children to know a little more about the world than I know. Thus, I would like to send my children to another school. I think the leaders are as they are because of personal power and prestige and not because they have the will of the *Gemeent* at heart. Else they would be concerned about the spiritual lives of the people and not about maintaining certain forms. There is a lot of corruption that should be cleaned up, and instead they haggle over little things. The concept of the *Nachfolge Jesu* [following Jesus] is lost, and . . . the materialistic concept of farming and gaining

33. Material gathered by the author during field research.

more land has crept in between and clouded the earlier concept. I am sure not all people are aware of the problems
of the Christian life and the need to make a commitment.
Oh, there are many who are genuine, but what is lacking most
of all in our *Gemeent* is pure and simple love. There is no
love or brotherhood among us any more. I can hardly go
to church any more since there is no fellowship or worship. It
is each man for himself, thinking that, by serving the
Gemeent, he is earning his salvation. Why they even put
great stock in the fact that they are Mennonites! They think
this gives them license and special privileges with the government, whereas they ought to make the New Testament their
primary base of living and not expect any privileges, rather
to take up the cross of Christ.[34]

There are evidences in the traditional settlements of increasing encounters with people of the outside world. Many
young people correspond with Americans and Canadians
whose acquaintanceships they have made in various ways.
Boys are increasingly fraternizing with non-Old Colony
groups. Others are defying the official rules of separation from
the world and are drawing in as much as possible of the
"world's" wisdom and experience: "John Enns, brother-in-law
of Abram Neufeld of Hochfeld, is a well-informed man. He
talked in an authoritative way of the death of Pope Pius XII,
of the rocket to the moon, of the Arab crisis, of the beginning
of the world, of the history of the world, and many other
things. He listens to a radio all the time and reads vociferously,
quoting an encyclopedia, German scholarly books on arche-
ology, and the like. He has not yet been banned, though he is
doing things that are strictly forbidden." [35]

Probably the most subtle and insidious tactic that the host
society uses to tempt the Old Colony out of isolation is its
quiet insistence on the attractiveness of its world. Old Colony
members themselves are aware of this force, as well they
should be, for the consequences are obvious. Among a random group of Canadian Old Colony teenagers, one can note
little that distinguishes its members from the larger society.

34. Material gathered by the author during field research.
35. Material gathered by the author during field research.

They wear decorated cowboy belts and pants. They install used car radios in their trucks and listen to Western music at high volume. They know many of the popular singers on the radio, and when someone's upcoming performance is announced, they are able to comment on the talents of the recording star. Some play the guitar and entertain village children in the evenings.

Conclusion

The Old Colony has made considerable adaptations to the environments in which it has settled, but not without significant consequences. The dynamics of the adaptations can be analyzed as well. Adaptations to the environment have been made only slowly. When survival seemed threatened, the necessary adaptation was made. Adaptations to the political environment have been particularly crucial for Old Colony environment. The Old Colony chose its "homeland" carefully, hoping to achieve freedom and support for its way of life. The history of the Old Colony reveals that in some ways it has realized its hopes, but often it has been betrayed by the political policies of the state. It is difficult to say whether the Old Colony's efforts to deal with a state on a basis of immutable integrity have been successful in any measure. It is obvious that the assumptions by which an ethnic minority deals with the state are different from those by which the state deals with the ethnic minority. The state is obviously pragmatic, whereas the minority is simplistic and ideological. Integrity thus may not be an applicable or meaningful concept.

Economic adaptation has been substantial and is probably one of the most powerful forces breaking down the walls of isolation. Clearly, the level of living determines how easily debts can be paid off, how easily surpluses can be created to buy more land for sons. Dependencies upon the outside world permeate the minority system and affect its very nature. Thus the Canadian Old Colony settlements in Manitoba and Saskatchewan are the most acculturated while at the same time their economic dependencies are greatest. Some relationship must obtain between these two factors.

Although the Old Colony deliberately chose some environments over others, the environments have had unanticipated effects on the Old Colony and have tended to change it in many ways. They have not, however, altered the basis of the Old Colony, its original religious ethnic solidarity, originating in its belief that it was called by God. A rational decision to *leave an environment* that might destroy it is not only possible but is also a reality. The Old Colony "sits loose" in its earthly habitation, ready to move if its life is at stake. (See Appendix O.)

Chapter 7

THE DAY OF AFFLICTION

The Old Colony system operates on the proposition that separation from the world—social isolation, in sociological terms —is the key to survival and growth. Isolation is threatened, as we have seen, by the host societies' making inroads into the Old Colony system. The internal dynamics of the Old Colony also exert an influence on group survival and are of great significance for its persistence. In the discussion which follows, these internal processes are not listed in order of importance necessarily, though some order of significance is implied in terms of the immediacy of influence.

The Population Dilemma

In 1958, in the Old Colony settlement in Mexico, John Reimer had four children and five grandchildren. In 1964, he had fourteen grandchildren. If his three daughters and one daughter-in-law continue to bear children as rapidly as most of the other Old Colony women have—his oldest daughter already has eight children—he will have approximately thirty-two grandchildren. (See Tables 7-1 and 7-2 for data on family size.)

The problems that the population expansion is creating are well illustrated in this family. The oldest daughter married a man from a large family which could not give the son any land. They have now bought eighty acres of land and are renting another eighty acres. The second Reimer daughter married a boy in the home village. Since his parents were not able to give him any land, he and his wife lived with the Reimers until they were able to buy a farm for him in another village. The couple has now moved onto the 120-acre farm, which they cultivate with the husband of the third daughter. The third son-in-law had no parental resources for starting a farm and was forced to work for Mexicans in Cuauhtemoc

Table 7-1   Number of Children per Completed Family Married in Manitoba Settlement between 1930 and 1935[a]

No. of Children per Family	No. of Families Having This Number
0	4
1	6
2	4
3	7
4	4
5	10
6	12
7	7
8	15
9	11
10	5
11	8
12	9
13	4
14	3
15	1
16	1
17	2
19	1
22	1
—	—
Totals 887	115
Average per family 7.7	

[a] Data based on completed families for whom data was available.

for some years (with some disastrous consequences, since he had internalized some Mexican attitudes which later caused severe tensions in the Reimer family). After he married, he worked for his father-in-law for a while and then moved to his brother-in-law's farm.

The Reimer son is married and lives at home. He is now twenty-four years old and will take over the property in several years. Unless the sons-in-law can find more land, the situation will become desperate for them in about ten years, when their own young sons grow to adolescence and need work (the oldest son-in-law already has faced this with his fifteen-year-old boy). If the four fathers do not find more land (land becomes available only as Old Colony farmers retire or as migration to new territories takes place), each grandchild

*Table 7-2 Number of Children per Completed Family Married in Manitoba
Plan, Mexico, between 1930 and 1935*[a]

No. of Children per Family	No. of Families Having This Number
0	6
1	5
2	4
3	2
4	3
5	3
6	12
7	9
8	10
9	7
10	9
11	9
12	14
13	10
14	8
15	4
16	3
17	1
18	1
19	2
23	1

| Totals | 1,128 | 122 |
| Average per family | 9.3 | |

[a] Sample of completed families for whom information was available.

will receive about 15 acres of land (the total owned by the grandfather's clan is 480 acres). The father of the extended family described above views the situation thus:

There is not enough land. It is a serious problem. We have organized a new treasury, which is for the purpose of buying new land for the landless. We are all to pay 2 per cent of our yearly earnings. It is not compulsory. Like it always is, there are many *meinungen* [views] among us. There is very little agreement. There are always those who are disagreeing with us. But I think about half of the people are co-operating in it. We have at least 200,000 pesos in the account now. And now there have been some referendums asking what shall be done with the money. Some say Honduras, some say Canada, some say Chiapas [an area in Mexico]. The Mexican government has offered us some new plots of land since they have noticed our exodus to Honduras. It is supposed to be woods and have adequate moisture. The Mexican government does not want to lose the Mennonites, for we have done too much for their country. Who else but an Old Colonist would go to live in such primitive conditions? It seems to be up to us to tame wild lands.[1]

Since the birth rate in the progressive settlements is relatively low, the population expansion is a serious problem mainly in the traditional Old Colony settlements. The availability of land in the outer fringes of the various settlements determines whether the effects of the population pressure are already being felt or are yet to be.

The traditional Old Colony settlements have some of the highest rates of reproduction in the Western hemisphere. When the Old Colony moved to Mexico in 1922, the best estimates indicate that 5,286 individuals made the move.[2] Of this number, 3,340 settled on the Manitoba Plan. In 1937, there were 4,976 in the Manitoba Plan alone. Twenty years later the population had increased to 8,678. The annual net increase in the population is 4.08 per cent. (This figure does not include the continuing migration of Old Colony members from Mexico back to Canada and to other nearby plans.)

For the total Old Colony settlement at Chihuahua, the population totaled 11,261 in 1943. In 1953 it totaled 18,287, and by the end of 1963 the population was 22,731. This amounts to a 5 per cent net increase each year. This figure may be even lower than the true figure because the migration to British Honduras in 1958 and the migration to Aylmer, Ontario, and to Matheson, Ontario, took sizable groups from the Chihuahua settlement.

The average Old Colony family has many children. The average marriage age for girls in the Mexican settlement is 20.64, while the average age for the boys is 21.7. The children

1. Material gathered by the author during field research.
2. Cornelius Krahn, "Old Colony Mennonites," *ME*, IV, 41–42.

Table 7-3   Marriage Age for Males and Females in the Manitoba Settlement in Selected Years[a]

Age	1920–25		1945–50		1956–58	
	M	F	M	F	M	F
17	0	0	0	1	0	0
18	1	6	0	4	0	3
19	1	6	2	7	0	6
20	4	5	2	3	1	3
21	4	4	7	3	1	3
22	6	1	4	7	4	2
23	5	2	6	2	7	0
24	2	3	6	2	2	1
25	3	2	2	3	3	1
26	1	0	2	1	0	0
27	0	1	1	1	0	1
28	2	1	1	2	0	0
29	0	0	0	1	1	0
30	0	0	1	0	0	0
31	0	0	0	0	0	1
32	1	0	2	0	1	0
33	0	1	2	0	0	0
34	0	0	0	0	1	0
35	1	1	0	1	0	0
36	1	0	1	0	0	0
Totals	32	33	39	38	21	21
Average	23.6	21.7	23.3	22.3	24.2	21

[a] Source: Official Church records

usually come early in marriage. In the Mexican settlement about 63.2 per cent of the couples have a child within the first year of marriage and continue to have children through the child-bearing years of the mother. In Manitoba the average number of children born to a mother is 6. In Mexico, at Chihuahua, the average number of children per completed family in 1950 was 7.61. (See Tables 7-1, 7-2, 7-3, and 7-4 for further details.)

The high birth rate means that the population pyramid has a broad base with many young children. Because the Old Colony people are beginning to avail themselves of medical assistance, the death rate is going down, especially among children. This means that the population of young children

Table 7-4   *Marriage Age for Males and Females in the Manitoba Plan, Mexico, in Selected Years*[a]

Age	1920–25 M	F	1945–50 M	F	1956–57 M	F
17	0	1	0	4	0	1
18	0	1	0	1	1	4
19	1	2	2	5	0	6
20	4	5	8	9	4	2
21	5	4	5	4	3	1
22	5	3	5	1	6	2
23	2	3	6	3	1	0
24	0	2	4	0	2	1
25	2	0	0	2	0	6
26	0	0	1	1	0	0
27	3	2	0	0	0	0
28	0	1	0	0	0	0
30	0	0	1	0	0	0
31	0	0	1	0	0	0
32	0	1	0	0	0	0
33	0	1	0	0	0	0
Totals	22	26	33	30	17	17
Average	22.3	22.4	22.2	20.4	21.4	19.5

[a] Source: Official Church records

remaining alive to contribute to child-bearing is increasing. Thus, it can be predicted that the rate of population increase is going to rise unless some form of birth control is adopted, a possibility which is not likely in the near future. "The Church is officially against birth control. We are supposed to have large families, as many as the Lord gives us. But there are a few families who have not adhered to the ruling; some have gotten into trouble for it. One of the brothers who run the store in Reinfeld got thrown out of the Church for one week and then was allowed to come back on confession of wrong for having had his wife undergo an operation to prevent her from having more children. This is the rumor and we have no reason to disbelieve it. They only have two children." [3]

In Canada, the situation is different, however. The rate of natural increase per year for the progressive settlements

3. Material gathered by the author during field research.

(Manitoba and Saskatchewan) has been about 2 per cent per year. The crude birth rate is about 28 per year. The death rate is about 5 per year. One author suggests that the Old Colony settlements in Manitoba and Saskatchewan have been losing population since the great migrations, though it is not clear whether the cause is mainly defection, low population growth, or both:

> In Canada among the Old Colonists of Manitoba and Saskatchewan, a good adjustment both to the environment and to other Mennonite groups is noticeable. According to Benjamin Ewert (*Mennonitisches Jahrbuch,* 1951, p. 22), the number of Old Colony Mennonites in Manitoba in 1950 was 1,165, of whom 551 were baptized members. They have six ministers and four places of worship. This would indicate that they have decreased in number. The total number in Saskatchewan is estimated at 2,000 with a membership of 1,000 with ten ministers and six places of worship. If this figure is correct, there are only over 3,000 Old Colony Mennonites in Canada today, whereas there should be about 20,000 if they had increased like their brethren in Mexico. This makes it evident that many of the Old Colony Mennonites in Canada are no longer counted as such.[4]

In any case, the Old Colony in Manitoba and Saskatchewan is barely holding its own in population growth, and therefore does not face the problems of the other settlements described above.

The consequences of the population expansion in those settlements where it does occur are momentous. First, there is increasing poverty because the amount of land available does not meet the growing need. There are instances of poverty and welfare cases in every settlement. Of course these people are helped by relatives and the Church, but these landless families are a drain on the well-being of the total Colony. Second, there is increasing distrust and unrest in the villages as the landed and the landless families interact and compete for what little land there is, as described by an Old Colony farmer:

4. Krahn, "Old Colony Mennonites," p. 42.

There is a noticeable conflict between the landed farmers who live in the village plots proper and those who live on village land on the edge. Each village has land which it will rent to a young fellow who is not able to find land. The understanding is that as soon as he finds land, he is to move off, giving someone else a chance to stay there till he finds land. The plots are about two acres, and the buildings are built by the renter. The *Anwohner* has to pay double the cost for sending his children to school and is limited to three cows that he can send to the common pasture. For these he pays double the price that the regulars pay, and if he sends any more, he is fined quite heavily, sometimes up to $20. The antagonism toward the *Anwohner* is because he exploits his free living. He has the best land and is not as poor as he puts on. How does he do this? By not paying for any village expenses, not having to pay any *Gemeent* taxes, by renting land from the Mexicans, and by buying the best land from the Mexicans. He finds out about the land since he has more time to run around, while the regulars have to be satisfied to farm the 160 acres that have been allotted to them.[5]

Moderate competition for land need not be deleterious, but great competition for land has disorganizing tendencies, especially when some families in the village manage to accrue considerably more land than many others. The "psychology of scarcity," as it applies to the demand for land, creates an almost obsessional emphasis on land—land must be had for its own sake—thereby distorting Old Colony philosophy and demoralizing those who seek to live by it.

The expanding population also produces problems of a noneconomic nature. For example, it has created an extended type of family relationship. Often the oldest child is already married by the time the youngest child is born. Thus, uncles and cousins grow up together in close relationships (it is very common to discover while visiting in an Old Colony home that children playing together have cousin-uncle or cousin-aunt relationships). Further, because of the difficulty of finding land or a separate house, the younger children especially

5. Material gathered by the author during field research.

must live with the parents after marriage and begin their families in the parental homes.

Another effect which the high population growth has is the loss of privacy. Old Colony members do not appear to value privacy, but it is not unreasonable to suggest that a lack of desire for privacy is an adaptation to a brute fact. In any case, the amount of time that is spent alone, with a husband or wife, or with a few others is limited because there are people everywhere! There is no privacy within the family. Girls do not have private rooms and are not able to visit privately with suitors. Boys usually share the same rooms. Village folkways direct that a visit can be made at any time; it is not necessary to knock at the door. There is no place or time which is sacred.

Migration is not really a workable solution to the population problem since migration often causes more problems than it solves. The migrations often are based on insufficient information and result, therefore, in loss of life and assets. The migration to British Honduras was consummated before the *Lehrdienst* could lead it; thus, migration took place in a very disorganized fashion. Inadequately prepared and uninformed of the problem of disease and weather in British Honduras, many children and adults died. The high proportion of returnees, many without resources, testifies to the failure of migration to provide satisfactory solutions. Furthermore, migrations almost invariably include dissident elements—overconformists and nonconformists alike—which have created havoc in the new settlements. (See Appendix E for an example of the kinds of problems which arose in just one case.)

Migration to new settlements has always posed the problem of leadership. This has been the case in moves to neighboring areas, such as from the Manitoba Plan to the Nord Plan in Chihuahua state and from the Manitoba and Nord Plans to the Casas Grandes settlement farther north. Migrations to more distant areas have posed still greater problems. Often an ordained man was not in the group that moved, and one had to be ordained from among his peers, all of whom he was not likely to please. In addition, distances between old and new settlements cut down on the number and frequency of visits by the bishops, and attempts to appoint bishops from among the migrants have not proved successful.

The decrease in communication between the mother and daughter colonies has tended to increase suspicions and rumors which have not helped the harmony of the total Old Colony. The distrust and suspicion expressed about the members of a migration such as the one to British Honduras surprise the outsider, and questions as to the reasons for them are not answered.

A final observation that can be made about the influences of the population density and population growth is that there is an overwhelming preoccupation with people in a competitive sort of way; that is, the intense Old Colony interest in people is peculiarly that of "keeping up" on the latest events of members of the Old Colony society. Because of the high population density and population growth, the culture necessarily deals with the problems of making a living. Overwhelmingly, the topic of conversation at almost any visiting session is the most recent economic gains or losses that have befallen Old Colony members. A second topic delineates the genealogy of a particular person. This, then, serves as the "thread of continuity" to bring other relatives into the picture.

The Educational Dilemma

The traditional Old Colony settlements have always remained true to a conviction that extensive formal education is the poison that will kill the Old Colony. The consequences of this restrictive education strategy, advocated particularly by the *Lehrdienst,* are not as affirmative as the Old Colony membership believes, however.

Lack of a formal liberal education has produced a people who are surprisingly receptive to rumor, folklore, and superstition rather than to the guiding philosophic principle by which the people are to be devoted to Almighty God. One rumor grew out of my presence in the Cuauhtemoc settlement. Having gone there from the States, I was connected, by rumor, with a relief organization that had operated to aid farmers during a drought that followed World War II. Although the group had been sent by the Mennonite Central Committee (MCC), its efforts were met by considerable resistance since it was feared that it would undermine the Old Colony system. Long after the MCC had been replaced by the General Conference Mennonite Mission Board, made up of new personnel, all "Americans" were still viewed as agents of the MCC and were, therefore, suspect. My landlord reported the reactions to my presence: "I have been hearing certain undertones that I have been harboring a stranger, 'one from the world' in my house. I have been accused of harming and undermining the Church. They have rumored that Redekop has turned my head so that I am believing all sorts of strange things. They feel that Redekop is an MCC worker and that he is trying a different approach in getting the confidence of the people. . . . I tell them to come see him in person and get the news directly from us, rather than feed on rumor." [6] Rumors grow out of misinformation as well as distrust, as a summary of an evening's conversation indicates: Much talk concerned the roads, the shape of vehicles, and modern inventions in the States. They talked about the new jet car that was to be ready by 1960. They also talked about an electrical road that would allow every car to tap the energy of electricity lying underneath the road bed. It is inconceivable that rumor can assist the Old Colony in achieving its objectives.

The Old Colony abounds with folklore which supplies part of the basis for belief and action in many areas of life. Although folklore usually helps to organize and integrate the society in which it has its roots, in the Old Colony it is developing in a manner which is sometimes injurious to the Old Colony belief and goal systems in those settlements which have attempted to resist the development of the educational system.

A sampling of the folklore follows: "One story that has originated among us is of a Mexican who was on his death

6. Material gathered by the author during field research.

bed but could not die in peace. He called continually for the priest and said he had something to confess. When the priest came, the dying man said that there had once been an opportunity for him to steal some money but he had not done it. After he had confessed this and received forgiveness, the man died in peace." [7] This lore may be more humorous than detrimental, but others do not square with the Old Colony belief system and can be said to be more harmful:

> There have been some people who have committed the unpardonable sin. I do not know what to think of it. What is it anyhow? I am told it is blaspheming the Holy Spirit. One fellow was brought to the *Gemeent* and severely sanctioned for the following thing. This farmer decided that his cow was coming fresh [having a calf]. The herdsman said no, for he knew which cows had bred. When the farmer maintained she was going to be fresh, the herdsman finally asked, "How was she bred?" "It must have been by the Holy Spirit," the farmer replied. This was reported and he was consequently excommunicated.[8]

Another instance of folklore that contradicts belief is as follows: "A Mennonite wanted to work on Sunday, but his son had received a conscience against it and had wanted to go to church. But the father used his authority and prevailed upon the son to help him cut some wood. The father sat upon a certain stump for a long time to rest and to smoke his big pipe. Some years later the son was cutting hay in the same area and the mower hit the stump. Warm, red blood gushed from the stump. The meaning apparently is that Christ was crucified by this man's actions." [9] And another: "Some men were in town drinking. They knew it was not right and [was] forbidden by the *Gemeent*. Then a storm came up, and their guilt began getting the best of them. Then one of them in a drunken stupor held up his bottle and invited the Holy Spirit in the form of the lightning and thunder to have a drink. The man froze in that position and died instantly." [10]

7. Material gathered by the author during field research.
8. Material gathered by the author during field research.
9. Material gathered by the author during field research.
10. Material gathered by the author during field research.

Folklore exists which pertains, among other things, to the history of Mexico, to the origin of the world, and, naturally, to Pancho Villa. One of the most spellbinding evenings ever experienced by the author was spent listening to a young, eloquent Old Colonist tell stories of the exploits of Pancho Villa. Folklore has it that the hills surrounding the Old Colony settlements are dotted with places where Pancho Villa buried his gold. It is there to be unearthed. Even now, on a moonlit night, if one looks into the hills, one can see a blue vapor over the places where the buried treasure lies, since buried gold exudes a gas which lights up at night.

Folklore is harmless when it conforms to the major outlines of the society, but when the content of the folklore tends to decrease understanding of the basic goals or when it tends to divert attention from the dynamic, it is harmful. In many villages, men and women who are impressed by folklore and believe in it, are directly in conflict with the Old Colony way.

Many of the folk stories accepted as true are based on superstitions and are, therefore, contrary to the "facts" of the real world as well as to the "facts" of the religious system that has traditionally guided the Old Colony as a society. Some are superstitious concerning the physical world. One Old Colonist insisted strongly that it is more healthful to sleep with one's head toward the north, because oxygen tends to flow in a southerly direction. He said that this was found in a book which "contained everything there is to know about the physical world." Some astrological books can be found among Old Colonists. These are largely German books, handed down from one generation to the next. One Old Colonist indicated one such book was not available in the States because the author was a very wise man who had been exiled because he was ahead of his time. There is a vast amount of superstition relating to physical health. They believe, for example, that cancer is the greatest killer, especially common because they eat too much pork. They exchange the tale that the Jews do not have cancer because they do not eat pork.

There are superstitions of a more "spiritual" nature in

which God is seen to intervene directly in the experience of man. Lightning, rain, drought, and other natural phenomena fall into this category.

Lack of adequate education obviously plays a role in the health of the Old Colonists. Some illnesses are more serious than they realize; others are less serious than they imagine. A medical doctor in the Mexican village of Rubio on the edge of the Manitoba Plan, who is held in high esteem by the Old Colony members, had the following to say:

Their queer ideas of sickness and health are further attributable to their ignorance. To an Old Colonist, every type of sore or illness is a form of cancer. They do not believe anything else. Their quack doctors are partly to blame for this. Dr. John Froese, for example, treats almost any type of superficial sore as cancer. I had a lady lately who had a sore on one of her breasts. Froese had put on a compress which contained a caustic, which was supposed to burn out the cancer. She was to apply this compress on every side of her breast, seven weeks on one side, seven on the next, till the whole breast had been covered, and the cancer was to be gone. I told her it was not cancer but the caustic that had done a great deal of tissue damage to her. Another fellow came to me with a sore on his forehead. He said it was cancer. He did not believe my diagnosis and maintained it was cancer. So he went to another doctor in Cuauhtemoc who told him the same thing. He still did not believe it and took a trip to the States, where several doctors gave him the same diagnosis—not cancer. So he came back and it healed. Now lately I saw him again, and he had a bandage on his forehead again. I guess he still thinks he has cancer.

They are very prone to telling stories which are not true. They will spread a story far and wide, always saying so and so said it, when in reality it is a myth. They believe in these myths for a long time, and I am convinced that it is ignorance that makes them superstitious. One story that has not yet died is that when the *Segura Social* doctor was in the village, he was attempting to poison me with a beer that contained certain poisons. I have tried to correct this impression, but have not been able. This shows that they want to believe certain things. Some stories are made up;

others are merely exaggerated tremendously. You never know whether you can believe their stories.[11]

The Old Colonist's lack of education frequently makes him the victim of deceit or exploitation. The following is one of many cases which have been documented.

John Dirksen, son of preacher John Dirksen of the North Plan, was in Chihuahua some time ago. At some corner a man approached him, speaking in English and said he was an American looking for a certain family who was living somewhere near Chihuahua. He was bringing them $7,000 as a gift from some rich American who wanted the family to have this gift. Dirksen, knowing Spanish, agreed to help for a little sum of money. After a while the "American" having discovered who Dirksen was, said there was some money for the Mennonites too. Then they went to a waiting room of an attorney and began to discuss how the money would be distributed. It developed to the point where the American convinced the Mennonite to lay down 1,500 pesos of his own as proof that he could be trusted. So the money was all laid on the table, and put in bags. Then the man said he wanted to see the attorney for a few minutes, that he should wait for him outside. Dirksen waited for a long time, then began to be suspicious and looked in his bag where he had deposited his money. It was empty. He was unable to trace hide or hair of the "American" and thus was out 1,500 pesos.[12]

Economic Factors

Numerous economic factors exert pressure on the Old Colony and will make its survival difficult, especially in the traditional settlements. One of these is occupational specialization, of which there is an increasing amount developing, forcing young fellows to look elsewhere for their livelihood. Reference has already been made in Chapter 3 to the proportion of young families in villages in the traditional settle-

11. Material gathered by the author during field research.
12. Material gathered by the author during field research.

ments who have no land and live in the *Anwohner* section of the village. A tabulation of the types of work engaged in, in the Mexican settlements, shows that there is considerable specialization. (See Tables 3-3 and 3-4 for the listing.)

These specializations are foreign to the Old Colony way of life for a number of reasons. First, they show that a way of life other than farming is possible and rewarding. The prestige that comes with being a machinist who can "turn anything on a lathe" is beginning to rival that of the successful farmer. Second, a more specialized and differentiated social structure is being created in the villages. The residents are increasingly designated as the "farmer," the "cheese maker," the "storekeeper," or the "carpenter," to name a few. Thus, the homogeneous society is being broken up into status and interest groups:

> Yesterday an *Anwohner,* Franz Neufeld, came to borrow some article from Henry Harms [a landowner]. Harms is a little antagonistic toward the *Anwohner,* for he says they feign poverty and often are richer than the farmers. Neufeld had hired Harms to do some bindering, but had kicked about the price. He had asked for credit and had paid later. Harms thought it should have been bearing interest while he was waiting for it. Neufeld said they were always picking on the *Anwohner.* Harms said the *Anwohner* were always trying to get the farmers to pay the *Anwohner*'s load too. Neufeld stated the farmers were always trying to keep them down, yet they wanted them to pay for the schoolteacher's wages and the like. And further, Neufeld said, "If we want to borrow money so we can move out onto farms, they will not loan it, so you can see they dislike us, yet want to keep us so they can exploit us." Harms then cited the case of two *Anwohner,* one who however owned eighty acres and threshed more oats than anyone else in the village.[13]

Third, these specialties, unlike farming, offer the practitioner a door to the outside world. The manager of the feed mill needs to know something about grain prices and trends. This need forces him to develop closer relationships with the "secular" person. Further, he needs to consult various legal

13. Material gathered by the author during field research.

and technical sources for information on how to run the mill, how to select ingredients for feed, and how to organize the mill. Finally, a mill must have a management and a labor force, and this introduces a concern for secular labor-management relations. Although there is not as yet labor-management tension to any noticeable degree, private discussions reveal the dissatisfaction with wages and working conditions.

Stratification, another economic factor which is having its impact on the Old Colony social system, is the result of internal competition for land and wealth. When a new settlement is laid out, each farmer usually is allocated 160 acres of land. Because of the differences in human ability and fortune, sizable differences in wealth develop which help to create severe strains on the religious norm of equality and the social norms of solidarity and mutuality. In every village there is a hierarchy of status based on wealth.

In Manitoba, a bishop owned over 3,000 acres of rich farming land. There are other Old Colony families in Manitoba who own no land and rent land from others or who work for other farmers. In 1950, there were 610 families in a representative sample of nineteen villages in the Chihuahua settlement in Mexico. Of this number, 486 families were landowners, leaving 114 families in the landless state. A typical village in Mexico shows the following spread in land ownership: the two highest acreages are 686 and 418; the two lowest acreages belong to two farmers who each owned 40 acres. In 1958, in the same village there were 35 families who owned some land and 23 *Anwohner*.

Wealth is not the only indicator of the stratification system and its implications but it is the single best variable. The implications of the increased disparity in wealth for the achievement of Old Colony ends are profound. The tendency for the individuals of similar conditions to coagulate and develop orientations conflicting with the rest of society is constantly present. This is illustrated in the tension between *Anwohner* and the landed pictured above. It is also illustrated in the tension between the richer and the poorer farmers in the village: "One of the well-to-do farmers in Hochfeld has a big irrigation system with big machinery to drive it. There is no ruling about who may dig large wells in the village. Everybody presumably may. It is common knowledge, however, that there is not nearly enough water in the ground to allow everybody to irrigate. Frank Fehr's sons said that it costs tremendous amounts of money to drill wells and set up the equipment to irrigate. Very few in the village could afford it, so only those that can afford them have wells." [14]

A visit with some Old Colony families one Sunday evening revealed some of the invidious comparisons based on the types of vehicles used. They stated that the marks of one lower on the ladder in the past had been one who could drive only a farm wagon for both Sunday and weekday use. Those who were more well-to-do had nice top buggies. Now it is much the same, only those who drive farm wagons made of modern cars on rubber are lower down, while those who drive buggies either on rubber or wood spokes are higher up. The presence of a stratification system and the tendency for it to become more pronounced unless it is equalized by migration indicate the precariousness of the way of life as understood by the Old Colony. A sudden drastic cessation of migration or the development of new industries and specializations within the Old Colony will profoundly increase the class differences in the system.

The other major economic factor which exerts pressure on the Old Colony is its increasing economic dependence on the host society, a factor which becomes more evident every year. Before the migration in Canada and in Mexico, until recently the technological development in the Old Colony was not very high and was, to a significant degree, self-sufficient. Field work was done largely with horses, and transportation was provided by horse and wagon. The amenities and necessities in the home were usually homemade. Banking was largely of the tea kettle or "cream can" variety.

In all the settlements the picture has changed considerably. Now all Old Colony settlements rely on mechanization to get their field work done; thus, a shortage, such as the fuel

14. Material gathered by the author during field research.

shortage which prevailed in Mexico in the summer of 1958, severely threatens the Old Colony economy. Transportation by horse and wagon is no longer sufficient to move produce, the sale of which depends upon delivery on specified dates. Increasingly, modern trucks are used. For example, the farmers who are raising large flocks of chickens and laying hens need feed often and quickly. For this reason, the Mexican Old Colony feed mills are forced to hire trucks or lease trucks and drivers from non-Old Colony people. The interaction that develops destroys the social isolation that is the backbone of the Old Colony system and creates tension among the Old Colonists. For example, a prosperous milling business was started by several young Old Colonists and several older men. The younger fellows bought a truck and drove it themselves. Then some farmers who had been buying feed began to boycott them because they were breaking one of the sacred rules of the *Gemeent.* This cut into the profits and future of the business considerably. So when an older stockholder took over again, he hired a full-time Mexican truck and driver and is now sending some of the Old Colony workers along with the Mexican to deliver feed.

In the home, the fact that refrigerators are becoming more prevalent suggests not only that eating habits and food preservation patterns are changing but also that there is increased dependence upon the market for fuel, electricity, and service.

Almost all banking is now done in commercial establishments. In Cuauhtemoc, one banker suggested that a large majority of the bank's business was with the Old Colony. The same banker said that his "biggest borrowing category are the young Old Colony farmers who want to start farming and need some money to buy seed, feed, and the like. The average loan is from 10,000 to 15,000 pesos."

The greatest area of interaction and interdependence of Mexicans and Mennonites is commercial and banking. Over 80 per cent of my banking business is with Mennonites, and the other three banks experience the same. A major part of all business in town is dependent upon the Mennonites and would need to fold if the Mennonites were not here. The greatest dependence that the Mennonites feel toward the

Mexicans is the merchandising. Mexicans, of course, are, in turn, just as dependent upon the Mennonites for business and patronage. Merchandising, banking, and ordinary work are the three things the Mexicans depend on the Mennonites most for. The greatest areas of contact are banking and doing business together—the Mennonites selling their wares and buying other things from the Mexicans. I learn to know many Mennonites very intimately since I have to be their financial adviser, though I never interfere in their affairs, since I want to be a friend to all.[15]

Although this demonstration of interdependence could be expanded, enough information has been supplied to show that the increased dependence on the larger economy has created networks of social interaction which break down the emotional, social, and cultural ethnocentric stances and force an exchange which, in the long run, will destroy the Old Colony way of life.

The Drive for Conformity

We have seen that one of the goals of the Old Colony belief system is that all members should live the Old Colony way of life. Ideally, every member should conform to the goal system and the norms provided to achieve the goals. The outcome, not understood by the Old Colony members, is that the achievement of this goal creates a conformity which is destructive to personal expression and creativity. (See Appendix L for an Old Colonist's view.)

This destructive conformity expresses itself in many ways. Nonconformists and innovators are excluded from the social system and ridiculed. One family in Mexico is clearly unorthodox in many ways, with wide interests such as reading books, keeping up on world affairs, and having hobbies. These interests have interfered with its farming operations so that it is not very well off financially. Because of its nonconformity the family was rejected so vigorously that it left the village and moved to a plot of land about three miles from the village. The village residents constantly make refer-

15. Material gathered by the author during field research.

ences to the family in a derogatory fashion, intimating that it is not able to make a living farming and thus turns to tinkering with machinery and to inventing. An objective observer would probably say that the family is very creative, with a wide range of interests including church history, music, science, and inventions—all of which are actually forbidden. The homemade shop of the family is amazing, considering the handicaps involved in creating it.

Another ramification of conformity is that it actually interferes with the achievement of Old Colony goals. This can be illustrated in many ways, of which only one will be alluded to here. As suggested above, ministers throughout the Old Colony (except for a few of the younger ones in Manitoba and Saskatchewan) read their sermons, which have been handed down from generation to generation. When a minister dies, his sermons are usually given to the young minister who was called to the ministry and did not have the time, education, or experience needed to produce good sermons immediately. Thus the practice of lending sermons was to help the young preacher over the rough "breaking in" period. This practice soon became institutionalized. Thus the average preacher probably adds one or two sermons to the collection and hands it on to someone else when he dies.

The effects of this practice are numerous: no new and creative thought is injected into the system; the traditional sermons are not relevant to the changing conditions which are inevitable, even in the Old Colony; and the sermon, both in form and content, becomes an exercise or ritual devoid of personal emotional involvement and commitment. It would seem that the Old Colony system is bound to degenerate as these forces are allowed to operate.

The Role of Tradition

Closely allied to conformity but on another level of complexity is tradition. The Old Colony's "charter" is determined from day to day on the basis of tradition. The response to many questions regarding behavior or belief is, "That is the way we have always done it." Obviously this is not a satisfactory reason in the long run, even in a highly traditional system such as the Old Colony, as perceptive Old Colonists realize:

> There is a big change coming. More and more younger people are defying the authority of the leadership. They are losing confidence in the old men. The elders are always saying, "Back to the old way," but we younger ones say there is no chance of going back. Time does not stand still but rather changes, and we have to change with it. The tractor is absolutely necessary for our survival here. But the tractor was wrong some time ago, and if we had not adopted it, we could not compete with the Mexicans or others. And the same goes for cars and trucks. Some time in the near future we will lose out if we do not adopt their use. The younger men who have not yet joined Church are eager to buy cars, and many of these will defy the leadership when they get into the Church.[16]

This statement illustrates the tension that develops when a pattern of behavior is enforced without an accompanying rationale that makes sense.

One of the greatest difficulties with a social system based on tradition is that the tradition becomes an end in itself and thereby deflects the society from proceeding on a course that will help it become what it hopes to become. The unreflecting enactment of a tradition tends to degenerate the tradition itself. The emphasis is on the enforcement of the objective aspects of the normative system without attention to the underlying purpose and motivation.[17]

One of the most telling illustrations of the force of tradition is the development of the so-called *a-au* controversy. (See Appendix J.) Because of the infiltration of the Low German pronunciations into the High German, many of the schoolteachers especially began to protest the corrosion of the High German. The *Lehrdienst* and the majority of the rank and file used the Low German pronunciation when using High

16. Material gathered by the author during field research.

17. See Robert Redfield's discussion of the unreflecting little tradition in his *Peasant Society and Culture* (Chicago: University of Chicago Press, 1956), pp. 67–104.

German, but a faction arose which staunchly maintained that the High German pronunciation should be retained. The tension narrowed down to the pronunciation of the letter *a*. Feeling ran so high that numerous Church meetings were held threatening excommunication of the "proud" folks, namely, those who held out for the correct pronunciation and would not back down.

The implications of the two usages for the Old Colony are illustrated in the transcriptions below:

> The first reason for pressing for uniformity in using the *au* is that there was such a confused usage of the *a* that it was necessary that something be done about it and that a uniformity be established. Especially those who used the *a* were so inconsistent in using it that it was funny to listen to. Further, to avoid parties of those going to hear the preacher who used the *a* and others going to hear their favorite preacher who used the *au*, it was decided that a uniformity be established. Several preachers agreed to relearn their *a* and change to the *au*. Many who had used *a* used it as a token of their advanced knowledge of the High German language, and this was to be avoided. It is also true that the *au* has been kept because it makes our German seem less like the worldly High German and hence differentiates us immediately from others who speak it. We want our group to have marks that will point us out as being different.[18]

One of the schoolteachers who was involved in the *a-au* controversy states:

> I have been forbidden to take communion because I have been teaching the *a* pronunciation instead of the *au*. I was asked to come to *Dunnadagh* because I taught the *a*. They told me I could not come to communion till I had repented. I have not done it yet. At Blumenort the same situation exists, but the teacher is an older man, and they do not want to hurt or attack him. They try to push the younger generation into the dirt. I am accused by many of not knowing the difference between the *a* and the *au* and thus confusing the children hopelessly. But the fact of the matter is that in German there are words using the umlaut or double laut,

18. Material gathered by the author during field research.

and they are too ignorant to know this. They [the preachers] have told me that if I would at least use the *au* in *Vater* and *Amen,* they would be satisfied. But that is not German. They are trying to make a Low German usage the absolute form.[19]

The problem of tradition is clearly perceived on the part of the more concerned and enlightened people, such as the schoolteacher who gave the following assessment of tradition in the Old Colony:

> The goal of the Old Colony is to follow Christ in living obedience. But there are so many intervening things by now that the image is blurred. I talked to a man recently about the same problem. I said we had been so concerned about copying the picture from the last generation that we have lost any resemblance to the original picture. Thus, we need to copy our *Gemeent* after the original which Menno Simons had, and we will be quite different. I guess this operates in all denominations. The first fever and life were perfect, but soon self-interest and pride got in the way and the original image was lost. I am sure our forefathers read and studied the Bible and prayed, but today there are hardly any who do that. Today the topic of conversation when families visit is not spiritual life or moral living or the goals of the Christian; rather it is gossip about the folly of another person, the mistakes he has made, or about the weather, the farm, and how one can get ahead to make more money. How the goals have become beclouded is obvious from the way moral things are treated in contrast to legalistic externals. When a man does a thing which is forbidden as part of the *Gemeent*'s rules of life, such as wearing a belt or buying a car, he is dealt with in no uncertain terms. But when a man is involved in serious moral deviations, little is done. . . . When externals that threaten the unity of the brotherhood are at stake, the discipline is severe; but when problems of evangelical living are considered, there is less concern.[20]

Finally, the force of tradition in a social system militates against rational management of change. Change, if and when

19. Material gathered by the author during field research.
20. Material gathered by the author during field research.

it comes, is literally forced upon the Old Colony and is always haphazard and tension-creating. An Old Colony minister in Mexico revealed the strain in the following conversation:

> There is a lot of disunity among our people now. I wish we could keep them together and keep things as we used to. Why could we not keep things as we always had them? It has worked so well. Why must our young people suddenly decide to jump over the traces? I guess we cannot keep the world from changing, but that is no sign that we must. I hope the Church does not split, for if it does, it will be difficult to re-cement. Why do the young people not understand and try to co-operate with the *Gemeent?* . . . Many are not satisfied with the schools. Why should this be? The movement to Honduras was an example of where the people did not listen but went on their own, and now there is a real chance that it will not succeed. If they only had listened to the counsel of the *Gemeent.*[21]

An Old Colony layman commented:

> Thus, we are having things gradually forced upon us. . . . Prohibition of rubber tires on tractors will be the first to go. The reason that rubber tires have not been condoned is that they know that if rubber-tired tractors are allowed, the automobile is not far behind, for those with cars will say that they use their car for exactly the same uses that the tractor drivers do now. But this business of catering to the weaker brethren has a limit. There is a limit to how much I must bow to the wishes and weaknesses of the other fellow. Though there is nothing immoral involved in some of the practices, as long as the Church thinks a certain way, we must think that way too in order to avoid any trouble.[22]

Conclusion

Five internal factors which are working for the dissolution of the Old Colony way of life have been listed and discussed. Others could be mentioned, but these appear to be the most

21. Material gathered by the author during field research.
22. Material gathered by the author during field research.

important. What can be said in an over-all way of the effect of these facts?

The first and most obvious conclusion is that many of the institutions and practices in the Old Colony system have unintended consequences which threaten the system. For example, it was shown that the educational system has the unintended consequences of creating a gullible and credulous population which will become victim to almost any bizarre event.

There are institutional discontinuities within the system which contribute to dissolution. The economic institutions which are concerned with providing subsistence for the Old Colony way do not support the religious principles and practices, as for example the inevitable integration of Old Colony farmers with outsiders, with the resulting loss of isolation and loss of faith in the Old Colony system. The various institutional systems thus do not seem to support each other in a way necessary for the system to prosper.

There is no adequate system of decision-making in the Old Colony which will enable it to meet the unending crises. The population dilemma, for example, is so grave that something must be done soon, but no mechanism is available to enable the members of the Old Colony to discuss the problem and decide what to do. Tradition has been the anvil upon which decisions were made. The *Lehrdienst* made the interpretations that dealt with spiritual matters, but the problem of population and its impact on the socio-religious system cannot be understood by the clergy because of its incapacity to think in nontraditional terms.

A traditional society, of course, has no philosophy or experience for dealing with change. There is no understanding of the fact of change, its implications, or the ways to meet it. Thus, the only reaction is the assertion of the authority of the past in an ever increasingly authoritarian manner, preparing the way for explosions and rebellions if a sophisticated response from the more enlightened members is not forthcoming. The presence of enlightened members is a dilemma in itself, for education and sophistication are signs of faithlessness and apostasy.

Figure 12. An Old Colony family in the Manitoba Settlement, Mexico (photograph by Rohn Engh)

Figure 13. An Old Colony mother, niece, and child

Figure 14. The traditional garb of Old Colony males in Mexico
(photograph by Ken Hiebert, courtesy of Mennonite Life)

Figure 16. An Old Colony store

Figure 17. A livery stable in Chihuahua, Mexico

Figure 15. The traditional garb of Old Colony women in Mexico

Figure 18. An Independence Day celebration in a Mexican village

Figure 19. Mexican laborers constructing an Old Colony trench silo

Figure 20. An Old Colony schoolboy (photograph by Rohn Engh)

Figure 21. A scene on a main road in Mexico

Figure 22. An Old Colony farmer-machinery importer

Chapter 8

THE PROMISE
OF DELIVERANCE

The first seven chapters have attempted to present the "facts" about the Old Colony. But what is the utility of facts? Facts "do not speak for themselves." [1] Facts do, however, provide the material for the formulation of good questions and possible answers to these questions. With Aristotle, we are interested in the relationship between facts, the causes of things, because as he says, ". . . we do not know truth without some knowledge of its causes." [2]

In the concluding chapters, an attempt has been made to put together the facts which get at the "truth" for the Old Colony and the "truth" of religious ethnic minority groups in general. Although no coherent theory of religious ethnic minority life can be presented, at least an "orientation" [3] is offered, which hopefully may lead toward a clearer understanding of the nature of minority life.

The Old Colony has been depicted as a social system which had a clear goal when it emerged, and which has strived ever since to retain its identity. The external and internal forces which are working toward dissolution of the Old Colony suggest a rather dim hope for its survival.

The future of the Old Colony as an ethnic minority is not easy to predict because the Old Colony is not a homogeneous society. As has been shown, the progressive settlements are in many ways greatly different from the conservative ones. Further, there is great variation in attitudes and behavior within the individual settlements. The issue is further complicated by the matter of interpretation of "survival." For

1. William J. Goode and Paul K. Hatt, *Methods in Social Research* (New York: McGraw-Hill Book Co., 1952), p. 13.

2. Aristotle, *On Man in the Universe* (New York: Walter J. Black, Inc., 1943), p. 11.

3. Robert K. Merton, *Social Theory and Social Structure* (Glencoe, Ill.: The Free Press, 1957), pp. 87–89.

the progressive settlements, survival would seem to mean "getting up to date" and becoming relevant to the larger world. The predominating conservative orientation in the other settlements maintains that survival is remaining forever as they have been.

The inroads made by the external social environment upon the internal environment have been discussed. But there is also the problem of the natural environment. Close analysis of the adaptations that the Old Colony has made to its physical environment reveals that adaptations have been made not to exploit the environment efficiently, but rather so that the traditional way of life can be perpetuated. The Old Colony is not interested in controlling the environment to amass a fortune.[4] Rather the environment is merely a series of limiting factors that must be dealt with in achieving the way of life considered desirable. The geographic determination of culture theory will find very little corroboration in the Old Colony settlements. A group like the Old Colony, which is concerned merely about surviving, will not be too greatly affected by the geographic and climatic conditions. The environment offers a limiting force, but does not dictate what a group must do in terms of a cultural form. (See Appendix O for a discussion of Old Colony adaptation to the physical environment.)

Another hurdle in determining the longevity of the Old Colony is the role that the self-fulfilling prophecy will play in Old Colony life. In the progressive Old Colony settlements, it is evident that statements about the need to become relevant are undermining faith in the Old Colony and are causing greater defections than would otherwise be the case. On the other hand, in the conservative settlements, statements about the decadence of the Old Colony system seem to work toward further decadence. However, and this makes prediction hazardous, such criticisms could serve to stimulate the Old

4. For a number of years an American Mennonite group has conducted agricultural experiments at Cuauhtemoc, with several experimental plots in the villages. The results have been so convincing that many Old Colony farmers are adopting some of the new practices in the face of strong disapproval from the *Lehrdienst*.

Colony to reaffirm its reason for being and begin to thrive. Before a prophecy is offered regarding the future life of the Old Colony, a sociological analysis of some salient aspects of the Old Colony social structure may prove useful.

Sociological Observations on Old Colony Survival

MEMBERSHIP

Belonging to a group is for members of most ethnic minorities far more important than adhering to the principles which brought the group into existence in the first place. Outward conformity to group standards so as to be accepted is the ultimate objective of an ethnic minority member.

This is nowhere more clearly illustrated than in the way young members of the Old Colony "skate on the edges" of accepted behavior and are restricted only by external pressures to conform. The drinking sprees mentioned, as well as other forbidden activities such as playing musical instruments, are not looked at in terms of their moral or ideological value, but rather in terms of how much these activities might get the young people into trouble with the authority figures.

This fact has important implications for the concept of the sect, as originally defined by Ernst Troeltsch. He suggests that the sect is composed of persons who voluntarily belong to a group because of its beliefs and commitments. The Old Colony is thus not a sect, at least not at present, according to the classic definition.

DEVIANCE

Another matter of great concern to the Old Colony system is the problem of deviance. Despite the fact that the Old Colony is not a homogeneous society, it does have a uniform value system which depends upon standardized behavior among its members. Since realization of the Old Colony's goals depends upon conformity, a great amount of energy is spent in controlling deviance. Much of the communication in the Old Colony concerns deviant behavior. A major emphasis is on restricting those expressions of human nature which do not clearly contribute to the goals of the Old Colony system. (See Appendix L.)

This society thus has a highly rationalized order, which according to Max Weber is a close connection and articulation of ends with the means to achieve them.[5] A clear set of objectives is outlined, and the ways in which these objectives can be met are prescribed. The same factor can be termed cultural integration, whereby there are certain cultural traits to which all must adhere.

The experience of the Old Colony throws some doubt upon the assumption, in much sociological thinking, that a society with a high degree of cultural integration is a "healthy" society. The Old Colony experience shows that the development of a rational structure creates tensions which are as difficult for the individual member as a lack of structure would be. (See Appendix N for mental illness and suicide statistics.)

In general, the goals and means are not greatly disparate. Thus the conflict the individual faces in reconciling the two is not as pertinent in this case as Merton and others have proposed. The problem is not so much one of accepting the goals and the conflicting means, but rather one of being motivated to accept either or both and to live up to them. The process of identification of an individual with group norms and the process of group morale and cohesion are yet little understood. The Old Colony may be a useful laboratory for achieving an increased understanding of the basic social process of group cohesion and solidarity.

DISCONTINUITY

Reference was made above to the fact that there was considerable institutional discontinuity in the Old Colony structure. That is, the patterns of behavior often conflict with the norms of various *institutions* so that considerable strains are imposed on the system. Reference was made to the fact that the economic practices tend to undermine the religious

5. Hans Gerth and C. Wright Mills (eds.), *From Max Weber: Essays in Sociology* (New York: Oxford University Press, 1946), p. 294.

goals of the Old Colony. Other illustrations of this fact can be seen. The lack of integration of the village life with the "religious" institutions is probably the greatest source of discontinuity.

In the Old Colony system, the individual is in reality governed by two groups of norms—those of the religious sphere and those of the village. As indicated earlier, the Old Colony is a theocracy, in which all of life ideally is lived under the command of God; there is theoretically no distinction between the sacred and secular. But in practice things work out differently. Village life, which includes all of the economic and social activities, has developed an autonomy of its own, which is not necessarily very closely integrated with the religious institutions. Thus, for example, interpersonal conflicts are often handled on a village level, with even serious difficulties never reaching the religious level.

The upshot of the institutional discontinuities is that institutions often work at cross purposes, which of course is self-defeating for the entire system. This discontinuity creates serious difficulties for the individuals who participate in all the institutions and find that there are contradictions among them. The schoolteacher is probably the best example of a person who gets caught in institutional discontinuity—he wants to be a good teacher and also a good pious person, but finds that these goals often contradict each other. Thus he is forced to choose which institution will retain his loyalty.

CONCRETE EXPRESSION OF BELIEFS

One of the processes which is most relevant to the study of the sociology of religion is the Old Colony's approach to expressing the belief system in concrete experience. Like every other group, the Old Colony has a set of beliefs which must be expressed in real life. The entire history of the Old Colony, from the perspective of their beliefs, can be described as a struggle to define what human behavior is sacred—what behavior best expresses the beliefs and understanding of God for the Old Colony.

The historical solution to the problem for the Old Colony has been to consider all social and economic behavior as an expression of the sacred belief system. It is believed that God called the Old Colony to be an agrarian group, for thereby most if not all of human activity could be considered sacred. All the various activities which contributed to keeping the Old Colony agrarian and to maintaining a rural way of life thus were expressions of the sacred.

The unintended consequences of the sacredness of all of life has been that nonmoral activities have been baptized with sanctity. Thus a particular cultural pattern, a subculture if you will, has become sacred.[6] The Old Colony way of life has come to symbolize and even to actually incarnate the will of God. The forms of dress, the patterns of behavior, the artifacts of farming and recreation have taken on religious and moral significance. A harmonica or belt is not only a symbol of pride, it *is* pride and therefore sin. Things are worldly not because they are composed of material, but because they have been defined as such through the long history of attempting to express belief in concrete behavior.

Equating the Old Colony way of life with the sacred is not necessarily irreligious or pagan. However, such a system does present problems in dealing with outside influences and perspectives which threaten the unity of the system. The controversy over the pronunciation of the *a* offers a very good illustration. This controversy would not have arisen if the importation of a foreign idea had not taken place. The issue thus is not a matter of determining whether God really uses the *a* or the *au* (i.e., its sacredness), but the implications for the unity of the system, which many leaders in the Old Colony well understood.

A further difficulty of the "sacred" society, which however the Old Colony has avoided, is proselyting. When a particular culture has been made sacred, the outsider has to accept the total package without questioning the assumptions; if he does,

6. Emile Durkheim, in *The Elementary Forms of the Religious Life* (London: George Allen and Unwin, Ltd., 1915), p. 229, says, "Therefore, the sacred character assumed by an object is not implied in the intrinsic properties of this latter: *it is added to them.* The world of religious things is not one particular aspect of empirical nature; *it is superimposed upon it.*"

he will eventually end up outside the group. The Old Colony has intuitively solved this problem by not concerning itself with gaining converts. It is possible that ethnic minority groups which do not proselyte do not do so for this basic reason.

A Prediction of the Old Colony's Future

It is undeniable that there are forces working toward the dissolution of the Old Colony, if the criteria of what the Old Colony was earlier are taken as bases for analysis. Retaining the integrity of the Old Colony is in question; according to an Old Colonist in Mexico:

> The biggest pressure that gets the young and coming genera-
> tion to join the Church is marriage. There is no marriage
> unless you are *Gemeent.* So you join Church in order to
> marry. Otherwise many young people might not join Church
> first, but might marry and later join if they felt the need,
> since Church does not mean much to many young people
> especially. We know many young people who join Church
> and promise all sorts of things, and do not know what they
> have said, and live contrarily. I must admit that I did not
> know all the things I was learning and committing myself
> to when I joined. It is the thing to do when you are of age
> and want to get married and you are therefore not aware of
> the tremendous consequences of the promises you have made.
> We feel that most people do not have a real idea of what
> belonging to the Church means, but do it out of custom.
> The Church has become a social organization rather than
> a religious group. The principles that keep us together are
> not spiritual, but social.[7]

One of the most recurrent complaints the observer hears when the Old Colony informants lower their defenses is the growing lack of unity in the Old Colony. The complaint is heard in the progressive settlements in Canada, but more commonly in Mexico and British Honduras. (See Appendix J for letter of Deacon Dyck.) In Canada, the concern is no longer keeping the Old Colony people conforming to the

7. Material gathered by the author during field research.

old patterns; rather there is concern that the Old Colony members may retain their spiritual purity. This emphasis indicates that the ethnic-minority dimension has largely vanished. A group of young people came to a minister in the Manitoba settlement in Canada and wanted to know whether it was wrong to play ball on Sunday: "I told them for a Christian it is not how far can a Christian go, but what is the middle of the road in this case? Why get your clothes torn on the fence when you can stay in the middle of the road? It is best to stay away from temptation. The disbeliever wants to see in the Christian a real difference and change of life, and yet we want to see how close we can go to what is evil. They had not thought of it in that way, and thought seriously about it." [8] [This minister's answer shows the change of emphasis in the progressive settlements.]

In the conservative Old Colony villages, the concern is with keeping a total unity—socially, economically, and spiritually. There the greatest fear is that the *Gemeent* is falling apart—unity is disappearing. This lack of unity runs through the fabric of the entire Old Colony. There is lack of unity between the individuals:

> There was considerable talk yesterday of getting a big ditch dug between the highest spot and the place where natural fall would take care of the water, but most of them talked in a sort of fatalistic vein, saying that it does no good, "As soon as the emergency is over, each is concerned about preserving his own way of life." Two farmers who had beans that were being threatened with inundation were talking about damming up the water so it would not flood their land. One said, "But if we dam ours, then the water will run over our neighbor's oats." This neighbor heard about this and came into the discussion quite perturbed, and said they had no right to detour the water over his oats. Then the first farmers asked, "Who has more right to a crop, you with your oats, or we with our beans?" They argued some more but came to no conclusion; so both parties began making a dam to keep the water off their fields.[9]

8. Material gathered by the author during field research.
9. Material gathered by the author during field research.

There is lack of unity in the relationships between villages, as the following account by an Old Colonist illustrates. This type of conflict can be duplicated in almost every village.

> There is a water hole right in the middle of the road from Hochfeld to the villages in the south. This hole lies in the middle of the road, but on Kronsthal property. First the Hochfelders wanted the Kronsthalers to fix it, but they would not, saying they had no use from it. Then the Hochfelders offered to fill the hole with nice gravelly dirt right near the hole, but the Kronsthalers would not allow it, saying they should get some gravel from the river bed some four miles away. This the Hochfelders refused, and thus the hole stays there, getting bigger and bigger each succeeding rain.[10]

There is evidence of tension between regional settlements, as was indicated above at several points, and is again illustrated below in connection with the same flood:

> The water from Hochfeld runs to the canal which was made by the Blumenhofers of the Swift Plan. The Swift Planners are responsible for the bridge over this canal, since they have to use it to drive to Cuauhtemoc or other towns; it is their only real route of communication. But the bridge has never been kept in very good repair, and has thus been a source of irritation for the Hochfelders. So last night, the statement was made, "I hope the water takes the bridge away, so the Swift Planners will have to build a better one, if they want to get to town. It is no worry of ours whether they get to town or not." [11]

And finally, there is evidence of a subterranean disunity as to the basic purposes and goals of the Old Colony, illustrated by a statement of a highly respected Old Colonist:

> The *Gemeent* is held together by the desire to abide by the will of the *Gemeent*. The leaders do exercise strong leadership, but that is not enough. It is unfortunate that there is such great disunity in the *Gemeent*. Some want to progress and move ahead, while others want to keep it as it was once decided. In Canada already it was decided to remain in a

10. Material gathered by the author during field research.
11. Material gathered by the author during field research.

certain condition, and those that adhered to this decision feel that we are betraying ourselves if we change. Those who were born here and know nothing of that commitment feel different, having had an entirely different history and experience. There are actually two *Gemeents,* one wanting to keep things as they are, the other wanting to go ahead. I do not know which is numerically stronger, but it is a bad thing for the life and morality of the Church. The teachings of the Church are adequately transmitted via the catechism and other things, but the people do not always understand, because of inability to understand High German, and because of the flightiness of youth. Most youth are more interested in buying a harmonica, a flashlight, and a bottle of schnapps than in things such as the Bible and religious topics. I find that there is a great disrespect for the older generation by the younger. They think we are crazy and tell us to stay with our own barley soup. Thus there is little order in the *Gemeent,* if they will not listen to what the older people say. The interests seem to be much different, for example in dress; the young fellows like nothing more than to go to town and buy a Mexican style hat and leather jacket. This is surely going with the world.[12]

But there are many hopeful signs of renewal which may allow the Old Colony to rally and cope with difficulties facing its survival. One of the most promising is the young and creative leadership that is slowly replacing the old. One such young minister, later elected bishop, stated:

I can not say that keeping the status quo is the best way to keep the *Gemeent* together. It might be far better to stress the ethical and moral aspects of the Christian life and then tell and teach the individual to draw his own lines. For this I say our people should be more educated. I think our schools should and could be a little better. But not too much, or the youth would lose interest in farming and leave for other occupations and places in which to live. A man can read and know too much, but he can also be too ignorant. Many of our families read nothing at home, not even the Bible. Others probably read too much and are always dissatisfied and uneasy. I guess there is not much you can do to

12. Material gathered by the author during field research.

get people to co-operate, except appeal to their good natures, and there are always black sheep among every flock.[13]

Other hopeful signs include the compromises being experimented with increasingly which involve "holding the line" yet allowing certain changes to take place. The pressure over the rubber tire issue could have reached the point of disruption if the compromise had not been reached. The result has been that an increasing number of younger farmers adopted rubber tires, but without being ejected from membership. On the other hand, through personal consultation, the "Young Turks'" basic allegiance to the Old Colony was explained and intensified, so that in the long run, this will have been beneficial.

A third sign of hope, among many others that could be mentioned, is the growing openness to the outside world evidenced by many people. Increasingly, people are suggesting that the isolation from other Christians and other peoples is in the long run only injurious. But this openness to outside ideas is a mixed blessing. This factor can well be the basic in the rejuvenation of the Old Colony, or it can mean its downfall, depending upon how the new ideas and patterns of behavior are integrated into the existing system. If the new traits are accepted wholesale without careful evaluation and integration, the Old Colony system may well disintegrate. If, however, the traits are integrated in order to help the Old Colony system better achieve its goals, this may well be a saving force.

According to the evidence, it appears to the author that the Old Colony faces the following fate:

The Old Colony as a viable ethnic minority is doomed in our contemporary world because of its intentionally obscurantist position. It is clear that those groups in history which have survived have exploited and anticipated cultural evolution, especially the evolution of new understanding and technology. Groups which refuse to accept change and progress cannot survive. Therefore the probable dissolution of the Manitoba and Saskatchewan Old Colony presents an enigma—

13. Material gathered by the author during field research.

have these two groups deteriorated and decayed, or have they taken the only course open to them? The fact that the Old Colony members in these two settlements exhibit more awareness of their history and purpose than almost any of the Old Colony in traditional settlements should give pause to anyone who says the Canadian Old Colony is disappearing.

The strategy of social and cultural isolation through migration is probably the most effective survival strategy, assuming that the obscurantist position alluded to above is defended. The conservative Old Colony has been amazingly successful in retaining a way of life with a minimum of change and loss. If the Old Colony can continue to find lands to retreat to that are sufficiently undeveloped, this segment of the Old Colony can survive for a long time. But here the illogic of isolation through migration emerges. The rest of the world is not standing still. The irreversibility of progress and the increase of world population in an inexorable fashion simply make the isolation strategy impractical and short-lived, as we have seen above.

There is considerable religious vitality in all the Old Colony settlements, contrary to the epithets hurled at each of the settlements by the other settlements, as well as by outsiders. The religious understanding and commitment are deeply intertwined with the social fabric, to be sure, but the judgment that the Old Colony is completely devoid of any religious experience, which was strong during its origins, is erroneous. There is a deep piety and amazing observable religious behavior on the part of many. A revival of the awareness of being God's people, and of responding to this awareness, is a distinct and pregnant possibility in the conservative Old Colony settlements, but not so likely in the progressive segments. The progressive settlements are trying to decide whether it is better to throw off the shackles of Old Colony tradition or to retain them. It is evident everywhere that the Old Colony faces a severe challenge.

There has been considerable weakening of the moral fibre of the Old Colony. There are meetings called with increasing frequence (*Browdaschafte*) to deliberate on the problems.

Among the younger generation especially there is a lessening of respect for the *Gemeent*. Further there is a laxity in enforcement of rules against deviation. There is beyond this a rift among the *Lehrdienst* as well as among the laity as to what must be done to preserve the unity of the *Gemeent*. The lay reaction to the meeting last Thursday was one of apathy. They feel the tendency is clear, that it is a matter of time until the "world has its victory," and the Old Colony will have lost its uniqueness. They are beginning to feel that it is illogical to create an island of worldly renunciation and rejections, while meanwhile in the Old Colony itself there is hostility and distrust and dissatisfaction.[14]

The Old Colony will face extinction in the foreseeable future. The progressive settlements will resemble respectable denominations in twenty years' time and will take their place alongside others in the Mennonite brotherhood. The conservative Old Colony settlements will probably survive for another half century or so. When they disappear as Old Colony settlements, they will probably not end up as religious denominations, but rather as assimilated natives of the nations in which they are found, unless religious rejuvenation takes place. The crucial variable for the recovery of the religious dimension of the Old Colony is the maintenance and expansion of contact with other religious groups, which seems highly unlikely unless the initiative is taken by the outside groups. Since the conservative Old Colony does not welcome the outside world, the chances of this happening are unlikely. There is a tactic that can be used which will work, and that is for outside concerned religious groups to begin making contacts on the basis of equality, not on the basis of considering the Old Colony as a pagan mission field.

The Old Colony society is a little society in a vast and complex world. It is one of many such little societies that have struggled for life throughout history. Many of these societies are now merely memories, recalled, as in the case of the Molokans, only by the street signs that marked their home. The Old Colony is a fascinating society, one which

14. Material gathered by the author during field research.

evokes admiration and respect. But it will probably die also. However, we have come to know that survival is not the test of whether a society was "wrong" or not viable. Thus, whether the Old Colony dies or survives, the anthropologist-sociologist must say that this society had its own "truth" and reality.

Chapter 9

AN ANALYSIS OF
ETHNIC MINORITY LIFE

The Old Colony ethnic minority is valid in itself as an object
of study. It adds to the knowledge of the types of social
systems possible within human society. But the Old Colony
is also valuable for the insight it offers into the social problems
and relationships of sectarian ethnic minorities. In this concluding chapter, some of the characteristics of the Old Colony
ethnic minority will be utilized to clarify conceptualizations
regarding the sect, the ethnic group, and the minority group.
Some propositions regarding the causes of cultural and
structural assimilation, based on Old Colony evidence, will
conclude the book.

The Sect

The concept of sect continues to be used in various ways,
especially in connection with ethnic and minority groups;
and this varied usage has not contributed to conceptual
clarity. The Old Colony is referred to as a sect in many
writings.[1] Many other groups of a similar nature are referred to as sects; included are such different bodies as the
Rosicrucians and the Black Muslims.[2] Considerable research
on religious groups has been conducted using the sect typology as the basic point of departure.

When, however, the sect concept that is variously used

1. According to the Troeltsch typology, Mennonites of various types
are classified as sects. See Ernst Troeltsch, *The Social Teaching of the
Christian Churches* (New York: Harper & Brothers, 1960), II, p. 691ff.
See also Elmer T. Clark, *The Small Sects in America* (New York:
Abingdon-Cokesbury, 1949). Clark classifies all Mennonite groups as
"legalistic" sects.

2. Clark classes the Rosicrucians as a mystic sect; see *Small Sects,*
p. 234. Peter I. Rose, for example, classes religious protest movements
among Negroes as "religious sects." See his *We and They* (New York:
Random House, Inc., 1964), pp. 139ff.

is closely scrutinized, it is discovered that the definition is not very clear; often the term is defined to suit the writer's needs. Thus there is research that utilizes the stratification aspects of low and high socio-economic conditions as the basis for the sect- versus church-type religious organization.[3] Other research utilizes the primary-secondary relationship continuum as a basic differentiation.[4] Still other research focuses on the theological and expressive aspects of religious experience as the bases for determining sect-type as opposed to church-type religious organization.

All of the above conceptualizations derive from the "classical" conceptualization proposed by Troeltsch. But the classical conceptualization is not adequate for contemporary analysis of religious groups. There are several reasons for rejecting the "classical" typology:[5]

1. The classical typology was created by utilizing the socio-religious development of Europe during the Middle Ages, the Reformation, and its development in American Christianity. A typology constructed on specific historical development cannot be universal in time and space since things change and history never exactly repeats itself. Thus it is constricting to work with a conceptualization which may no longer be a faithful reflection of reality. It is logical therefore to propose that a new typology be devised which reflects the contemporary religious scene.

2. The church-sect typology has been constructed in such

3. See, for example, Russel R. Dynes, "Church-Sect Typology and Socio-Economic Status," *American Sociological Review* (October, 1955). This article is based on other writings which stress the economic nature of sectarianism such as Liston Pope's *Millhands and Preachers* (New Haven: Yale University Press, 1942).

4. See, for example, Gerhard Lenski's classification of associational versus communal involvement in *The Religious Factor* (Garden City, New York: Doubleday and Company, Inc., 1961), especially pp. 192–233. Lenski suggests that the radical sectarian dynamic was characterized by "its attempts to create through church-related organizations a substitute for secular social relationships, especially those of the extended family" (p. 222).

5. Calvin Redekop, "The Sect Cycle in Perspective," *MQR*, XXXVI (April, 1962), 160.

a way that it is tautological. That is, circular reasoning is involved in defining the form of religious experience in the church-sect mold. For example, the sect is characterized as upholding voluntary membership and discipline. Actually discipline may be the cause or requisite for voluntary membership. One aspect of the definition may be the antecedent of another aspect of the definition and thus evidence confusion of cause and effect.

3. The characterizations of the church-type and the sect-type have not been mutually exclusive. That is, many of the traits that have been attributed to the sect are also present in the church-type religious organization. For example, the sect would normally be placed at one extreme of a continuum of mutual discipline and exhortation, while the church would be placed on the negative end of the scale. Mutual discipline can and does certainly exist in the church-type social structure. Most of the other characteristics reserved for the sect are also prevalent in the church-type organization.

4. From a scientific perspective, adoption of a theory as final is usually seen as stagnation—an intellectual hardening of the arteries. Numerous attempts have been made recently to revamp the typology so that research on social aspects of religious experience can go forward. A recasting of the way religious experience can be analyzed should be helpful in understanding the religious life of human nature.

The old typology fell into the fatal error of defining sectarianism in a particular sociological form; a particular pattern of culture and social organization made the group sectarian. But no groups could be classified as falling even approximately into this mold, since each group is unique in its form and content. A more viable approach is to conceive of the behavior of religious groups as having many dimensions. The only dimension relevant to sectarianism is that which deals with openness to change and new experience. The quickest way out of the morass of the relationship between sectarianism and religious groups is to take an operational view of religious groups—how do they behave?

A religious group which is closed to change and is concerned only about preserving its traditional beliefs and religious behavior is sectarian in its behavior. (The discarding of the noun "sect" in favor of the adjective "sectarian" helps solve the problem.) All religious organisms evidence the sectarian trait in varying degrees at varying times. The Catholic Church has evidenced sectarian traits at many junctures of its history, as have most other denominations. The Old Colony has evidenced a sectarian nature in much of its history in all of the settlements.

The Old Colony emerged on the basis of a sectarian stance toward the world and toward the religious expression of its time, including the Mennonite parents from which it sprang. But the Old Colony was not a "sect." It has rather been a social system that emerged on the basis of a sectarian impulse, and the experience of the Old Colony has been guided to a large extent by the sectarian motive—the attempt to stop change and to reaffirm the old ways. (Cf. the ordination sermon cited above—Appendix C.)

The Old Colony is an ethnic minority which grew out of a particular cognitive view of the world—a view which is a reaffirmation of the static dualistic nature of reality. There is a kingdom of God and a kingdom of this world. There is no intercourse between these two worlds, and there is no point in encouraging communication between the two. This is the sectarian spark that caused the Old Colony to emerge.[6] The sectarian motif has remained in the Old Colony from its beginning. Thus the question as to whether the Old Colony has changed from sect to church is beside the point. operate The point is that the Old Colony has continued to under the sectarian frame of mind which was described in Chapter 1.

The Old Colony provides us with material for the following propositions about "sects": 1) the emergence of a religious movement often is based on "sectarian" dynamics; 2) the sectarian dynamic is a frame of mind which is authoritarian, dualistic, and resistant to change; 3) the sectarian dynamic almost universally results in ethnic groups—a social system

6. See Calvin Redekop, "The Sectarian Black and White World," (Ph.D. dissertation, University of Chicago, 1959).

that develops a way of life derived from the sectarian perspective; 4) the sectarian orientation is never an all or nothing situation—all social groups have some sectarian traits.

The Ethnic Group

The Old Colony has been described as an ethnic group throughout the book. Through historical events, it has come into being as a cohesive group with beliefs, behavior, and memories that are quite distinct from those of other groups. The sectarian impulse almost invariably prompts the emergence of ethnic groups. In fact, it appears as one of the most important factors in the emergence of ethnic groups. The roster of "sects," "cults," and pentecostal groups comprises a large section of the entire realm of ethnic groups.

The conflict with the existing mores and beliefs, which is often based on sectarian motives (as defined above), has produced the Old Colony, "a group with a shared feeling of peoplehood." [7] When individuals with similar reactions to a certain factor find each other and form a cohesive group, a common tradition develops. One generation cannot create an ethnic group. There is a sense of a shared past and future which is at the heart of the ethnic group, and this comes only with shared experiences handed down from generation to generation.

The concept of the ethnic group has been most adequately stated by Milton Gordon:

Common to all these objective bases [common national or racial identities], however, is the social-psychological element of a special sense of both ancestral and future-oriented identification with the group. These are the "people" of my ancestors, therefore they are my people, and they will be the people of my children and their children. With members of other groups I may share political participation, occupational relationships, common civic enterprise, perhaps even an occasional warm friendship. But in a very special way which

7. Milton M. Gordon, *Assimilation in American Life* (New York: Oxford University Press, 1964), p. 24.

history has decreed, I share a sense of indissoluble and intimate identity with *this* group and *not that one* within the larger society and the world.[8]

The Old Colonist in all the settlements would echo this stance, though not many could state it in this way! Because of the common stance toward the world and toward religious behavior and belief that has been adhered to for generations, the Old Colonist has become a part of an ethnic group— a people with a past and a future.

The confusion in the literature regarding ethnic groups is almost as great as that regarding sects. Ethnicity has been used in reference to all persons with a common language or cultural system.[9] It has further been used to refer to a nationality origin or religious affiliation. As Gordon so clearly points out, these objective factors may be present in the ethnic group under discussion, but central to the concept is the common "sense of peoplehood." An ethnic group is one whose members identify with *this* group and not with *that* one. It is a group which lives life on a primary relationship level because the common history and common future bind them together in a transcendent purpose and separate them from others. It is this binding force which distinguishes the Old Colony system.

This study of ethnic groups would be much enhanced if the admonition of Everett C. Hughes were heeded. He maintains that the whole field of ethnic minority relations ought not to be discussed primarily on the basis of a "combination of . . . language, religion, customs, institutions or 'cultural traits' . . ." but rather on the basis that "people in it and the people out of it know that it is one; because both the

8. *Ibid.*, p. 29.

9. See Lenski, *The Religious Factor*, p. 28, in which he defines ethnic groups as groups based on national origins. Will Herberg, in *Protestant, Catholic, Jew* (Garden City: Doubleday and Company, Inc., 1955), pp. 13–14, defines the ethnic groups as those achieving an identity by language and national origins. His thesis, that as the language and national origins identification disappears the religious takes its place, still focuses on an objective factor, unlike the definition by Gordon.

ins and the outs talk, feel and act as if it were a separate group." [10]

This orientation will be most useful in studying the life of ethnic groups. Most studies of ethnic groups assume that an ethnic group has disappeared when its culture and social organization have changed through assimilation. But this view has been challenged by numerous recent authors, the foremost being Gordon and Hughes. Thus Hughes can say that French Canadians are ethnic group members even though they wear English tweeds. Glazer and Moynihan [11] suggest that new ethnic groups are emerging on the basis of common experience. Ethnic groups do not vanish just because their culture becomes like that of the larger society.

Ethnic groups remain as long as there is a social structure existing among members who identify with a common past. Cultural assimilation can take place but structural assimilation does not necessarily follow. Cultural assimilation refers to the adoption of cultural traits by the ethnic group, including religious beliefs, political behavior, economic practices, etc. Cultural assimilation is the standard process for an ethnic group, except as the larger society adopts some of the traits of the ethnic group in which case it is a two-way acculturation. [12]

Structural assimilation is the key variable in the study of ethnic-minority relations and refers to the process in which members of the ethnic group begin to interact socially with persons outside the ethnic group instead of with members of the ethnic group. Thus cultural assimilation has taken place in the Old Colony as Old Colony members adopt practices and beliefs from the Canadian, Mexican, or British Honduras host peoples. Structural assimilation takes place if and when the Old Colony member begins to interact socially with the Mexicans, for example, more than with his own Old Colonists and marries a Mexican.

10. Everett C. Hughes, *Where Peoples Meet* (Glencoe, Ill.: The Free Press, 1950), p. 156.
11. Nathan Glazer and Patrick Moynihan, *Beyond the Melting Pot* (Cambridge, Mass.: Harvard University Press, 1963).
12. Gordon, *Assimilation in American Life,* pp. 74ff.

In the Old Colony, cultural assimilation has taken place in all the settlements, for in all the settlements ideas, behavior, and artifacts have been taken over from the host society and its peoples. Little if any structural assimilation (that which breaks down the ethnic group) has taken place in the traditional Old Colony settlements, since they have taken the isolation tactic to keep away from other people. The progressive Old Colony settlements in Manitoba and Saskatchewan are becoming structurally assimilated, as was shown by the intermarriage which takes place and the interaction in the villages and in the churches. This interaction will of course undermine the ethnic nature of the Old Colony, as has been illustrated above.

The importance of this conceptualization of ethnicity for the Old Colony is that to some extent the Old Colony has been overemphasizing the significance of cultural assimilation. The philosophy of the Old Colony has been that cultural assimilation would mean the end of the ethnic group. However, as has been shown above, recent scholars show that an ethnic group does not disappear with the adoption of a foreign culture. Cultural assimilation does not need to lead to structural assimilation. However, the Old Colony people must be given credit for a certain amount of sophistication in realizing that cultural assimilation often paves the way for structural assimilation.

What is central is the fact that structural assimilation will change the inner nature of the ethnic group. The French Canadians have changed culturally but still remain French Canadians. The *sectarian* character of the Old Colony thus is highlighted in that the Old Colony feels that change in the style of life, as well as loss of ethnicity, is to be avoided at the peril of losing all. A sectarian ethnic group is thus a group which believes that all change (cultural) will dissolve the group, whereas a nonsectarian ethnic group will not resist change as much.

Again, Everett C. Hughes, in a perceptive article, stated that an ethnic group is not ethnic because it retains a certain culture or behavior system: "It took me a long time to discover that the French Canadian who speaks English best is generally pretty stoutly French in sentiment and way of living, and that sometimes one who speaks but little English has often suffered severe lesions in the integrity of his French culture and loyalty." [13]

The Old Colony is an ethnic group which has emerged on the basis of sectarian dynamics. It continues to be an ethnic group because of the common history which is largely sectarian. But, and this is crucial, the sectarian impulse could vanish from the Old Colony system without necessarily destroying the Old Colony as an ethnic system.

The Minority Group

In the first chapter, the Old Colony was designated as an ethnic *minority*. A definition was provided which suggested that a minority group "is a group which, regardless of where it is on the class ladder, faces barriers to the pursuit of life's values that are greater than the barriers faced by persons otherwise equally qualified." [14] But this definition is derived from a broader "classical" definition proposed by Louis Wirth: "We may define a minority as a group of people who, because of their physical or cultural characteristics, are singled out from the others in the society in which they live for differential and unequal treatment, and who therefore regard themselves as objects of collective discrimination. The existence of a minority in a society implies the existence of a corresponding dominant group with higher social status and greater privileges. Minority status therefore carries with it exclusion from full participation in the life of society." [15]

This definition has served as the basis for the study of minority groups for several decades. Wirth proposes that the stance of the minority regarding the dominant group may take four forms: assimilation, pluralism, secession, and dom-

13. Hughes, *Where Peoples Meet,* p. 157.

14. John Milton Yinger, *A Minority Group in American Society* (New York: McGraw-Hill Book Co., 1965), p. 22.

15. Louis Wirth, "The Problem of Minority Groups," in Ralph Linton (ed.), *The Science of Man in World Crises* (New York: Columbia University Press, 1945), p. 374.

ination. Yinger explicates these four stances as follows: "Let us disappear as a group, judge us only as individuals—assimilation; let us maintain our group identity, based perhaps on language, religion or culture, so long as we give full allegiance to society—pluralism; give us our freedom, let us establish our own society where we can practice our way of life without hindrance—secession; we are wary of being dominated, and we shall do everything we can to reverse the present status arrangement, by militant means if necessary—domination." [16] If this description is applied to the Old Colony, the Old Colony is a secessionist minority.

However, it is apparent when applying the definition of a minority and its stance toward the dominant group to the Old Colony, that the Old Colony is not completely described. The Old Colony does not fit the minority definition of Wirth, because the Old Colony has not been "singled out from the others . . . for differential and unequal treatment" as such. The Old Colony has been "invited" to share the culture of the dominant group, and the unequal treatment has been the result of *refusing the "invitation"* of the dominant group. The Old Colony feels itself discriminated against, not because it is being refused entry into the dominant society, but on the contrary, because it wants to be left alone. Consequently, Wirth's statement that "minority status therefore carries with it exclusion from full participation in the life of the society" is not applicable to the Old Colony.

The stance of "secession" which was suggested above as the Old Colony stance also needs some qualification. The Old Colony wants the freedom to live its own "life without hindrance" but it wants the dominant society to provide certain amenities and protection. This has been suggested in the description of the way the Old Colony officials prior to immigration attempted to establish a type of paternalistic relationship with the receiving state. The Old Colony does not want to "secede" from the larger society. It wants the freedom to live its life with the encouragement and assistance of the dominant group. The point is, most minorities would

16. John Milton Yinger, *Minority Group in American Society*, p. 31.

like to decide what the relationship should be between the dominant society and themselves, or at least have a mutual voice in the discussion. Everett C. Hughes has stated the case for a full-orbed view of the minority-dominant relationship by describing the differences in the French Canadians and the Negroes.

> The two minorities are alike in that they have gone from a rural condition to an urban and see themselves as thereby put into a position of increased disadvantage. . . . But they see opposite remedies. The Negro Americans want to disappear as a defined group; they want to become invisible as a group, while each of them becomes fully visible as a human being. . . . The French Canadians, on the other hand, struggle not for survival as individuals—in which their problems are those of other Canadians—but for survival as a group with full social, economic and political standing.[17]

The Old Colony, and many other minorities, wants to have the freedom to decide whether to be left alone or to assimilate. Many minorities feel they have been "singled out" and given "unequal treatment" not because they are rejected by the dominant group, but precisely because they are denied the freedom to decide whether to assimilate or to secede.

An adequate definition of minority groups, therefore, would require the stipulation of the intentions of the minority and of the majority. It would also require a modification of the "stances" which Wirth suggests minorities can take vis-à-vis their dominant society. A revision of Wirth's definition which includes the qualifications discussed above is as follows:

> A minority is a group of people who [have a clear idea either individually or as a group of what status they would like to have in the society and because this conflicts with the intentions of the dominant society or] because of physical and cultural characteristics [which the dominant society has some negative preconceived notions about] are singled out from

17. Everett C. Hughes, "Race Relations and the Sociological Imagination," *American Sociological Review*, XXVIII, No. 6 (December, 1963), 883.

the others in the society in which they live for differential or unequal treatment, and who therefore regard themselves as objects of collective discrimination. The existence of a minority in a society implies the existence of a corresponding dominant group [which determines what status the minority will have without the consent of the minority]. Minority status [therefore] carries with it the exclusion [not] from full participation in the life of the society [but from the participation in the decision as to what the relationship shall be].[18]

This revised definition enables us to include as minorities various groups, as diverse in intentions and status as the Negroes and the Old Colony, or the Jehovah's Witnesses and the Black Muslims.

A minority group in one instance, therefore, is a minority because it is rejected by the dominant society into which it wants admittance. Another group can be a minority group because it wants to be left alone but is not, as the Old Colony illustrates. Thus the stance toward the dominant society should be considered another category, beyond the four Wirth suggests. The fifth stance, which typifies groups like the Old Colony, might be called the "beneficiary" relationship, wherein the host society does the bidding of the minority.

The crucial variables in the study of minorities therefore are: 1) the attitudes and intentions of the dominant society; 2) the attitudes and intentions of the subordinate group; 3) the access to the power needed to achieve the objectives. But the access to power is the source of trouble for most if not all minority groups—that is, the power to decide what the relationship shall be is what is not available to minorities.[19]

18. For an application of this definition to several other groups, see Calvin Redekop and John A. Hostetler, "Minority-Majority Relations and Economic Interdependence," *Phylon,* XXVII, No. 4 (Winter, 1966).

19. This situation has been perceptively stated by Hughes, *Where Peoples Meet,* p. 883: "The two minorities (the Negro and French Canadians) are alike. . . . But they seek opposite remedies. The Negro Americans want to disappear as a defined group. . . . The French Canadians, on the other hand, struggle not for survival as individuals . . . but for survival as a group with full social, economic and political standing."

The Paradox of Pluralism

There is thus bitter irony in the life of many ethnic minorities. Some want to retain their own identity and separateness and are barred from doing so, while other ethnic minorities would like to lose their identity and are not able to.[20] The Old Colony illustrates the first situation, while the Negro ethnic minority illustrates the second.[21] The "paradox of pluralism" is the condition in which the group in question does not have the power to decide its own fate.

The objectives of the group, and the resources it has at its disposal, are crucial variables in the life of minorities and at the heart of the "paradox of pluralism." Thus a minority group can take two positions toward its continued existence as a minority: 1) it can want to remain a separate group; 2) it can want to become assimilated. But the host society also has the similar two possibilities in regard to the minority: 1) it can desire to have the group become a part of the larger society; 2) it can refuse to accept the minority group. The paradox exists for those groups which fall into one of two categories where the will of the host and the minority group conflict (I and III in the diagram, p. 238).[22]

20. See Rose, *We and They,* pp. 130ff, for a typology of the relationship between majority image of minority and the minority's acceptance or rejection of the image. This deals only with those groups that are rejected by the host society, however, and does not deal with the power element.

21. Discussion of the American Negro as a minority group desiring assimilation into the majority must except that portion of the Negro population which has recently rejected the stance of assimilation. Black Nationalists, those Negroes who have chosen to disaffiliate with the North American society which has rejected them and to revive their African heritage, take something closer to a secessionist stance. It is difficult to estimate the percentage of Negroes wishing to separate from the majority society of North America, but it is probably safe to say that the Afro-American group is still a small minority of the American Negro population.

22. See Redekop and Hostetler, "Minority-Majority Relations and Economic Interdependence," for an expansion of this idea.

Paradox of Pluralism

| | Host Attitude toward Minority | |
	Desires Group	Rejects Group
Ethnic Minority Intention Wants Acceptance	Swedes II	Negro I
Wants To Retain Identity	III Old Colony	IV Dukhoubors

The situation depicted in Quadrant I is the area of greatest conflict: the group that wants acceptance almost by definition has accepted all the values of the society and therefore will be able to challenge the host society the most, since it uses fire to fight fire. The paradox of wanting what one should want but is not allowed to get compounds the basic paradox.

The relationship in Quadrant II is not a paradox at all since there is unanimity as regards the values, goals, and techniques.

Groups finding their situation illustrated by Quadrant III will experience great conflict, but not as much as those groups in Quadrant I; for since the value system may not be at all similar, the minority always can resort to emigration if the pressure gets too great. This is not the case in Quadrant I. The tactics of the host society need not be considered coercive alone, but can include other enticements to get the group to accept membership in the larger family.

The conditions in Quadrant IV can produce moderate tension; but since the host society has the power to "evict" the minority group if it wants to, there is a limit to how much tension can emerge.

There is a final irony in the paradox of pluralism which affects the groups which fall under the paradoxical sections of the graph. The power to determine the future of the status of the ethnic minority is different in the two quadrants. In

Quadrant III, the minority has the power to decide to lose its identity and thereby merge with the larger society. It also has the power to decide to remain a minority.

The ethnic minority in Quadrant I, however, really has the power neither to decide to remain as it is, nor to resolve on change. The power to decide whether the minority will be accepted in the larger society or not resides with the host society. The power to remain an ethnic minority is also in the hands of the host society, since the minority group has already decided it wants to be a member of the host society; and in the case of the Negro, no decision was necessary because of the established similarity in culture as shown above.

The Old Colony ostensibly, therefore, is not so bad off! It can decide to "throw in the sponge" any time it wants to and become accepted into the larger, more homogeneous society. But since it has no intentions of relinquishing its objectives, for all practical purposes the status of the Negro ethnic minority and that of the Old Colony ethnic minority are the same. Neither group is achieving the objective it would like to achieve. And neither has anything to say about the "rules of the game."

But there is a difference! The resistance to the acceptance of the Negro minority is based on more complex subconscious forces than is the case in the Old Colony. The forces which are causing the deterioration of the Old Colony ethnic minority are more simple and innocent; there is less intentional subversion of the Old Colony than the intentional and very complex rejection of the Negro on the part of North American society. In any case, minority life is not necessarily the life of pain to be avoided. In the case of some minorities (such as the Negro) it is a shackle to be sloughed off; but in the case of groups like the Old Colony, minority status is something to rejoice about, for it substantiates a basic tenet of its charter stated by a Mexican Old Colonist: "We must stay separate from the world. The Bible says we are to remain pure and uncontaminated by the world. The Bible says we are to be persecuted by the world." [23] For some minorities, the olive branch would mean

23. Material gathered by the author during field research.

death, for it would undermine the ethnic character of its being, as shown above. Everything depends upon the objectives of the minority group.

The future of the Old Colony has been shown to be rather dark. What is the status of the minority in the larger framework of social organization? From the above discussion, the conclusion is logically thrust upon us that the key variable of "power" resides with the majority and that, in the end, the minority will disappear. In a perceptive article, Robert Bierstedt states: "Utilizing only the most extreme and rigid cases [rigidly organized hierarchical organizations] for illustration, . . . it can be demonstrated that they [minorities] are not immune from the pressures of majorities. . . . One is tempted to say that no association, no matter how rigidly organized, is able to withstand the permanent pressure of a majority and that an organized majority is the most potent social force on earth. There is a certain authority in a majority which no hierarchy can wholly obliterate." [24]

The Causes of Assimilation

Resistance to assimilation into the host society by a minority has been the central theme of this book. Cultural and structural assimilation have been defined and described in relation to the Old Colony experience. *How* assimilation works has been seen, but the problem of *why* a group experiences cultural and structural assimilation has not been answered, nor can it be in this book. Propositions about the causes for cultural and structural assimilation, which need much more testing in future studies, can be suggested.

CULTURAL ASSIMILATION

Numerous studies have proposed forces which cause cultural assimilation. Diffusion of culture as the "migration of elements or traits from one culture to another" [25] without the

24. Robert Bierstedt, "The Sociology of Majorities," *American Sociological Review*, XIII (1948), 707.

25. Bronislaw Malinowski, *The Dynamics of Culture Change* (New Haven: Yale University Press, 1945), p. 18.

active participation of persons in social systems is not an explanation of cultural acculturation. No trait has been adopted in the Old Colony without having been deeply entangled in its social process. If the Old Colony can be considered representative of other societies, cultural change always must involve the social system.

The concept of a "superior culture" or a "cultural compulsive" is not applicable to every case where two culture groups meet, nor does it explain acculturation. Malinowski proposes that cultural change takes place when an aggressive culture clashes with a passive one.[26] Raymond Firth proposes that modern cultural developments have a compelling power over more primitive ones.[27] He goes so far as to say that these "cultural compulsives" have often been "forced upon people who in the initial stages have been unwilling to accept what has been given to them." [28] Both of these explanations are at least partially refuted by the Old Colony. The Old Colony is a "passive" culture according to Malinowski, and it has not adopted the culture of the "aggressive" society—at least not wholesale. The Old Colony experience shows that the range of Firth's "cultural compulsives" is very narrow.

The best explanation for acculturation in the Old Colony, and in those groups which are similar to the Old Colony, is that acculturation depends upon the type of relationship that exists between the two groups in question.[29] Thus in a relation such as that between the Old Colony and the host society, the presence of an intentional minority will determine the type of acculturation that will take place.

In the Old Colony then, as the description above has amply demonstrated, acculturation will be controlled, allowing only those traits to be accepted which will not disrupt the system.[30] Adoption of traits is determined by the values of the social

26. *Ibid.,* pp. 18ff.

27. Raymond Firth, *Human Types* (New York: Thomas Nelson & Sons, 1956), pp. 18ff.

28. *Ibid.,* p. 189.

29. See Melville Herskovits, *Cultural Anthropology* (New York: Alfred A. Knopf, Inc., 1960), pp. 478–79.

30. Joseph Eaton, "Controlled Acculturation: A Survival Technique of the Hutterites," *American Sociological Review,* XVII (1952).

system and the social structure. The determination of the desirability of a trait and the ability to enforce the decision thus predicts acculturation in societies like the Old Colony.

STRUCTURAL ASSIMILATION

Structural assimilation (the entrance of diverse groups into primary relationships) is a very complex phenomenon. It involves the acculturation of values as well as of behavior and material artifacts.[31] But as was shown above, this is not sufficient for structural assimilation to occur. Why does structural assimilation occur? In reference to the type of relationship existing between the Old Colony and the host society several propositions can be advanced.

Structural assimilation depends upon the cohesion of the group. The greater the cohesion of the social system, the less structural assimilation there will be. Stated in terms of behavior, the greater the interaction of minority members with each other, the less will be the chances of structural assimilation with outsiders. The cohesion of a group is based upon the effectiveness of communication between members of the group. The greater the amount of interaction and communication, the greater will be the cohesion of the group.[32] The Old Colony exhibits a considerably high degree of interaction, and thus has high cohesion. The greater the number of common beliefs and practices, the greater the cohesion of the group.[33] The Old Colony evidences a relatively large number of common beliefs and practices. It is clear that these contribute to high rates of interaction, which in turn will contribute to a resistance to structural assimilation. Groups that manage therefore to maintain a great number of common beliefs and practices will achieve high cohesion. But the final question—that of how the common beliefs and practices are achieved in the first place—brings us back to the beginning again. The answer lies beyond the scope of this book.

The factors and forces that have been described above which

31. Gordon, *Assimilation in American Life,* pp. 67ff.
32. Emile Durkheim, *Suicide* (Glencoe, Ill.: The Free Press, 1951), pp. 208ff.
33. *Ibid.,* p. 170.

are "boring" at the heart of the Old Colony can all be success-fully resisted if the "will to live" remains. Structural assimi-lation is the sign that the "will to live" has died. At this point, there is no hope for the group. The quest for the answer to the source of the "will to live" remains to haunt us as we see the Old Colony slowly disappear.

The Old Colony illustrates a process that has been in oper-ation for many centuries: on the basis of a religious principle, usually sectarian in nature, an ethnic group emerged which attempted to put into practice the original principles. As the ethnic group struggled to retain its identity, its way of life collided with that of the larger societies; thus the minority relationship appeared. The minority status has always carried with it unfavorable odds.[34]

Ethnic minorities such as the Old Colony will pass away, but new ones will emerge, for man is continually becoming possessed by a vision which is different from others around him, as the Old Colony has so well illustrated.

34. See Wirth, "The Problem of Minority Groups," for general statements which propose this cycle.

Memorandum Concerning
*Mennonite Schools**

We Mennonites, of the Reinland-Mennonite Church or the so-called Old Colony, who have immigrated into Canada, feel obligated to express our thanks to the kind and honorable Dominion government as well as to the provincial government for the truly benevolent protection and assistance which we have received; because of this we pray to God: "O Lord God, bless our king, the leaders of the land, and all the officials and executives in Canada as you have in the past, in that you directed your intents and desires so that we could exercise our religious rights, including the right to have our own schools under the protection of the government in joy and peace. Now give them wise hearts and your Holy Spirit, that they may rule wisely in all Canadian and British nations."

Such similar prayers are offered publicly every Sunday in all of our congregations for the British government, under whose protection, thank God, we are privileged to live.

We have learned that the possibility exists that a revision of the provincial school acts will be presented to the legislative house. This revision has the intention of revoking the privileges of having our own independent schools, which the Mennonites have enjoyed since the time of our immigrations.

Our concern that this possibility exists has prompted us to present to you, honorable members of parliament, the following facts which we humbly request you to consider.

It has been our tradition in our old home, Russia, that all our children learned reading, writing, arithmetic, religion, industry, and cleanliness, in such a manner as to meet the requirements of the agricultural way of life to which we have belonged.

One of the requisites upon which the decision to migrate to Russia was made was that we should have the freedom to educate our children in our own schools in our own way; and it was the loss of this freedom, plus the loss of freedom from military service, that caused us to decide to emigrate from Russia.

As we began considering immigration to Canada, we were

* Translation by the author.

invited to visit Canada at her expense. Our delegated representatives responded to the invitation in 1873, and while they were in Canada, they were magnanimously offered the privileges we sought, if we would choose Canada as our home. The conditions of this offer were detailed in a letter dated July 23, 1873; we consider this letter a holy document stating the basic policy of our freedom on the behalf of the Canadian government. Among other things, this letter states, "The unrestricted right of practicing your own religion is protected by law for the Mennonites without any restrictions or limitations whatsoever, and the same goes for the education of your children in the schools." We believe that the government understood clearly that the requirements concerning the schools were very important to us since the Minister of Interior stated in his letter of 1873, that the "reason for the possible emigration from Russia is the question of military service. It is also related to the school issue. A new law requires that the Mennonites must teach their children in Russian in the schools, and that the schools shall be conducted according to Russian regulations, which the Mennonites simply could not reconcile with their conscience." This was an accurate description of our reasons for leaving Russia.

The Minister continues to expound on the conditions of the agreement: "The responsibilities for this people, as outlined in the letter to the Mennonite delegates dated July 23, 1873, are:

1. . . . . .

2. . . . . .

3. The right to conduct their own religious schools."

On the basis of these promises, we migrated to Canada. And since we believed, as we still believe, that the word of the government is unchangeable, since the nation is ordained by God, we proceeded to construct our own schools and have continued to do so, even though it has caused us considerable hardship. We did this without requesting any support from the provincial government.

Our children are being trained in our schools in the three main disciplines: reading, writing, and arithmetic. The children can read with competence religious as well as secular materials; they can also write clearly and understandably and do the computations necessary to conduct with ease the bookkeeping and recordkeeping required in their business activities. In short, they receive exactly what is necessary to enable them to qualify for the life of agriculture to which we are committed.

Our schools total twenty-two. The buildings are roomy, well ventilated and lighted, warm, and comfortable. We have "teacherages" in connection with the schools. These two buildings are very close together so that there is easy communication. The teachers are all well trained with high characters. The schools are open about seven months. The children attend schools regularly, between the ages of seven and thirteen for girls and seven and fourteen for boys, while many attend before they are seven and some after they are fourteen.

The clergy assumes the responsibility of seeing to it that the parents send their children to school regularly and that the schools are effectively conducted. We believe that all of our children, with the exception of those who are weak or sick, are consistently being educated and trained. It is a precept of our church that the parents must train their children. There are no illiterates among us.

We do not want to bore you with our mode of thought and behavior, but we would like to clarify for you the foundations of our school system. While we are called the Reinland-Mennonite Church, we are a church (*Gemeinschaft*) which does not hang together merely on a religious basis, but also in secular things; our faith decrees that we obey the commandments of the Holy Spirit not only in religious things, but in secular activities as well. Therefore, we are obligated to obey the commandments of the word of God so that we do not harbor a contentious spirit, that we do not fight among ourselves but turn the other cheek, that our word shall be yes or no, and that we do not go to court, rather give our cloak to him who asks our coat.

Insofar as we are in charge of our children's education, we have the responsibility on our conscience to teach them both the religious and secular truth as one whole, so that the children may be holy, good, honest, industrious, unselfish, and co-operative in their relations with God and their fellow men. Thus we intend to prepare our children to discharge their responsibility to God and man and to the world. We are a people of the land. We live on the land and plow the fields, and our schools are constituted to train our children to become good farmers—progressive, ambitious, simple, friendly, helpful, and full of good works toward all men.

We are not prone to talk about the results of our school system, since we don't want it to sound like boasting, but with your permission, we must talk about them so that you will get a clear and complete truth about the matter. We will pass by the intimate religious aspects of our common life, since we assume you will not want us to discuss it because it is basically a personal matter of a relationship to God, even though it is related to the other relations in life which are open to the world.

In view of this, we will take the liberty to discuss the consequences of the common educational practices.

(a) We teach our children to be obedient and faithful to the king and his government as ordained by God, and we assure you that our people are truly patriotic to the land that is giving us these great freedoms of conscience.

(b) Our children are taught to live the life of the farmer, the natural life on the farm; and their spirits and bodies, as well as their activities and habits, are all adapted to farm and rural life. The consequences of this are that from generation to generation our people continue the simple life of the country and do not anticipate moving to the towns or cities. They are taught to love peace, and we can truthfully say that they are peaceful.

(c) Our children are taught to live in community, to stick together, and to help each other in all responsibilities and activities of life. And we want to inform you that the people are carrying this teaching out in practice. We work together in the normal activities and work responsibilities; we help each other in that we seek the material well-being of each other; we assist those who want to become self-reliant and independent. We work together in order to encourage frugality; we have our own savings and trustee system—the *Waisenamt*. The trustees receive the members' monies from the members and loan it to others, giving 5 per cent interest and receiving 6 per cent. We trust the integrity of the borrower, and we are happy to tell you that we have not had any losses so far.

In all the productive aspects of life, our children are taught to live simply, selflessly, and we are able to say that with few exceptions our people carry this teaching out.

(d) We take care of our poor and sick, the weak and the mentally feeble, whoever or whatever they may be; and we are not consciously allowing anyone to become dependent or lazy. We believe that we have not cost the government anything in court or police costs, hospitals or prison expenses.

(e) We live in peace with our non-Mennonite neighbors, since we respect them; their behavior reflects their inner feelings since they do not look down on us, but treat us very kindly.

(f) We have, through the grace of God, following the freedom which was promised us through the government when we settled in Manitoba, had the liberty to conduct our own schools. We have followed the agreements which were made between our representatives and your government and have transferred this to the persons who have been working in the schools.

The material responsibilities have increased considerably, but we have been and are still willing to carry our full share and more of the tax burden to support the nation and government, and in this connection we ask to be permitted to say that during the war we tried to give to every worthy cause, in order to show our thankfulness for the freedom of conscience we enjoyed.

It could be concluded from the above that we have a very high opinion of ourselves, that in the light of our accomplishments we are praising ourselves. We want to remind you, however, that we do not take this view, since we are very much aware of our own weaknesses and confess them in humility before God and men.

We request that our memorandum concerning our way of life and the schools not be used as the basis for your decision. We do request of you that you conduct an objective and impartial study concerning the social, economic, and moral aspects of our brotherhood, and that you decide on the basis of your findings what should be the fate of the schools. We have only one request in this connection: that you would be so good as not to evaluate our school system on the basis of individual parts, that is, in areas where one school may depart from the provincial schools, without considering the ultimate objectives which we try to achieve through our schools. . . .

We respectfully ask you before the agreement of 1873 is changed to make a comprehensive, just, and impartial analysis of our school system in light of the goals of our brotherhood.

We humbly submit that the agreement mentioned above has been a great blessing for our brotherhood and through us for the entire nation, and that in no way has it been a detriment to anyone in the entire nation.

We respectfully remind you further, that both parties to the agreement are bound to honor it and to carry out all the requisites contained therein.

We assume that the people of the province of Manitoba will respect the agreement that the Dominion government enacted with us, and that we may continue to enjoy the freedom which we have thus far enjoyed, for which we are thankful in advance.

A copy of the agreements between the Mennonites and the Minister of Interior as completed in July, 1873, is enclosed.

We close with emphasis on our willingness as a brotherhood to support the government in the future as we have in the past.

May God bless the government for its graciousness and goodness!

> The Honorable Members of the
> Legislative Assembly of Manitoba

February, 1919

> For the Reinland-Mennonite Church
> signed, Johann J. Friesen, Bishop
> signed, Franz F. Froese, Trustee

Appendix B

*Letter of Special Concessions
to the Old Colony Church**

To the representatives of the Old Colony Reinland-Mennonite Church, Rev. Julius Loewen, Johann Loeppky, Director Benjamin Goertzen, and members Cornelius Rempel, Klaas Heide, and David Rempel.

In reply to your letter of January 29, 1921, in which you express the desire to establish yourselves in this country as agricultural settlers, I have the honor of giving you the following information in answer to the specific questions contained in the letter referred to above.

1. You will not be forced to accept military service.
2. In no case will you be compelled to swear oaths.
3. You will be completely free to exercise your religious principles and to observe the regulations of your church without being molested or restricted in any way.
4. You are fully authorized to establish your own schools, with your own teachers, without any hindrance from the government. Concerning this point our laws are exceedingly liberal.
5. You may dispose of your property in any way you may desire. This government will raise no objections to the establishment among the members of your sect of any economic system which they may voluntarily want to adopt.

It is the most ardent desire of this government to provide favorable conditions to colonists such as Mennonites who love order, lead moral lives, and are industrious. Therefore we would deem it a pleasure if this answer would satisfy you. The aforementioned privileges being guaranteed by our laws, we hope that you will take advantage of them positively and permanently.

Sufragio Efectivo No Reeleccion.

Mexico, February 25, 1921

The constitutional President of the United States of Mexico

A. Obregón

Secretary of Agriculture and Economic Affairs

A. I. Villareal

* Translation by the author.

Letter of Clarification to Old Colony Inquiry
*Concerning Basic Freedoms**

In reply to your request of October 27, presented by your representatives Arturo J. Braniff and Johann E. Wiebe, I have the honor to inform you that you can at any time rely upon legal protection for your life and property.

Furthermore I want to assure you that you are allowed to conduct both school and church in the German language.

Sufragio Efectivo No Reeleccion.
Mexico, D. F. October 30, 1921
Sign. A. Obregón
Sign. A. I. Villareal
Secretary of Agriculture and Economic Affairs.

* Translation by the author.

Appendix C

Ordination Sermon
of Bishop Froese, Written
January 5, 1937, by Jacob Froese, Reinfeld*

As I indicated in the introduction, we have assembled here in order to renew our covenant with God, which we made with the holy baptism before God and many witnesses. This covenant was to remain true to God and the *Gemeinde,* to serve the Lord in holiness and justice, as it pleases Him. We have also met here to renew our obligations to help in the construction (building) of the body of Christ, namely the *Gemeinde.* Therefore the Apostle sees as the goal of all believers the building of the body of Christ— that is, the true church of God. We ask ourselves: "What can the individual contribute to the body of Christ?"

1) to be aware of your responsibility to the body of Christ— you are responsible to the head of the church. Jesus Christ is the Head of the Church. He has a special relationship with His Church on earth as stated in Ephesians 1:22. The Church is His body and He wants to rule it with his spirit. He does not want to use force; rather through the power of His grace does He want to lead His body. In order to feel a part of the body, you need to feel your relationship to the entire body. What are you doing to build the entire body? You want to be strengthened, but what are you doing to strengthen others?

2) Secondly, the Church, the body of Christ, is the temple of the eternal God according to II. Corinthians 6:16. Whoever destroys the body of Christ destroys the temple. Temple desecration was always considered a specially punishable crime. How can we desecrate the body of Christ? First, we can destroy through self-seeking. A body feels best when all the extremities naturally obey and serve the entire body. A healthy arm or leg does not make itself noticeable. Only sick members are noticed. The spiritual life of the Christian shall be revived and renewed in church fellowship. In general this view is not contested, but we do not show it with our actions. If someone does not feel his responsibility, then he is not a member of the eternal body which is

* Translation by the author.

dependent on Christ. If you refuse the offering of fellowship, then you do not belong to the Head, which is Christ, and you are a foreign object in the living body. Members that expect something special for themselves create pain for the entire body. A member that seeks its own gain is so easily offended when it is passed by in any way. Thus conflict often develops in a church. A member that seeks his own gain cannot bring a gift or sacrifice, and without sacrifice, it is not possible to build.

Second, we can destroy through domination. To want to dominate is the opposite of service. There is only one lord of the Church, Jesus Christ. All others are servants. The more humbly we relate to others, the closer we will approximate the image of Christ.

How do we beware of desecration of the temple? We can avoid desecration through the building of the temple. Therefore, let us grow in all ways into the Head, which is Christ. He works so that the body shall grow. We are here commissioned to help in the growth of the body of Christ through the growth of its individual members. Serve one another each with the gift he has received. (1. Peter 4:10.) The head craves each service in love. We must serve one another; then one part of the body is connected to another and is dependent on it. It is clear that the church fellowship is as strong as each member.

Beloved brethren, we all know that we are engaged in the building of our Church (*Gemeinde*) and that you all, brethren and sisters, are being enlisted to assist. We can all contribute, especially through prayers, because the prayers of the righteous have great effect when they are earnest. Yes, our Church is not what it was years ago. Then it was a strong Church. But around fifteen years ago, because of the school problem, the Church decided to leave the country and to find a new home in a foreign land. The position of the leaders at that time was that the entire Church was to emigrate.

But through various hindrances numerous people stayed behind, while others could not decide so quickly to leave their beloved home in which they had lived so many years in peace and blessing. So they lingered though always with the idea of ultimately migrating to Mexico to join the Church. This was the reason why we did not immediately try to re-establish the remnant into a congregation here, since the majority continued to plan to move to Mexico. But with the years this desire to emigrate disappeared, especially through the disturbances that the Old Colony experienced in Mexico from the indigenous people. Their persecution included robbery, forceful entry into homes, and even murder. So that soon some families began to return. Then the question emerged here whether we could not raise up our Church again, and again conduct our services according to our old practices. Thus we began in all our weakness to hold meetings and consultations numerous times. The question was raised, "What will the Church in Mexico say if we re-establish our Church here?" This question concerned especially the ministers, for if and when we embarked on a selection and ordination of ministers, what would the Mexican ministers think of it? We were afraid of what they would think if we selected our own preachers here and began to revive our congregational life. In the meantime the situation in Mexico had worsened to the extent that a delegation from the Church in Mexico returned to Canada to search for an area where they could settle down in peace and quiet. Thereby the last reason fell for considering Mexico our home, and thus the question of the reviving of the Church was followed with greater urgency in order that we could guide our children, so that they could be shielded as much as possible from the world, its fashions and pride. It was further hoped that we might all unite together in humility and heart before God; for in the years in which we had no shepherds and teachers, many things happened which were not pleasing to the will of the highest, and in fact were very displeasing to Him. Yes, the word in Proverbs 29:18 was true for us—where there is no prophecy, the people perish.

Thus in the summer of 1936 we held numerous *Bruderschaften* (membership meetings), encouraged by the letter from the bishops in Mexico saying they were not negatively disposed in the issue and that, in fact, they wished us success in building the Church.

Therefore, we want to unite in rebuilding ourselves, as it is stated in Judas (*sic*), verse 29 [20]: "But you, my beloved, build yourselves up through the Holy faith through the Holy Spirit and prayer. And keep yourselves in the love of God and wait upon the mercy of our Jesus Christ, for eternal life." As it is stated in Hebrews 10:24 [and 25]: "And let us encourage each other with love and good works and not forsake the fellowship of the congregation, mutually admonishing one another, all the more, since the day of judgment is approaching." Oh, beloved brethren and sisters, according to the evidence, we are living in the last time, and signs are being fulfilled so that we can with truth say with the Apostle John: "Children it is the last hour. Oh that we might all be ready, as the wise virgins if suddenly in the middle of the night the voice will say, 'The Bridegroom comes! Go to meet him.' "

Therefore with all sincerity, prepare for this time in the holy fear of God, so that this hour may not overtake us. Therefore it is also necessary that we prepare the Church as the temple of God, as the Body of Christ, and that we do not let sin reign over us, nor serve it, but rather try to evade sin. Therefore we cannot allow a person who considers himself a brother or sister, but who lives in sin and according to the flesh, to remain in the Church. As Paul writes in II Thessalonians 3:6, "We beg you beloved brethren, in the name of our Lord Jesus Christ, that you withdraw yourselves from the brother who lives after the flesh, and not after the words that came from us."

Let us try to live according to the pure doctrines, as they are stated in our articles of confession, and to live according to His word as much as God gives us the power to do so through His love. But beloved, we ask for much understanding and prayer for us as the poor shepherd boys. For we are needy; we are poor and weak servants. We ask you to remember us constantly in your prayers, as we read that the Apostle Paul asked three times that the Church remember him. We need much more, since we are inexperienced and unknowledgeable in the service of the Lord. It is like it is stated in Romans 7:18 [and 24]: "The Will to do good, I have, but the good, I cannot achieve. Miserable man. Who shall deliver me from this death?"

Beloved brethren, let us intercede for one another. If someone stumbles, or falls, let us help him find the right with the gentle spirit and pure unfeigned love as the poet says: Should a weak fall somewhere, then the strong will come to the rescue, man helps others, man plants peace and joy, come, be more closely tied each to the other the strong and the weak. Let us take courage. The road is getting shorter, one day follows another, and soon the flesh falls into the grave.

Just a little courage, just a little more faithfulness to the eternal goal, just endure a little longer and we will reach home, where man will rest eternally. How wonderful it will be when we all meet before the Father. Therefore let us weigh the matter—it is well worth considering—what hinders us and what drags us down? World, you are too insignificant. We are marching into eternity through the suffering of Jesus. It shall be Jesus only. Amen.

Appendix D

*Brief Description of Some of the
"Unfriendly" Acts the Old Colony
Has Experienced in Mexico
(Chihuahua Settlement)* *

Stealing and Robberies

There are no statistics available on the amount of stealing that takes place. At certain times in certain areas, the villages have organized "police forces" to guard the village at night. The village is usually invaded from the rear, with the Mexicans sneaking up through the fields to the barns. Dogs normally alert the village, but often a diversionary tactic is used—alerting the dogs at one end of the village and then attacking the other end. At certain times, the Mexican police have "deputized" Old Colonists to arrest Mexicans found trespassing. Cases where organized gangs have broken into houses are known. One such case occurred in the village of Hochfeld several years before the author resided there. Livestock is the main object of robberies, though grain and machinery have also been taken.

Bodily Violence

A number of murders have been committed in the Mexican settlements, and the following took place in the Chihuahua settlements (Manitoba, Swift, and Nord Plans). In 1931 a farmer, aged twenty-nine, was shot by some Mexican thieves when they were caught in the act of stealing. The farmer died a month later. In 1933 a husband, wife, and son were murdered in their home. The culprits were never found, nor was a motive discovered. It is generally agreed, however, that it dealt with revenge for land lost to the Old Colonists. In 1934, a schoolteacher, aged forty-nine, was murdered by a Mexican, who was shot down by Mexican police and Old Colonists when he was cornered in a ravine. In 1953, a farmer, aged fifty-one, was killed when he challenged some Mexicans as they were stealing his grain. In 1962, a father, mother, son, and daughter were murdered in a

* Author's comments.

wild orgy which involved firing at long range and wounding the father and son and killing the mother and daughter in the house. The presumed killers were apprehended and have been incarcerated.

Appendix E

Notes on the Old Colony
*Emigration to British Honduras**

When the first people went to British Honduras in 1958 there was no preacher among them. The first families bought some Ford tractors with rubber tires because they felt the tractors were absolutely necessary to transport the supplies from the river ports great distances inland to the settlement.

When a substantial number of people had settled there, the Bishop from Chihuahua came and held an election, and a conservative preacher Jacob Fehr was elected. He immediately said the rubber tires had to go. He stated publicly that he had promised God and the *Gemeent* that would try to keep the *Gemeent* as it had always been (one Old Colonist remonstrated by saying that "If we had always remained as we were, we would still be in the Catholic Church"). But the rubber tires did not go. Even the stalwarts allowed themselves to be hauled around by the "faithless" brethren. The *Vorsteher* was sympathetic to the minority who had rubber-tired tractors, so the bishop replaced him by an orthodox man. A minister who sympathized with the majority was told to quit preaching, but he refused and continued to shepherd the minority, which began to meet separately. The bishop thereupon refused to give instruction to the young people applying for church membership and refused to baptize them.

Then the minority wrote to the bishop of the Old Colony in Manitoba, Canada, and requested him to come and minister to the minority which was being excluded by the majority. The bishop responded and came and baptized the youths. This resulted in further recrimination. The orthodox said the unorthodox had not paid their dues with the wood that they were clearing from the church lands (see letter below) which the church had paid for, while the unorthodox claimed they had not received credit for road work they had done for the church with their rubber-tired tractors. Reports of the fighting reached the capital of British Honduras since the bishop had attempted to reach an agreement with a lumber firm to withhold payment to the dissident group. But the firm had refused to agree, since they dealt with

* Transcription by the author.

others purely on a business basis and could not become involved in religious affairs.

> The Elders of the Reinland
> Mennonite Church,
> Blue Creek,
> July 21, 1962

The Belize Estate and Produce Co., Ltd.
Belize
British Honduras

Sirs:

We hereby give you notice that in case of felling of mahogany logs with our people from Blue Creek, kindly retain the 4¢ per foot royalty to be paid to the church at the disposal of our secretary Isaac Wieler to pay the taxes from our lands. All receipt orders must bear our seal.

> With best regards,
> Forest Mas [Master] for
> Mennonite Colony,
> Blue Creek
> Signed, Peter C. Thiessen
> Bishop, Jacob Harms

Appendix F

*Sample of Questions and Answers in Catechism**

Chapter 3. How the Triune God has Created All Things
    Section 2: The Creation of the Angels
        Question 9: Are there any creatures that were created in Heaven?
           Answer: Yes, the Angels—Hebrews 1:6-7; Colossians 1:16.
        Question 10: What are Angels?
           Answer: They are ministering spirits—Hebrews 1:7, 14.
        Question 11: Why has God created the Holy Angels?
           Answer: That they may praise the almighty God and benefit.
        Question 12: Have any of the Angels fallen?
           Answer: Yes, some left their position and were placed before the great judgment and are chained in eternal darkness—Jude, 6.
        Question 13: What are they called?
           Answer: Evil Spirits or the Devil—Luke 7:21, Mark 5:12.
Chapter 4. Concerning God's Reign and Support

* From *Katechismus—oder—Kurze und einfache Unterweisung aus der Heiligen Schrift* (27th ed.; Winnipeg, Manitoba: The Christian Press, n.d.), pp. 11-12 (printed in Elbing, Prussia, in 1783 for the first time). Translation by the author.

Appendix G

Notice Sent July 29, 1958, to All the Villages
in the Three Plans by Two Vorsteher*

1. There are still many people who have not paid for their land tax last year. It amounted to one peso and sixty-five centavos per acre, and should have been paid long ago. The treasury is now empty, and we are not going to borrow money and pay interest just because some are not paying their dues. There is no sense why this must be.

2. There are still people whose land was not paid for when the original settlement took place. This is a shame. We urge you to pay this up as soon as possible, else we will be forced to take the land from you.

3. There are still some people who signed an agreement to rent land at Yermo under a 5 year plan. Many returned without fulfilling their obligations. Will you please take care of this matter. Those who signed should be feeling their responsibility to clear this matter up.

Note: This can be paid on ————, of Gnadenfeld. [Below this the notice had a handwritten note that the local village dues were to be paid to a local man, but his name was not given.]

---

* This is a full translation of the note. The names of the *Vorsteher* were not included. Translation by the author.

Appendix H

Sibling Relations of Married Couples in Hochfeld, Manitoba Plan, Chihuahua, Mexico*

There are a total of forty-four families in the village, one of which is a widow with children. There are three parents who do not have siblings in the village. One set of relationships† includes ten siblings, each the husband or wife of a couple. There is one set of relationships which includes nine siblings, two sets which include six siblings, while three include five siblings. There are two sets which include four siblings. Three sets include three siblings, while eight sets include only two siblings. Four sets of siblings account for over half of the parents in the village. Those families having the least number of siblings tend to live on the ends of the village, while those with the most siblings tend to live in the middle of the village.

* Author's comments.

† A set of relationships refers to the brothers and sisters in one family who are now married and living in the village.

Letter to Federal Government of Mexico
Concerning the Segura Social *Question**

Honorable Judge Antonio Aris Mena,
Director, Mexican Social Security
Mexico, D. F.

Thank you for the reception you gave us, accompanied by the Honorable Colonel Carlos T. Serano. Since that time we have met numerous times with various groups which constitute our colonies, concerning the directive you gave us that we should come to an understanding with the local officials, which you are directing so well, concerning the implementation of the social insurance (*versicherung*) in our work areas. In this attempt, many hindrances have emerged. The majority of our representatives are of the opinion that the social security system is not applicable to our situation for the following reasons:

1. The law concerning social security springs from Article 123 of the Constitution of the Republic, which provides the basic norms so that the congress of the Union may not impose regulations on various groups and gives freedom to those who are not covered under day laborers, hired help, house servants, craftsmen, and those in other types of labor.

2. Our colonies are organized by families in farmsteads; we set up small private families and provide all the self-employed labor for these households. The children help, but are not employed in the sense of being paid.

3. Neither according to the law or in fact do we consider ourselves corporations.

4. In terms of money we limit ourselves to our own resources and have intentionally avoided any assistance from official sources. In spite of the fact that we have need, we have reserve funds which are situated in private banks in the city of Cuauhtemoc and Chihuahua.

5. In relation to the schools and public roads, we inform you that we provide for the necessary education and for repair of roads. We are convinced that the social security will not apply here. We do

* Translation by the author.

not want to appear to lack understanding in regard to your good intentions, and we respect the good will of the Lord President of the Republic. So in order to show our good intentions, even though we can not enter the social security program, we propose the following things in order to reach a working agreement:

a. We will enter into a formal agreement with the Social Security in which we will base our relationship on the Article 99 of the law and on the exceptions of the paragraphs, and on the exceptions of paragraph 1 and 2 of the same law. Our Church accepts the exceptions that are contained in the third and fourth places in the above article which hinder us. Therefore we commit ourselves to mutual assistance which is at the basis of our religious beliefs and is the main ground on which our trust resides by which we conduct our financial affairs.

b. We will attempt to register a minimum of 1,500 persons. We will pay a yearly sum which will be agreed upon by both sides as reasonable in light of our financial conditions.

c. The agreement shall be in force January, 1957. We will undertake the registration of our own people. We will set up the machinery to collect the dues in a way which seems most efficient to us. We will take the responsibility of taking care of our members who have registered and paid their dues, when they are hospitalized in Cuauhtemoc, or in Chihuahua, or in the City of Mexico, D.F. All these conditions were proposed to Mr. Dr. Manuel Moreno Islas on March 22, 1956.

d. The time limit of this agreement cannot be abrogated without agreement of both parties. Any other determination, which deviates basically from this agreement which we here propose, will demand a concurrence from your office; the agreement which we propose has taken considerable work and negotiation among our people, since the social security issue is very distasteful to our people. The above solution stems in large measure from the insightful assistance of Mr. Colonel Carlos T. Serano, who has encouraged us to try to achieve a good understanding with the federal government.

Article No. 2

This law concerns the explication of paragraph 1 (accidents at work) and professional sicknesses. Paragraph 2 concerns sicknesses not applicable to professions and maternity cases. Paragraph 3 concerns incapability for work, overage for work, or death. Paragraph 4 concerns unemployment.

Article 99

This institute can enlist either individuals or groups in aspects of the article which would apply (Article 6) and would include the self-employed professionals and independent workers in the crafts and all such. Pader Executive Federal, with prior study and by order of the institute, will determine the date and the conditions at which the workers for the state, for family businesses, house work, and land laborers will enter, and we will list the people that fall in these classes.

Article 123

Guarantees us that the Social Security institute is tax free and will not derive support from other governmental agencies except that it may use office space in public services such as water or sewage in localities.

Respectfully,

Cuauhtemoc
June 27, 1956

Colonia Manitoba
Gerh. J. Rempel

Colonia Norden
Jacob Martens

Colonia Swift
Franz F. Klassen

Colonia St. Clara
Heinrich Friesen

Colonia Jagueges
Johann D. Friesen

An Essay Concerning the Letter *"A," Reflecting the Tension and Strife Now Rife in the Church**

Since there is at present great attention focused on the letter "a" I have decided to write down my thoughts on the matter. To begin, those concerned in the matter maintain they are not doing anything wrong and ought to be given the freedom to continue as they have done. Certainly there is nothing of great importance in the dead letter, as long as it remains an innocent letter, namely that each speaks it as he has learned it from his forefathers. Much more weight should be given to what is read. Thus for example a couple reads, one to the other, though one learned the a one way and the other the opposite way. They lay no weight on the different pronunciation, but focus on the content. Neither declares himself to be more educated than the other. There are however some *Vorsteher* and ministers who are relearning the pronunciation so that they will not create a stumbling block when they preach from the chancel. Thus they try to place the emphasis on the content of the word, rather than the form. So far, everything was done in innocence and needed to have caused no harm.

But today it has become a battle. For example in one village live people from both orientations. One party believes they should retain the pronunciation as the "fathers" taught them, and to this they have added even more the "worldly" pronunciation. They practice this in private but do not admit it in public. The other party has learned it differently and wants to retain its practice. This is the position of all the ministers and the majority of the *Gemeinde,* and thus this party is very strong.

Thus, to arbitrate in this case is no easy matter. It demands from the beginning great caution in handling the case. If the greater segment maintains that the minority is becoming proud and thereby makes the matter significant, then this is against the teachings of the Church. That it is wrong on the other hand to teach the "worldly" pronunciation the minority will not accept, according to the Word of God, since so much significance can not reside in the dead letter. Only if both parties can remain in the simple

* Transcription by the author. The essay, dated September 20, 1942, was found among the documents of Deacon Isaac Dyck after his death.

obedience and do what they have been taught can peace return. For the tree is known by its fruit, and this we see in the bishops and ministers. They are simple people like others. Since the problem has become tense and the minority has the key to the problem, they should do like ministers Franz Dyck and David Wiebe who yielded to the desires of the majority for the blessings of the Church and to avoid the derision of the world.

Appendix K

*British Honduras–Old Colony Arrangements**

Memo of Agreement between the Member for Natural Resources of the Government of British Honduras and Representatives of the Mennonite Churches of Chihuahua, Mexico, subject to approval of the Executive Council of British Honduras and to the Mennonite Church of Chihuahua.

1) The Member for Natural Resources welcomes the immigration of the Mennonites to this country. His government has decided to:
   a) grant the Mennonites the privilege of running their own schools in their own language
   b) exempt them from making the customary immigration deposits
   c) give protection of life and property in peace and war.
2) The Member for Natural Resources undertakes to request the approval of the Executive Council to grant the following concessions to the Mennonites:
   a) Freedom from direct civil service such as the bearing of arms, doing work or wearing uniforms. It is understood that in the event of war the Mennonites will contribute to the war effort by producing the necessary food.
   b) The privilege of not taking an oath or a sworn declaration in the courts or in government affairs. Instead of an oath or sworn declaration a solemn "I . . . do solemnly, sincerely and truly declare and affirm that the evidence I shall give shall be the truth, the whole truth, and nothing but the truth."
   c) Freedom of movement to enter or to leave the country after complying with normal immigration and currency exchange regulations.
   d) Freedom to organize economic and social systems and administration in accordance with the laws of the country.
   e) Freedom to bring into the country the old, infirm, and invalid members of the Mennonite community, provided that these individuals do not become a charge on the government of this country.

* Transcription by the author.

f) Exemption from a future security or compulsive system of insurance. It is understood that the Mennonites will pay the normal duties, taxes, fees and charges by law established, such as customs duty, land tax, property tax, income tax.

3) The Mennonites will finance their immigration, pay transportation, paying for purchase of lands, cost of establishing farming community and other related costs, and they will in no way become a charge to the government or the people of this country.

4) The Mennonites will bring into the country capital investment in cash and kind amounting to over one million dollars, B. H. currency.

5) The Mennonites will produce food not only for themselves, but for local consumption and for the export markets.

6) It is clearly understood that the Mennonites will not conclude purchase-sale transactions for land until conditions set out in section 2 of this memo of agreement are granted to the Mennonites by the British Honduras government.

George Price
Member for Natural Resources, and
Leader of the Majority Party in the Government of
British Honduras, Belize,
British Honduras,
September 2, 1957

Appendix L

"Your Brother Is as Good as You" *

This poem was written by a George Kroeker, who was not living with his wife, was considered a bit peculiar by other Old Colonists, and was looked down on by the majority of them. He has written and distributed numerous poems in the villages. This poem obviously was written as a defense against the ostracism he was experiencing as a result of his deviant behavior.

> Your brother is as good as you
> For he also seeks peace for his soul
> For he also has his burden of sorrow
> In the same measure as you do.
>
> He hopes, plans, worries and works
> With all his might, just as you do.
> He hopes for regards and success
> In his work, also as you do.
>
> Your brother has sorrows unexpressed
> In his own Gethsemane.
> There he sighs and often weeps.
> He agonizes and prays, as you do.
>
> And though he may be a bit queer,
> Even as you are in your own way,
> Does this allow for the judgment
> That he is not as good as you?
>
> Though he be often unfriendly and cross
> Are you not the same, as much as he?
> Therefore, love him and agree
> Your brother is as good as you.

* Translation by the author.

Appendix M

"Es Geht Zu Weit" (It Is Going Too Far)*

We are now in such a time
That man hears—"it's going too far!"
Yet where is it going?
Forward or backward?
The Christian does not have the courage
To discern this continually.
That which was unknown earlier
Is forbidden out of hand.

Others maintain that too many
Human rules are in the way.
This is also dangerous
For the Christian in the World.
Thus, for our farming practices
Nothing apparently is of help.
We are told what to do
Even though it is unreasonable.

We are looking to one thing:
Just so we follow that
Which we humans have determined.
Nothing else matters,
Even if it be much worse—
Betting, lying, lust, and greed
Hate, ridicule, and more,
All against Christ's teaching.

Yes, there is no sin any more
That man can't find today.
However, if someone's tractor wheel
Has rubber around it,
Soon there is judgment
Concerning the evil thing.
If he does not change it soon
He finds himself in the Ban.

* Translation by the author, with intention of retaining meaning
rather than form.

He who does not glory in such laws
Will begin to hear the warning:
Obey what we have made
Or stand in shame tomorrow!
But God's teaching and law
We do not hold so high,
Though God has commanded
Hear and Obey my Word!

The Lord much despises
All self-made laws.
In Matthew fifteen already,
He clearly speaks thereof.
Also in Mark, chapter seven,
He warns of the use of the Law
Of human origin,
And continually in his teaching.

And Paul remembers it,
In Colossians two, verse twenty-one,
Where man reads
That it is human teaching
When he leans more on custom
Than he does on Christ's law
And refuses the neighbor
This and that as too costly.

That thing do not touch
Else you have done evil
Also you shall wash your hands
Before you have your meal
This believed also these others
And felt, "It's going too far."
If man without washing
Sits down to the meal.

It seems to me we understand nothing,
Even though He speaks so clearly
Through His word which is eternal
And will not end with the world.
Must we always
Seek our Salvation
In the things that will perish
And will not remain?

But what the Scriptures state
Man should ponder always.
He who trusts anything else
Will build on sand.
But what motivates man,
The people in Christendom?
Does she depend on the shadow
Which can not do a thing?

For example, can we see
A church newly built,
Pews partly of new wood
And partly of old wood
But what matter? Man paints
The benches with grey paint;
All is covered over
Including the chancel.

Thus everything looks conformed,
Everything looks joyful,
Finally all the work is done
That causes man so much concern.
Sparing no time or energy
They work early and late—
Should not in this place
God's Word and Glory Rule?

Mental Illness and Suicide Data for
*Manitoba and Mexico**

A. Mental Illness

    1. Manitoba

At present there are three mentally ill—two females, age forty and sixty, and one male, age twenty-two. These have been committed to Brandon Mental Hospital.

In 1962 an Old Colonist from Mexico was brought to Brandon from Mexico for treatment.

One family moved to Manitoba from Mexico to receive help for the mother who was ill. They have since returned to Mexico.

Three boys in Brandon are from the Mexican Old Colony, but little information was available on them.

One Manitoba Old Colonist is an outpatient at Brandon and is receiving help from a psychiatrist.

Doctors familiar with Old Colony people suggested that mental disturbances are greatest among women, mainly because of depression related to child-bearing.

    2. Mexico

Few cases are known. One man went berserk and used profanity constantly. He was beaten severely by several "faithful" who wanted to "drive the devil out." They were chastened by the Church.

Another Old Colonist went berserk, became violent, and finally was put in a Mexican jail. He has not been helped and is still there.

A third Old Colonist became emotionally disturbed, evidencing bizarre behavior such as wanting to sell his wife for $10. He has apparently improved.

One Old Colony woman, apparently a mentally marginal woman, became a prostitute among Mexicans.

Another woman, considered "brilliant," also became a prostitute among Mexicans and is reputed to have made considerable money at the trade.

* Author's comments.

B. Suicides

   1. Manitoba

   One mother killed herself before the migration to Mexico. She was forty-five and had children.

   One male took his own life because of brain damage (arterial sclerosis), according to the doctor.

   2. Mexico

   One father hanged himself in 1943 (until 1958 there had been only one suicide in Mexico, according to the Bishop of the Manitoba Plan).

   One mother hanged herself in 1964. She was diagnosed as a manic depressive personality.

Appendix O

*A Note on the Physical Environment
of the Old Colony**

The Old Colony physical environment has been rather similar in
Prussia, Russia, and Canada. The basic climatic variables, latitude
and altitude, were generally very similar. The migration to Mexico
constituted a departure from the latitude, since the Mexican settlements were between the 25th and 30th parallel. The altitude was
extremely different, since both Chihuahua and Durango settlements were very high, around seven thousand feet above sea
level. The migrations to British Honduras and Bolivia constituted the greatest changes, since both are within twenty degrees of
the equator and are subject to entirely different climates. British
Honduras and Bolivia are different, however, in that British Honduras has an altitude of less than three hundred feet, while Bolivia,
where the Old Colony is settling, is at least five thousand feet in
elevation.

Not only has the climate been drastically different in the recent
migrations; the soil types and the resultant farming conditions
have been varied. Most of the soils have been Pedocals (Russia,
Canada, Mexico, and Bolivia), though with rather great differences in productivity due to the difference in rainfall. British Honduras has the greatest variation in soil type and rainfall and consequently demands the greatest changes in types of farming—
dairying, chicken raising, fruit and vegetable raising, with no grain
cultivation. The productivity of the Mexican soils is so low because
of the lack of rain (irrigation is just beginning to be introduced)
and because of the Old Colony reluctance to use fertilizers (referred to in the text).

The seasonal variations have been remarkably similar in all of
the settlements. The winters were cold, long, and hard in Russia
and Canada. In Mexico they are long and dry, while in British
Honduras they are rainy. The Bolivian winter resembles that of
Mexico, though it is not so cold. There is thus a long unpleasant
and inefficient winter, so that all the productive work must be done
in the summer months. The topography again has been similar
for the Old Colony from Russia to Mexico, but British Honduras

* Author's comments.

and Bolivia have presented great changes. In British Honduras the settlements have had to carve clear land out of the dense subtropical forests, with all the accompanying problems and difficulties. In Bolivia, there is a scrubby forest which has to be cleared for settlement. In Russia and Canada a gently rolling "steppe" was prevalent, while the terrain in Mexico and Bolivia has been rather rough, and British Honduras again is flat.

The adaptations to these rather drastic environmental factors have been amazingly few and inconsequential. Old Colony dress patterns have changed hardly at all in any of the settlements. Aside from the shift in the progressive settlements, the women still wear the heavy petticoats, dresses, and aprons, regardless of the climate. They braid their hair and cover it with a shawl over which a hat is worn. Babies are wrapped in heavy blankets, summer or winter, in all the settlements. Bed covers are heavy comforters filled with goose down and are used throughout the year, in all the settlements alike. It is almost impossible to sleep under these covers unless one has become thoroughly used to them. The men wear dark overalls and dark shirts. Sunday clothes are heavy, dark, and warm.

Eating patterns are very similar, though some adaptations have been made. The food is largely home grown and home cooked in all the settlements. Home-baked breads, potatoes, soups, chicken, pork, sausage, ham, and occasional beef are eaten. Fresh vegetables are eaten in season. The diet is very starchy, usually including potatoes and bread. A few Mexican dishes have been adopted, especially beans. Since refrigeration is not condoned, the foods are either fresh or canned, but never frozen.

The shelters of the Old Colony in Mexico resemble the basic form used in Russia and Canada, with steep roofs and design. There is one significant change—the walls are made of adobe, for the Old Colony soon discovered that wood was very expensive and that adobe was much better as an insulator than wood. The houses are being separated from the barns in British Honduras because of the problems of mosquitoes, flies, and other vermin. Some of the houses in British Honduras have no window panes, only screens.

The greatest change resulting from environmental factors has been in the farming methods. In the early years of the Mexican settlement, the Old Colonists tried very hard to raise their traditional wheat, but without success. A serious crisis developed before they turned to beans and corn. The feeding of livestock also had to change because of the temperature and other changes. With the experience of needing to make changes in Mexico, the migration to British Honduras has not faced the crisis of changing farming methods. The farmers there are already very busy selling milk to Belize and raising tropical fruits such as bananas.

The Old Colony has adapted to the changing environments not to exploit the environment or to develop a harmonious rhythm with it, but rather so that a traditional way of life could be perpetuated. This is concretely illustrated by the soil rotation and soil enrichment practices. The Mexican Old Colony farmer typically has a three-crop rotation system—corn, oats, and beans. Summer fallow, if it is practiced at all, follows the oats crop. Fertilizer has not been applied, though in scattered villages a few energetic and daring younger farmers apply it. On the whole, however, the average yields are extremely low. An oats crop yielding thirty bushels an acre is considered a bumper crop.

The Old Colonist shares none of the American attitude toward exploitation of the land for profit, nor does he share the more mystical attitudes toward the land found in Oriental and some European countries. He sees the land, and the entire environment, as a context within which he achieves his objective, which is to live as God has called him to live—as interpreted through the Old Colony social system of which he is a part.

Bibliography

Allen, Gordon, and Redekop, Calvin. "Individual Differences in Survival and Reproduction Among Old Colony Mennonites in Mexico: Progress to October, 1966," *Eugenics Quarterly,* Vol. 14 (June, 1967).

Burkhart, Charles. "Music of the Old Colony Mennonites in Mexico," *Mennonite Life,* Vol. 3, No. 3 (1948).

Bushong, Allen D. "Mennonite Settlement in British Honduras," *Association of American Geographers,* Vol. 50 (September, 1960).

Dreidger, Leo. "A Sect in a Modern Society: A Case Study, The Old Colony Mennonites of Saskatchewan" (M.A. thesis, University of Chicago, 1955).

————. "From Mexico to British Honduras," *Mennonite Life,* Vol. 13, No. 4 (January, 1958).

————. "Hague-Osler Settlement," *Mennonite Life,* Vol. 13. No. 1 (January, 1958).

————. "Saskatchewan Old Colony Mennonites, *Mennonite Life,* Vol. 13, No. 2 (April, 1958).

————. "Old Colony Mennonites Are Moving Again: From Mexico to British Honduras," *Mennonite Life,* Vol. 15 (October, 1960).

Engh, Jeri, "A Happy Simple Life," *Words of Cheer,* Vol. 90, No. 41 (October, 1965).

Francis, E. K. *In Search of Utopia.* Glencoe: Free Press, 1955.

Fretz, J. Winfield. *Mennonite Colonization in Mexico.* Akron, Pennsylvania: The Mennonite Central Committee, 1945. Publication Number 2.

————. "Mennonites in Mexico," *Mennonite Life,* Vol. 2, No. 2 (April, 1947).

————. "Cuauhtemoc," *Mennonite Encyclopedia,* Vol. 1.

Harder, Sara Lehn. "Mennonites Along the 'Peace,'" *The Canadian Mennonite,* Vol. 13, No. 45 (November 9, 1965).

Hostetler, John A. "Pioneering in the Land of the Midnight Sun," *Mennonite Life.* Vol. 3, No. 2 (April, 1948).

Jantzen, Carl R. "Social Disorganization Among the Old Colony Mennonites in Mexico" (research paper presented to the Department of Sociology, Bethel College, North Newton, Kansas, May, 1957).

Krahn, Cornelius. "Old Colony Mennonites," *Mennonite Encyclopedia,* Vol. 4.

————. "The Old Colony Mennonites," *Mennonite Weekly Review,* Vol. XXIX, Nos. 4, 6, 8, 10, 14, 20, 30, 32 (1951).

Redekop, Calvin. "Analysis of an Ethnic Minority Struggling for Existence in Two Cultures," *Year Book.* Philadelphia: American Philosophical Society (1966).

————. "Decision Making in a Sect," *Review of Religious Research,* Vol. 2, No. 2 (Fall, 1960).

———. "The Sect From a New Perspective," *Mennonite Quarterly Review*, Vol. 39, No. 3 (July, 1965).

———. "Toward an Understanding of Religion and Social Solidarity," *Sociological Analysis*, Vol. 28 (Fall, 1967).

———. "The Old Colony: An Analysis of Group Survival," *Mennonite Quarterly Review*, Vol. 40, No. 3 (July, 1966).

Redekop, Calvin, and Hostetler, John A. "Minority-Majority Relations and Economic Interdependence," *Phylon*, Vol. XXVII, No. 4 (Winter, 1966).

———. "Education and Boundary Maintenance in Three Ethnic Groups," *Review of Religious Research*, Vol. 5, No. 2 (Winter, 1964).

Redekop, Calvin, and Loomis, Charles P. "The Development of Status-Roles in the Systemic Linkage Process," *Journal of Human Relations*, Vol. 7, No. 2 (April, 1960).

Redondo, Regino Diaz. "El Dificil Regreso; Los Menonitas Piensan Emigrar," *Excelsior* (July 4, 1965).

Sawatzky, Leonard. "Colony Leaders Must Realize that Present Trends Lead to Disaster," *Canadian Mennonite*, Vol. 14, No. 14 (March 29, 1966).

Schaefer, Paul J. *Woher? Wohin? Mennonnite!* Altoona, Manitoba: Mennonite Agricultural Advisory Committee, 1946. Parts 3 and 4.

Schmiedehaus, Walter. *Ein feste Burg ist unser Gott*. Cuauhtemoc, Chihuahua: G. J. Rempel, Blumenort, 1948.

———. "New Mennonite Settlements in Mexico," *Mennonite Life*, Vol. 4, No. 4 (October, 1949).

Smith, C. Henry. *The Story of the Mennonites*. Newton, Kansas: Mennonite Publication Office, 1950.

Stoesz, A. D. "Agriculture Among the Mennonites of Mexico," *Mennonite Life*, Vol. 2, No. 2 (April, 1947).

Warkentine, John. "Mennonite Agricultural Settlements of Southern Manitoba," *Geographical Review*, Vol. XLIX, No. 3 (July, 1959).

Wiebe, Cornelius W. "Health Conditions Among the Mennonites of Mexico," *Mennonite Life*, Vol. 2, No. 2 (April, 1947).

"Mennonites Vex Mexican Hosts," *New York Times*, October 30, 1955.

"Mennonite Life Goes to Mexico," *Mennonite Life*, Vol. 7, No. 1 (January, 1952).

"Old Colony Mennonites and Hutterites," Record Groups No. 85, Records of the Bureau of Immigration . . . , Files 54623/130 and 54623/130H, April 21, 1919–November, 1931, National Archives of the United States, 1934.

INDEX

A-au controversy: and power of tradition, 206; schoolteacher involvement in, 207; and unity, 216; focus of, 271; cause of, 271; emphasis upon, 271

Acculturation: explained, 241

Adobe: in Mexican homes, 284

Agreement: with provincial government, 159; of 1873, 249–50; not kept, 263; with British Honduras government, 273

Alcoholic beverages: beer, 131; whiskey, 136. *See also* Drinking

Alms fund: use of, 65

Altkolonier Reinlaender Mennoniten Gemeinde (Mennonites in West Reserve), 10

America: minorities in, 1

Anabaptists: fleeing Switzerland, 1; coming to America, 1; as a minority, 4; under persecution, 4; in conflict with reformers, 4; on obedience, 4

Architectural forms: in Mexican colonies, 143

Assimilation: determination to avoid, 158; transportation as factor in, 175; tactic used to encourage, 181; in progressive Old Colony, 223; cohesion as deterrent to, 229, 242; cultural, 231, 232; structural, 231, 242; as process, 234; tenet against, 239; resistance to, 239–40

Astrology: in Old Colony settlements, 197

Authority. *See* Power

Automobile: use of, 138; in traditional settlements, 139; purchase of forbidden, 151; radio, 182;

youth desire for, 206. *See also* Transportation

Ban: as a deviancy control, 67, 277; defined, 68; enforcement of, 111

Banking: Old Colony leadership in, 177; interaction with Mexicans, 203; loans to young farmers, 203; business with Old Colony, 203. *See also* Capital; Money

Baptism: as rite of passage, 33; problems connected with, 51; administered by bishop, 63; admonition during service of, 102; denial of, 141; of minority, 259

Behavior: control of, 102; compared to society, 130; ethical, 131; undesirable, 134. *See also* Ban; Sanction

Beliefs: validation of, 31; lack of logic in, 153; historical, 168. *See also* Belief system

Belief system: of Old Colony, 29; punishment for doubt of, 39; source of *Lehrdienst*'s authority, 178; concrete expression of, 215, 216; sacred, 216; common, as basis for cohesion, 230, 242

Beneficiary relationship: defined, 236

Bergthalers: mentioned, 10; success in school upgrading in Manitoba, 10–12

Bible: as textbook, 9; use in decision making, 45; concerning rubber tires, 48; Old Testament, 60; New Testament, 60, 181; use of, 64; study of, 130, 147;

Designed by Edward D. King

Composed in Granjon by The Colonial Press Inc.

Printed offset by The Colonial Press Inc. on
60–lb. Warren 1854

Bound by The Colonial Press Inc. in GSB, Natural, S/400